Interdisciplinary Teaching Through Physical Education

Theresa Purcell Cone, MEd
Brunswick Acres Elementary School, Kendall Park, New Jersey

Peter Werner, PED
University of South Carolina, Columbia, South Carolina

Stephen L. Cone, PhD
Rowan University, Glassboro, New Jersey

Amelia Mays Woods, PhD
Indiana State University, Terre Haute, Indiana

Human Kinetics

Library of Congress Cataloging-in-Publication Data

Interdisciplinary teaching through physical education / Theresa Purcell Cone ... [et. al.].
      p.   cm.
    Includes bibliographical references (p.) and index.
    ISBN 0-88011-502-5
       1. Education, Elementary--Curricula. 2. Interdisciplinary approach in education. 3. Physical
education and training--Study and teaching.   I. Cone, Theresa Purcell, 1950-
    LB1570.I5669   1998
    372.19--dc21   98-7515
                                                        CIP

ISBN: 0-88011-502-5

Acquisitions Editor: Scott Wikgren
Developmental Editor: Judy Patterson Wright, PhD
Managing Editors: Joanna Hatzopoulos and Henry Woolsey
Assistant Editor: Jennifer Miller
Copyeditor: Karen Bojda
Proofreader: Myla Smith
Indexer: Joan Griffitts
Graphic Designer: Robert Reuther
Graphic Artist: Judy Henderson
Photo Editor: Boyd LaFoon
Cover Designer: Jack Davis
Photographer (interior): All photos by Tom Roberts unless otherwise noted.
                Photo on page 213 by Theresa Purcell Cone.
Illustrators: Mary Yemma Long and Robert Reuther
Printer: United Graphics

Human Kinetics books are available at special discounts for bulk purchase. Special editions or book excerpts can also be created to specification. For details, contact the Special Sales Manager at Human Kinetics.

Copies of this book are available at special discounts for bulk purchase for sales promotions, premiums, fund-raising, or educational use. Special editions or book excerpts can also be created to specifications. For details, contact the Special Sales Manager at Human Kinetics.

Printed in the United States of America   10 9 8 7 6 5 4

Human Kinetics
Web site: www.HumanKinetics.com

United States: Human Kinetics, P.O. Box 5076, Champaign, IL 61825-5076
800-747-4457
e-mail: humank@hkusa.com

Canada: Human Kinetics, 475 Devonshire Road, Unit 100, Windsor, ON N8Y 2L5
800-465-7301 (in Canada only)
e-mail: orders@hkcanada.com

Europe: Human Kinetics, 107 Bradford Road, Stanningley
Leeds LS28 6AT, United Kingdom
+44 (0) 113 255 5665
e-mail: hk@hkeurope.com

Australia: Human Kinetics, 57A Price Avenue, Lower Mitcham, South Australia 5062
08 8277 1555
e-mail: liahka@senet.com.au

New Zealand: Human Kinetics, P.O. Box 105-231, Auckland Central
09-523-3462
e-mail: hkp@ihug.co.nz

Contents

Preface

One cold day when the sixth graders came in from outdoor play period several children were discussing what could be the matter with their large rubber and soccer balls. When they took them from the cupboard they had seemed to be "blown up hard enough" but after being used on the playground for a short time they were too soft. The teacher ended the conversation by saying, "Play period is over. Put your balls away and get ready for science class. We are starting our unit on air today."

This passage was taken out of a book written by V.E. Herrick in the 1930s. Yet how true is it today? As a teacher, what would you do in this situation? Would you see the relationship and bridge the gap between science and physical education? Or, like this teacher, would you focus on your discipline and miss the opportunity to draw relationships between subjects?

The world is full of examples of situations in which people in everyday life use relationships among conceptual information. Children look up at clouds and see alligators, mushrooms, and other wonderful shapes. Cooks read recipes and use fractions to make delectable dishes. Canoeists use knowledge of fluid dynamics, leverage, and Newton's third law of motion to propel their canoe in different directions. Consultants in decorating stores mix paint and suggest wall coverings with an eye for design to make the home a pleasant place to live. Michael Crichton in *Jurassic Park* combined his knowledge of archaeology, genetics, and mathematics to fabricate a story that captured the imaginations of millions. The world is full of relationships. As teachers, we need to take advantage of these opportunities to give meaning to what children learn.

From what leading child development experts teach us, we can safely say that children have different learning styles, they are concrete learners, and they learn actively by doing. Regarding learning styles, some children are visual learners. Others are verbal learners. Others learn best through the tactile-kinesthetic sense. Others learn best through a combination of these sensory mechanisms. Because children are concrete learners, we need to be able to take conceptual information that is often abstract and present it in a practical, hands-on manner. Because children learn by doing, we need to provide a learning environment in which we actively engage children in learning experiences.

The ideas that relationships exist among school subjects and that children are concrete learners and may learn best through practical, active learning experiences are part of the educational reform movement of the 1990s. Interdisciplinary teaching has become a notable approach to the delivery of elementary school curricula. Many teachers at the elementary level welcome the opportunity to teach across the curriculum and recognize the interdisciplinary approach as a natural way for students to learn. A comprehensive education provides children with opportunities to learn in multiple ways that are developmentally appropriate. It offers a way for educators to enhance and enrich student learning through the integration of two or more subject areas. The skills and knowledge taught in physical education can easily be integrated with the content areas of mathematics, science, language arts, social studies, and the arts. Movement, the heart of physical education, actively engages students in learning-by-doing situations that are relevant and contemporary. The interdisciplinary approach to teaching challenges educators to design experiences that make learning meaningful, fun, and rewarding for the student.

It is common to find interdisciplinary efforts by teachers in language arts, mathematics, science, and social studies. Many books have been written that provide teachers with ideas on how to integrate these subjects. What has not been available until now, however, is a book that focuses on interdisciplinary learning with additional emphasis on active, concrete, practical learning experiences with human movement as the central core.

The purpose of this book is to introduce the reader to learning experiences that use active learning to help teach concepts addressed throughout the elementary curriculum. The intended audiences are elementary physical education teachers, elementary and early childhood teachers, and faculty and students in professional preparation programs who are interested in promoting a broader understanding of the connectedness we share within our disciplines.

The book is divided into two parts. Part I of the text presents the theoretical need for and benefits of interdisciplinary learning, identifies the various models of interdisciplinary programs, and provides strategies for implementation. Included in the discussion of implementing an interdisciplinary program are ideas for getting started, building a support network, and assessing interdisciplinary learning. Part II of the book includes five chapters that describe in detail how learning experiences may be developed in each of the academic disciplines of language arts, mathematics, science, social studies, and the arts. Within each of the disciplinary chapters is a framework, or scope and sequence of concepts, that are taught to children at each grade level. Four complete learning experiences with detailed lessons are included. Each learning experience has a name, identifies an intended grade level, and follows an interdisciplinary model. Objectives, equipment, and an organizational pattern are listed and followed by an in-depth description of the lesson. Each learning experience ends with assessment suggestions, what teachers should look for in student responses, ideas on how teachers could change the lesson to further expand the concept, and suggestions for teachable moments. Each chapter also includes short descriptions for additional learning experiences based on the breadth of concepts taught to children in each discipline. Each additional learning experience is named and gives the major concepts to be learned, an appropriate grade level, and a vignette for teachers on how to develop the concept. The book concludes with reference materials that have proven invaluable for the authors in developing their interdisciplinary work, which are offered to the reader as sources for developing further interdisciplinary learning experiences.

Acknowledgments

As with any major professional work, the authors are grateful and indebted to a whole host of support people who have made this project possible. We particularly wish to thank Christine Hopple (formerly of Human Kinetics) and Scott Wikgren of Human Kinetics for their encouragement and vision to publish this work. As the editors, Judy Wright and Joanna Hatzopoulos provided many suggestions to make this work more logical, complete, and readable.

Our appreciation is extended to the students at the Brunswick Acres Elementary School in Kendall Park, New Jersey, and to faculty members Kathy Guzzo, Don Sweeney, Pat Taylor, and Barbara McWilliams for their help, suggestions, and willingness to explore the realm of interdisciplinary learning. A special thanks to the many undergraduate and graduate students at the University of South Carolina who served as sounding boards in the development of materials included in this book. We would also like to recognize the children at the Center for Inquiry, Richland District 2, Columbia, South Carolina, who frequently participated in these lessons and offered their ideas and reactions to the learning experiences. We would like to thank the students and faculty at Keene State College for the perspectives they offered and their commitment to interdisciplinary approaches to learning. And a special thank you to Gordon Leversee, Delina Hickey, Judith Sturnick, Bob Golden, and Ann Waling for making this project possible.

Most of all, we are eternally grateful to our families for all their encouragement and support through this lengthy writing process:

Sophia Purcell and Bill Beetel

Mary, Lauren, and Amy Werner

Marjorie and Warren Cone

Amy, Lisa, Tim, and Meredith Cone

Jeff and Jack Woods

How to Use This Book

You are invited to join us as we explore the possibilities of interdisciplinary learning. This book has been written for novice as well as veteran teachers willing to take risks and enjoy the benefit of professional and personal growth. We offer this book as a means to help you understand the richness and complexity of this approach to teaching and learning. Our goal is to provide you with some background information, strategies for developing and implementing interdisciplinary learning experiences, and some concrete examples that you will find useful and interesting.

We suggest you begin by reading the foundational information presented in chapters 1 and 2. This information will provide you with a sense of how we view interdisciplinary teaching and learning when physical education is integrated with other subjects. Familiarize yourself with the national standards. They will provide you with the basic curricular framework on which you will be able to ground your ideas for developing your own interdisciplinary learning experiences. The three selected interdisciplinary teaching models developed by the authors are unique to this book. As you review each model, keep in mind that the models are guides on how to organize your content, how to collaborate with others, and how to create meaningful activities that affect student learning. You can use the ideas and models in the book to initiate a conversation and build support with another teacher, your administrator, your students, or parents.

Use the tables and figures as a quick reference. They give you a good overview of the "what and how" of interdisciplinary teaching and learning. You can see that table 2.1, "Strategies for Developing an Interdisciplinary Learning Experience," gives you seven strategies to help you develop an effective interdisciplinary experience. We have included examples of three assessment instruments for you to try as is, to adapt, or to use as a starting point to create your own. Remember to tie the assessment directly to the objective.

The second part of this book includes five chapters that describe how physical education is integrated with language arts, mathematics, science, social studies, music, theater arts, and visual arts. Each chapter uses a common format, with a brief introduction followed by the K-6 scope and sequence of each subject. Next, complete learning experiences illustrate the application of the interdisciplinary teaching models in a practical setting. A quick look at the focus and delivery of each learning experience is offered. Teachers should feel free to use these lessons as described or to modify them to meet the needs of their situation.

Each complete learning experience includes a ready-to-use lesson containing all the components needed to get started. Each learning experience is in the following format:

- Name of the learning experience.
- Suggested Grade Level.
- Interdisciplinary Teaching Model. Describes one of the three selected interdisciplinary teaching models presented in chapter 1: connected, shared, or partnership. Specific skills and concepts used as the focus of the experience are listed with their respective curricular area.
- Objectives. The specific skill and concept outcomes to be learned by the student as a result of participating in the learning experience.
- Equipment needed to complete the learning experience.
- Organization in which students will be working: individual, partner, small group, or large group.
- Description of the total learning experience, explained as if teacher was actually presenting the learning experience to children.
- Assessment Suggestion. Examples of different assessment instruments that can be practically applied during or following the learning experience.

- Look For. Key points for you to keep in mind when informally observing students' progress in the learning experience.

- How Can I Change This? Ways you can vary the organization of the students, introduce new skills or concepts, or change the level of difficulty, thus allowing all students to be challenged at their ability levels.

- Teachable Moments. Opportunities either during or after a lesson to emphasize a specific skill or concept related to what has occurred in the learning experience.

The final sections of chapters 3 through 7 contain additional ideas for developing learning experiences. These brief descriptions offer ways in which you can use movement to integrate the skills and concepts being taught. The sample learning experiences are intended to give you a starting point for developing your own complete learning experience. Because teachers and schools differ in background, levels of expertise, equipment, and facilities, this section provides a broad range of ideas.

Now it's your turn. Take the ideas and run. Good luck!

Fundamentals of Interdisciplinary Programs

Ring the bells that still can ring.
Forget your perfect offering.
There is a crack in everything.
That's how the light gets in.
—Leonard Cohen

Part I comprises two chapters that offer the rationale and theoretical perspectives underpinning the use of human movement to teach subject area skills, topics, and concepts. Interdisciplinary programs may be used to supplement, support, or enhance the teaching of basic skills and concepts taught in an elementary school's physical education program. They can also stand on their own as a viable curricular approach to cross-disciplinary learning in which human movement interweaves with other subjects to demonstrate how knowledge is interrelated among school subjects.

Chapter 1, "Introduction to Interdisciplinary Learning," defines the theoretical aspects of interdisciplinary programs and explores the advantages and disadvantages of interdisciplinary learning. An historical perspective on interdisciplinary programs in physical education is followed by a presentation of the national standards for physical education, dance, and teacher preparation. An overview of the interdisciplinary teaching model continuum identifies a variety of models that follow an integrative approach. The chapter concludes with detailed descriptions of three selected interdisciplinary teaching models developed by the authors: connected, shared, and partnership.

Chapter 2, "Successful Interdisciplinary Teaching," addresses the more concrete or practical aspects of successful interdisciplinary teaching. The chapter describes the process for reviewing information, selecting the interdisciplinary teaching model, developing lesson plans, and addressing the logistics of implementation. A section on assessment of interdisciplinary learning using alternative strategies is included, with three examples of assessment instruments. The chapter closes with a vital section on developing a successful support network of administrators, parents, students, and colleagues.

CHAPTER

Introduction to Interdisciplinary Learning

This chapter provides an introduction to interdisciplinary learning and outlines a framework and theoretical background for integrating subject areas in a school's curriculum. The purpose of this chapter is not only to give you information on interdisciplinary learning but also to motivate you to try this exciting approach to teaching and learning. The chapter includes the advantages and disadvantages of interdisciplinary learning, a historical perspective of interdisciplinary learning efforts in physical education, and the impact of school reform on interdisciplinary learning initiatives. We have also included three selected interdisciplinary teaching models that range from simple to complex and describe several approaches for integrating the skills or knowledge of two or more subject areas.

What Is Interdisciplinary Learning?

Interdisciplinary learning is an educational process in which two or more subject areas are integrated with the goal of fostering enhanced learning in each subject area. Implementing an interdisciplinary learning program brings teachers together to create exciting learning experiences for students and to discover new ways of delivering the curriculum. The concept of interdisciplinary learning acknowledges the integrity and uniqueness of each subject area, yet recognizes the interrelationships among subjects.

Interdisciplinary learning in education is not new. There are numerous examples that illustrate teachers' efforts to integrate a variety of subjects such as the language arts with mathematics, the visual arts with social studies, mathematics with science, or music with physical education. A vivid example of teaching across subject areas is given by Whitin and Wilde's (1992) *Read Any Good Math Lately?* The book highlights children's books that focus on selected mathematical concepts in an integrated way. Heidi Hayes Jacobs, author of *Interdisciplinary Curriculum: Design and Implementation* (1989), says that "there is no longer as much discussion among educators about whether to blend the subject areas, as about when, to what degree, and how best to do it" (Association for Supervision and Curriculum Development, 1994, pp. 1-2). Integration of the curriculum emerged from what educators knew about learning, child development, and how school prepares a child to be a productive member of the community. Children's interest in their environment is not subject specific; it crosses many disciplines.

Interdisciplinary learning is nourished by the content offered in multiple subject areas. The specific content of each subject is composed of skills and knowledge that constitute what is integrated. Skills are the abilities or techniques a student learns and uses to perform a movement or demonstrate a concept or idea, such as throwing, measuring, and drawing. And knowledge is defined as concepts, principles, theories, beliefs, or topics inherent to each subject area. There is no one model that describes all the ways interdisciplinary learning can be delivered. The College Board's (1996) newsletter presented excerpts from Elliot Eisner's 1996 keynote speech at the University of Oklahoma. Eisner tells us that the curriculum can be structured using an idea as a focal point; a central theme can be the focus of several disciplines that each examine that theme. He also describes another approach, which is to develop problems that need more than one disciplinary frame of reference to be solved. You may also find that implementing an interdisciplinary learning experience requires rearranging the order of your teaching to coincide with a concept being taught in another subject area. The opportunities are endless, and interdisciplinary learning serves as a continual source of energy feeding the educational process.

Advantages of Interdisciplinary Learning

Interdisciplinary learning experiences enhance and enrich what students learn. Proponents of interdisciplinary programming believe that children learn best when using this approach. Wasley (1994), a senior researcher with the Coalition of Essential Schools and author of *Stirring the Chalk Dust: Tales of Teachers Changing Classroom Practice,* makes a strong argument for interdisciplinary programming by addressing the issue of relevance. She observes that by breaking through disciplinary boundaries, teachers can make the curriculum more relevant because they can embed knowledge and skills in real-life contexts. An interdisciplinary approach mirrors daily life, in which we are constantly called on to cross disciplines. As a result, this approach to learning is more readily embraced by students, and they are excited about learning. One of the most often cited works is Gardner's (1983) *Frames of Mind: The Theory of Multiple Intelligences*. Gardner provides convincing evidence that humans possess multiple intelligences: linguistic, musical, logical-mathematical, spatial, tactile-kinesthetic, intrapersonal, and interpersonal intelligence. He contends that children deserve to have all seven intelligences nourished so they may function at their full potential. He also notes that each person has different strengths in each of the intelligences and those strengths affect their learning mode. When the multiple intelligences are used to teach a skill or concept, it naturally becomes an interdisciplinary learning experience.

According to Piaget (1969), young children are in a preoperational stage of learning operations and gradually move into a concrete stage. This means that children profit from concrete, practical, active learning experiences that bridge the gap between abstract concepts and the hands-on real world. Through exploration and play, children learn about their world. Further, Tarnowski (quoted by Wilcox, 1994) tells us that the "interdisciplinary nature" of children's own play should become our model for planning and teaching.

Interdisciplinary learning speaks to children with different learning styles and often combines the modalities of seeing (visual), hearing (auditory), and doing (tactile-kinesthetic) allowing children the opportunity to use their strengths to learn what they are taught. Children make sense of the world through expressing their thinking in a variety of ways. "For the young child, movement is the first and foremost vehicle through which a child is able to communicate their feelings about themselves and their world to others." (Fraser, 1991) Movement as a language is a natural and powerful way to express ideas and demonstrate understanding. A child's ability to be proficient at using movement as a means of communication and learning is directly related to the range of movement experiences he or she encounters. It is through the physical education program, as part of an interdisciplinary approach to learning, that students gain the essential kinesthetic learning experiences that will enhance their ability to learn both movement and other subject areas through movement.

Additional support (Bucek, 1992; Gilbert, 1992; Friedlander, 1992; Gallahue, 1993; Connor-Kuntz and Dummer, 1996) for interdisciplinary programs emphasizing a movement orientation includes the following:

1. Using movement promotes active involvement in learning (versus passive learning) that leads to increased understanding.
2. For young children, movement is a natural medium for learning. As children learn fundamental concepts such as height, distance, time, weight, size, position, and shape, movement gives meaning to an abstract system of language symbols.
3. Movement stimulates development of the motor and neurological systems.
4. Movement can be experienced as a means of expression and communication.
5. Movement activities motivate children and capture their interest.

Teachers, like students, benefit from interdisciplinary learning because it builds understanding of other subject areas and fosters appreciation of the knowledge and expertise of other staff members. It facilitates teamwork and planning as teachers work together to weave a theme across several subject areas. In addition, students benefit when they see teachers working in different subject areas, teaching in different classroom space, and making similar points across subject areas. Their learning is reinforced in a powerful and meaningful way. As a result of participating in and observing a variety of interdisciplinary activities in the school, students begin to realize how the skills and knowledge in one subject area can transfer into another and ultimately be applied to life experiences.

Disadvantages of Interdisciplinary Learning

Despite all the interest in interdisciplinary programming, some educators and parents raise concerns or cautions. The concern most often voiced is that moving from a discipline-based curriculum to one using interdisciplinary learning will cause important content to fall by the wayside. Teachers, especially at the upper grade levels, fear that the "purity" of their subject areas and the logical scope and sequence will be lost in integrated units. They may be reluctant to change content priorities and unwilling to adapt content to be taught in a new way. The concern over losing important content in one's own subject area is very real. Jacobs (1989) emphasizes that teachers should integrate disciplines only when doing so allows them to teach important content more effectively. By providing a context in which students can see relationships among information and skills learned across subject areas, interdisciplinary teaching can improve students' retention.

Another common concern is that one subject area will be allowed to greatly overshadow another when pursuing integrated work. Trade-offs are inevitable and inherent in any inter-disciplinary learning endeavor. Along with difficult decisions about what to integrate, teachers' concerns include planning time for their own interdisciplinary efforts and arranging a common planning time with other teachers. Collaboration involves dealing with inter-personal issues that require blending different teaching styles, agreeing on a theme topic or activity, dividing the work to prepare materials, and committing resources of time and energy. Flexibility and compromise are essential for successful implementation, which means trust and teamwork need to be developed or must already exist. Teachers may be concerned that they do not possess adequate knowledge in another subject area and will not be able to find ways to interrelate concepts and skills. There are few assessment technique models for teachers to follow that specifically address interdisciplinary learning. In addition, school districts may not offer opportunities for professional development in interdisciplinary teaching and learning and can present barriers that limit attendance at conferences and workshops outside the school district. Inadequate professional development will result in poor preparation, unclear objectives, and superficial activities that students may find confusing. The students' enthusiasm and motivation drops off, teachers become frustrated, and administrators withdraw support of future efforts. Even after thorough planning of an exciting interdisciplinary lesson or unit, a teacher can encounter logistical barriers involving restructuring schedules, finding an adequate space to conduct activities, organizing materials, and securing the use of audio and visual equipment, computers, and other technical support.

The time and effort needed to create a quality learning experience for children requires a commitment and a willingness to take a risk. Not all experiences will enjoy immediate success; however, this should not be a reason for abandoning the attempt at integrating the curriculum. Take the time to reflect on your efforts and make the necessary changes to increase the opportunity for a successful learning experience.

Historical Perspectives on Interdisciplinary Programming in Physical Education

In 1929 Horrigan wrote that teachers of physical education were facing a new problem in the elementary schools. Units of work developed in the classroom used all subjects as far as possible to broaden the child's learning experiences. If physical education were to maintain a significant place in the total education pattern, it too would have to make a definite contribution to teaching units.

Since that initial call for teachers to integrate subject matter across subject areas, there have been several cycles in which this type of work has received attention in physical education. In the mid- to late 1960s Humphrey's *Child Learning* (1965) and Miller and Whitcomb's *Physical Education in the Elementary School Curriculum* (1969) focused on an integrated approach to a total school curriculum by illustrating applications of physical education in language arts, mathematics, science, social studies, art, and music. In the early 1970s Cratty's *Intelligence in Action* (1973) and *Active Learning* (1971) focused on a more generic approach to interdisciplinary learning by including games and physical education activities to enhance academic abilities. By the late 1970s Gilbert's *Teaching the Three Rs Through Movement Experiences* (1977) and Werner and Burton's *Learning Through Movement* (1979) encouraged teachers to pursue a more conceptual approach to interdisciplinary learning by providing examples of movement experiences based on problem solving and guided discovery.

The 1980s were a decade of back-to-basics and discipline-based education with the focus on defining the specific content to be learned in a particular discipline, not on integrating subject areas. Led by the Getty Foundation, work in the visual arts emphasized four areas from which the content of discipline-based art education is drawn (Eisner, 1988). These four content areas are art making, art criticism, art history, and aesthetics. In physical education the content is learning about how the body moves using locomotor, nonlocomotor, and manipulative skills in combination with movement concepts related to space, effort, and relationships. Another way to view the content of physical education is by categorizing it under the broad areas of games, dance, gymnastics, and health-related fitness. In essence, the 1980s served to identify the content of what physical educators teach and reaffirmed physical education's place in the curriculum as a disciplinary subject based on an identified body of knowledge.

As we move through the 1990s and toward the 21st century, there seems to be a resurgence of interest in interdisciplinary teaching. Robin Fogarty, author of *The Mindful School* (1991a), calls interdisciplinary teaching "a wave that is gaining momentum in the United States, Canada and Australia" (Association for Supervision and Curriculum Development, 1994, pp. 1-2). She goes on to say that it is a trend, not a fad. Leading educational organizations such as the Association for Supervision and Curriculum Development (ASCD), the National Dance Association (NDA), the National Association for the Education of Young Children (NAEYC), and the National Association for Sport and Physical Education (NASPE) support the idea of interdisciplinary teaching. As an example, the documents on developmentally appropriate practices of both NAEYC (Bredekamp, 1987) and NASPE (1992a, 1994) support interdisciplinary learning with specialists working with classroom teachers to deliver an integrated curriculum. In addition, NASPE's (1995b) *Standards for Beginning Physical Education Teachers* and NDA's (1994) *National Standards for Dance Education: What Every Young American Should Know and Be Able to Do in Dance* re-

quire that teachers have content knowledge that allows them to incorporate concepts and strategies into other subject areas.

The popularity of interdisciplinary programming in physical education has been evidenced in leading journal articles for physical education teachers and on national convention programs. For example, the topic of an integrated curriculum was a special feature of the December 1994 issue of *Teaching Elementary Physical Education*. In that issue, in addition to providing several examples of interdisciplinary activities, Stevens (1994) called for the collaboration of physical education and classroom teachers. She goes on to say that if "two disciplines can find a way to work together both areas can be reinforced by helping students learn academic concepts from a movement perspective." Werner (1994b) wrote about the concepts of whole physical education in the preschool feature of the *Journal of Physical Education, Recreation and Dance*. Several articles on dance education (Bucek, 1992; Friedlander, 1992; Gilbert, 1992) show how an interdisciplinary approach to dance can enrich the experiences of children. A national newsletter for preschool teachers called *Kids on the Move* (Pica, 1995) often illustrates movement concepts with other subject areas. Clements and Osteen (1995) also emphasize interdisciplinary work with preschool children through the use of movement narratives that draw heavily on integrated themes. At the 1995 United States Physical Education Conference in Orlando, three programs featured interdisciplinary work. The National Conference on Early Childhood Movement Experiences sponsored by the Council on Physical Education for Children in Washington, DC, in May 1995 sponsored a whole section of six programs devoted to interdisciplinary programming. Programs at regional (Cone and Cone, 1998) and national conventions (Purcell and Werner, 1996) and articles in national journals continue to reflect an emphasis on interdisciplinary learning as we move toward the 21st century.

Curricular Frameworks for the 21st Century

As we near the beginning of the 21st century, parents, educators, business leaders, and politicians have been examining the educational system in America. They have asked questions such as "Will our children be ready to meet the demands of the 21st century?" and "What do our children need to know and be able to do to prepare for the future?" As a result, educational reform has received support from the highest levels of government. The nation's president and governors met at an education summit and established goals for the nation. From this effort has emerged a movement to establish nationwide education standards.

The development of national standards does not establish a national curriculum or a predetermined course of study nor does it dictate specific teaching methodologies. Rather, the standards offer a road map for competence and educational effectiveness that focuses on student learning results. The expectation is that students in every school should be able to reach these standards with adequate support and sustained effort. With the passage of the Goals 2000: Educate America Act in March 1994, educational standards were written into law.

Using the Goals 2000: Educate America Act as an impetus, national and state associations in each of the subject areas have established standards with accompanying benchmarks that indicate what children should be able to know and do at selected grade levels. Key concepts in each of these curriculum frameworks include support for interdisciplinary learning in which teachers work together to deliver an integrated curriculum. For example, the *National Standards for Arts Education* (Consortium of National Arts Education Associations, 1994) contains specific content standards that focus on making connections between the arts and other disciplines. The *National Standards for the English Language Arts* (National Council of Teachers of English and International Reading Association, 1996) described that the language arts are interdisciplinary in nature and that they provide students with the means to access and process information and understanding from all other disciplines.

National Physical Education Standards

Just as standards and curriculum frameworks have been developed at national, state, and local levels for language arts, mathematics, science, the arts, and social studies, so too have they been developed for physical education and

dance. The National Association for Sport and Physical Education (1992b) published *The Physically Educated Person,* containing a section "Outcomes of Quality Physical Education Programs" in response to needs expressed by NASPE members, other educators, and concerned citizens for a national platform on which to base judgments of quality about physical education programs. Outcomes with appropriate benchmarks at grades K, 2, 4, 6, 8, 10, and 12 indicate the ways in which students should be transformed by school programs by providing guidance for *what* students are able to learn as well as *when* it is reasonable to expect that they have learned it.

Following the publication of the physical education outcomes document, a Standards and Assessment Task Force was appointed by NASPE to develop national content standards and assessment material. *Moving into the Future: National Standards for Physical Education* (NASPE, 1995a) established seven content standards (table 1.1) with accompanying sample benchmarks for each standard at the grade levels previously noted. Assessment guidelines were also designed to expand and complement, not replace, the original physical education outcomes document. While none of the national physical education standards directly address the concept of interdisciplinary programming, there is ample indirect support. For example, the application of movement concepts and principles to the learning and development of motor skills supports the many scientific principles that have application in physical education. Learning to understand and respect differences among people provides support for learning across gender, racial, cultural, and other differences such as religion.

National Dance Standards

Dance education is an integral part of a comprehensive physical education curriculum, yet it also appears in education as a component of an arts education curriculum. It can exist in both places. However, it should always be taught primarily as a means of expression and communication through creating dances, learning to perform dances, and responding to one's own dancing or the dancing of others. In this book, dance education has been included as a content area in the physical education curriculum. All students should have the opportunity

Table 1.1

CONTENT STANDARDS IN PHYSICAL EDUCATION

A physically educated person

1. demonstrates competency in many movement forms and proficiency in a few movement forms.

2. applies movement concepts and principles to the learning and development of motor skills.

3. exhibits a physically active lifestyle.

4. achieves and maintains a health-enhancing level of physical fitness.

5. demonstrates responsible personal and social behavior in physical activity settings.

6. demonstrates understanding and respect for differences among people in physical activity settings.

7. understands that physical activity provides opportunities for enjoyment, challenge, self-expression, and social interaction.

to participate in learning experiences that focus solely on the skills and concepts intrinsic to dance education and in interdisciplinary learning experiences linking dance education to another subject area. Many dance education skills and concepts naturally correlate with music, visual arts, theater arts, and language arts and can easily be tied to mathematics, science, and social studies.

In 1994 the National Dance Association, in conjunction with the American Alliance for Theater and Education, the Music Educators National Conference, and National Art Education published a set of national standards for arts education (Consortium of National Arts Education Associations, 1994) describing what students should know and be able to do in the arts. Specifically, the dance education standards (table 1.2) are a guide for developing meaningful learning experiences in dance education and for suggesting levels of achievement for grades 4, 8, and 12, much like the presen-

tation of physical education content in the NASPE (1995a) document. The dance education standards address the movement concepts and skills that are universal to teaching all types of dance forms, such as creative dance, folk dance, and social dance. They also describe the basic choreographic principles, processes, and structures appropriate for elementary students and emphasize using critical and creative thinking skills when learning to perform and respond to dances. A strong interdisciplinary focus that speaks to performing and understanding dance as a part of history and culture, maintaining a healthy lifestyle, and making direct connections between dance and other disciplines is evident in several of the standards. We suggest that using the dance education standards will help you develop specific objectives, activities, and assessments not only for learning experiences in dance education but also for interdisciplinary efforts with other colleagues.

Table 1.2

CONTENT STANDARDS IN DANCE EDUCATION

1. Identifying and demonstrating movement elements and skills in performing dance

2. Understanding choreographic principles, processes, and structures

3. Understanding dance as a way to create and communicate meaning

4. Applying and demonstrating critical and creative skills in dance

5. Demonstrating and understanding dance in various cultures and historical periods

6. Making connections between dance and healthful living

7. Making connections between dance and other disciplines

National Teacher Preparation Standards

As national standards have been developed for our nation's schools, organizations such as the National Council for the Accreditation of Teacher Education (NCATE) have been developing new standards for the preparation of teachers. In cooperation with NCATE, the Teacher Education Task Force appointed by NASPE has created beginning physical education teacher standards (NASPE, 1995b). Among the 10 standards, which outline a comprehensive teacher education model, are principles that focus on content knowledge, pedagogical knowledge, teaching and learning styles, and collaboration. Within the principles of content knowledge is a requirement that teachers understand how to relate physical education content with other subject areas. Instruction for diverse populations of learners will require teachers who are well versed in strategies that include direct instruction, problem solving, discovery learning, cooperative learning, independent study, and interdisciplinary instruction. Collaboration fosters teachers' relationships with colleagues, parents, and community agencies to support learner growth and well-being and calls for teachers who value learning about all aspects of a learner's experience, including other subject matter areas. From this document it is clear that the teacher of the future will have to be well versed in interdisciplinary programming.

The Continuum of Interdisciplinary Teaching Models

Over the last decade, experts in curriculum design have identified a variety of models that follow an integrative approach. A model provides a guide or a framework. Teachers can organize their ideas following a particular model to give them an idea about how involved a particular lesson or unit might become with respect to interdisciplinary work. Nielsen (1989) provided a hierarchical concept continuum that flows from simple or more concrete concepts such as climate and animals to highly abstract concepts such as change, patterns, and variation. The author held that a conceptually

based approach to curriculum development and implementation would better help young students to integrate information and develop a set of clearly defined links between themes, topics, and subject areas. Fogarty (1991b) provided an even more complex model with 10 variations along a continuum. Variations begin with an exploration within individual subject areas (fragmented, connected, and nested models) and continue with models that integrate several subject areas (sequenced, shared, webbed, threaded, and integrated models). The continuum ends with models that operate within learners themselves (immersed model) and across networks of learners (networked model). Fogarty's hope for these models was to provide teachers with a solid foundation for designing curricula that help their students make valuable connections while learning.

You will in all likelihood discover, adapt, or create various models during your interdisciplinary journey. You may already be familiar with the intradisciplinary concept of merging content within one subject area. In this approach, you make links within a subject area, tying one skill to a related skill or linking one concept to another (see figure 1.1). Fogarty states that the effort is to deliberately relate curricula within the subject area rather than assuming that students will understand the connections automatically. "Connecting ideas within a subject area permits the learner to review, reconceptualize, edit and assimilate ideas gradually and may facilitate transfer" (Fogarty, 1991a, p. 15). Fogarty also notes that the intradisciplinary approach is useful as a beginning step toward an integrated curriculum. Teachers feel confident looking for connections within their own subject area; as they become adept at relating ideas within the subject area, it becomes easier to scout for connections across subject areas.

Three Selected Interdisciplinary Teaching Models

Although each of Fogarty's models is helpful, the multiplicity of choices is somewhat overwhelming. We have experimented with a variety of approaches to interdisciplinary teaching and have developed three models that func-

Subject area	Skill or concept	Link
Physical education	Ready position	Volleyball, dance, tennis, basketball
Science	Life cycles	Plants, animals, humans
Language arts	Story structure	Reading or writing, fiction or nonfiction

Figure 1.1 Intradisciplinary links.

tion on a continuum from simple to complex (see figure 1.2).

The three interdisciplinary teaching models—connected, shared, and partnership—provide approaches for integrating the skills and concepts of two or more subject areas. These models will help you clarify your intent and objectives for using interdisciplinary teaching. They are not meant to be finite models that serve every type of interdisciplinary teaching experience, but rather guides to integration with meaning and purpose. You may develop interdisciplinary learning experiences that do not fit neatly into one of the three models, and you may need to overlap or adapt the models to meet your particular situation.

The connected model uses a simple approach in which content from one subject area is used to augment or supplement the learning experience in another subject area. For example, you are teaching folk dances from Mexico in a physical education lesson, and you use a map

to show where the country is located as a means of connecting it with social studies. The shared model emphasizes the linkage of similar topics, concepts, or skills from two or more subject areas taught collaboratively with another teacher. To continue the folk dance example using a shared model, the concept of Mexican cultural traditions would be taught concurrently in the physical education and social studies lessons. The folk dances emphasize the cultural traditions and the social studies lesson focuses on how traditions are part of holidays. The even more ambitious partnership model provides a strategy for complex unification of content from two or more subject areas. To carry the example further, both teachers plan and team-teach a unit on Mexico including lessons on the folk dances, cultural traditions, games, music, visual art, and foods.

Another way of viewing interdisciplinary teaching and a vivid description of the continuum of these models is using the image of

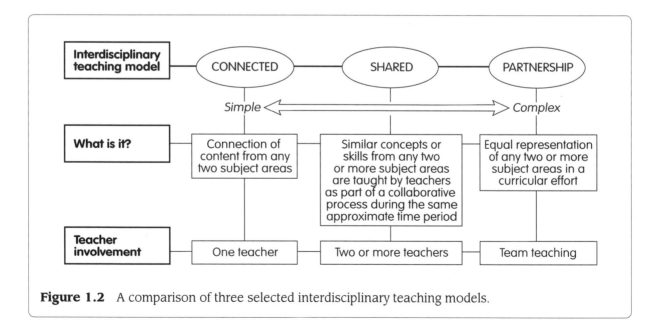

Figure 1.2 A comparison of three selected interdisciplinary teaching models.

"fruit cocktail." The connected model demonstrates the rudimentary form of fruit cocktail in which each fruit retains its individual identity. In the partnership model you experience an integration more like "fruitcake" than fruit cocktail. The disciplines persist in recognizable chunks that make sense, but they are imbedded in a pervasive and unifying batter in which raw materials are unrecognizably transformed. Each of the models is designed to give the teacher the structure needed to link one subject area to another. In your planning process, select a model or models that offer the most appropriate means to achieve the goals you identify for the learning experience.

The Connected Model

In the connected model (figure 1.3) the skills, topics, and concepts of the physical education curriculum are the primary focus of the learning experience, and the content from another subject area is used to enhance, extend, or complement the learning experience. This model, commonly used by teachers because they are comfortable with it allows them to independently plan, schedule, and choose the subject area content for the connection. They can schedule the lesson at a time when it fits into the learning sequence they have planned for the year; choose the subject area and specific skills, topics, and concepts they want to use; and do the planning on their own time.

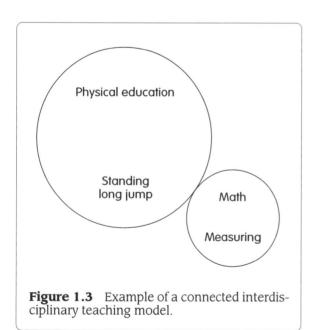

Figure 1.3 Example of a connected interdisciplinary teaching model.

However, they may want to consult with a colleague about resources and accuracy of information.

This model can be used in these ways:

• When you introduce a new skill, topic, or concept, you can use the content from one subject to further explain or illustrate the skill, topic, or concept you are teaching. For example, when introducing the proper technique for a jump, you can use the scientific principle of how a spring works to illustrate the jumping action. You use imagery when you use the notion of a moving spring to make a point about jumping. You cross the bridge from imagery to interdisciplinary teaching when you present the scientific principle of how a spring works as covered in the science curriculum.

• You can use the connected model to stimulate interest in a lesson and demonstrate how the content you are teaching is relevant to the student. For example, at the beginning of a rope-jumping unit, the class reads a poem that expresses the frustrations and joys experienced when learning to jump rope. The teacher makes a connection between the language arts and physical education subject areas through use of the poem.

• You can use the connected model to enhance a lesson by applying a skill from another subject area. For example, students have just learned the techniques used in a standing long jump. They then use the math skill of measuring to see how far they jump.

• The content of a physical education lesson can be used to supplement or reinforce skills, topics, and concepts used in other subject areas. A gymnastics lesson can be connected to a writing lesson when students write sentences using words emphasized in the gymnastics lesson, such as tripod, cartwheel, or straddle.

The Shared Model

A shared model is when two subjects are integrated through a similar skill, topic, or concept that is part of the content for both subject areas (see figure 1.4). The model requires agreement between the teachers on the skill, topic, or concept and on the timeline for teaching. The timeline can result in simultaneous presentations in the respective classrooms, or one subject area may precede the other by a short time

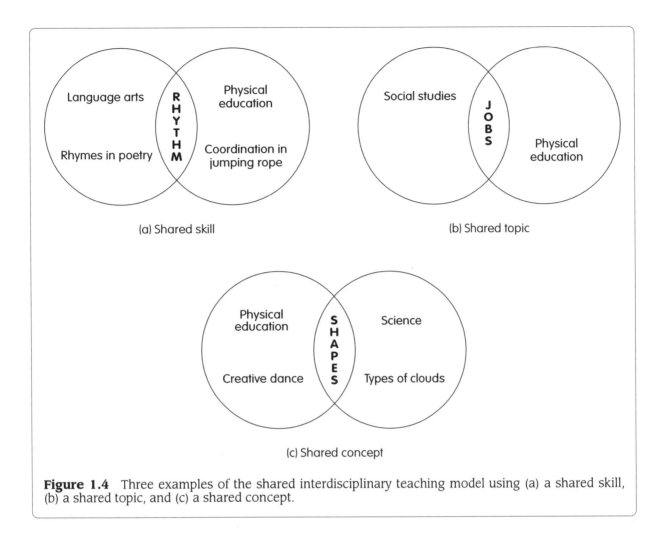

Figure 1.4 Three examples of the shared interdisciplinary teaching model using (a) a shared skill, (b) a shared topic, and (c) a shared concept.

in teaching the common skill, topic, or concept. The shared model may require the teachers to adjust their sequence of teaching to include the new "shared" content. The integration helps students understand how skills, topics, or concepts can cut across subject areas. The students' learning is reinforced in a meaningful way as they view teachers presenting similar ideas in different classrooms on a parallel timeline.

This model can be used in these ways:

• To help teachers take the first step in collaborating with another teacher. The teachers discuss the content they plan to teach during the year and identify common skills, topics, or concepts. Once the content has been identified, they align the sequence of teaching to deliver the common lesson or unit at a similar time. For example, in a social studies unit, students are learning about how communities work together, and the students develop a homework hot line to help other students in the school. At the same time in the physical education class, students are learning about teamwork and participate in team-building activities. The subjects share the concept of how people work together to help one another complete a task.

• To reinforce a selected theme. Several teachers may choose a broad theme for a grade level or as a schoolwide project. Teachers in all subject areas find a way to teach different aspects of the theme (see figure 1.5). However, a theme may not be equally important across all subject areas. As an example, you might use the theme of change. In science, students study the changing seasons; the visual art lessons focus on how changing your perspective while viewing a sculpture changes what you see; the language arts emphasize the process of changing a piece of writing to fit different audiences; and in physical education, change will be addressed through studying how the sport of basketball has changed over the last 100 years.

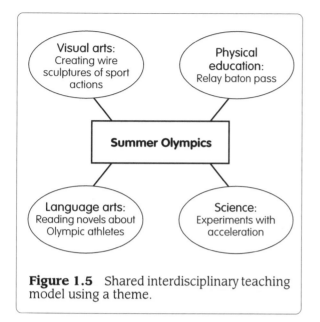

Figure 1.5 Shared interdisciplinary teaching model using a theme.

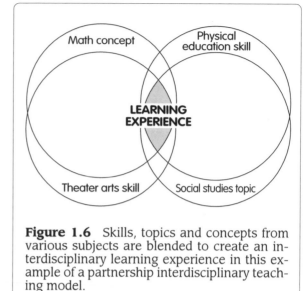

Figure 1.6 Skills, topics and concepts from various subjects are blended to create an interdisciplinary learning experience in this example of a partnership interdisciplinary teaching model.

• To select a skill, topic, or concept from one subject area to share in both subject areas. For example, in figure 1.4*b*, the shared topic is *jobs,* which is taught in the social studies curriculum but is not typically part of the physical education curriculum. This use of a shared interdisciplinary teaching model extends the physical education curriculum by adding a new area of content.

The Partnership Model

A partnership model is defined by the equal representation of two or more subject areas in a curricular effort. The skills, topics, and concepts of two or more subject areas are blended together so that learning takes place simultaneously in all subject areas. Teaching is collaborative and is often accomplished through a team-teaching model. The teachers teach together at the same time in the same classroom, collaborating to deliver an agreed-on content within the curricular areas. This model takes considerable planning, a willingness to seek common areas of agreement, the identification of a time block for teaching in this manner, and a significant effort to identify links between specific curricular areas. It often leads to uncharted territory, challenging teachers to view their curriculum from a new and different perspective. The result is a curriculum in which students will gain a better understanding of the interconnectedness of all subject areas (see figure 1.6).

This model can be used in these ways:

• To demonstrate the value of understanding the relationship between two or more subject areas that would have otherwise been taught as discrete subject areas. Students have an opportunity to apply their knowledge in a different context, thus demonstrating their complete understanding of what they have learned. The application of the mathematical concept of fractions infused with the teaching of the correct mechanics for badminton strokes is one example. A teacher could describe the backswing of the stroke as a fraction of a circle or assess the number of successful serves using fractions. Before the learning experience, both teachers share their content with each other and together create a new way to teach the targeted content.

• To give teachers the opportunity to restructure or refocus curriculum to provide students with the chance to learn through a new lens. For example, when teaching patterns, the physical education and music teachers create a joint learning experience to enhance the children's understanding of patterns. The teachers select the ABA structure or ternary form as the focus of the experience. The students create movement sequences, such as twist, stretch, twist, and compose music in the ABA form to accompany their movement sequence (see figure 1.7).

• To facilitate an integrated event. This type of event usually involves total immersion by

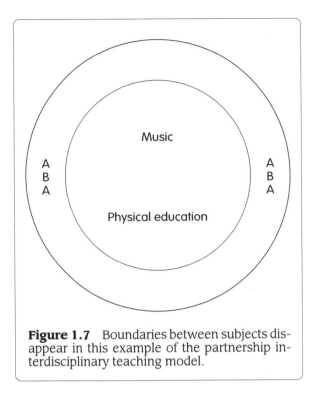

Figure 1.7 Boundaries between subjects disappear in this example of the partnership interdisciplinary teaching model.

all faculty, students, and staff of the school. For example, the school decides to celebrate a particular event and focuses all activities around a theme. The entire school community participates through activities, food, costumes, and customs associated with the event and coordinates learning experiences representing various subject areas. Faculty and staff work with many different students in a variety of activities.

Summary

Interdisciplinary learning is an educational process in which two or more subject areas are integrated with the goal of fostering enhanced learning in each subject area. It adds new meaning and perspectives to the content and reflects how knowledge and skills are used in daily life. Interdisciplinary learning experi-

ences enhance and enrich what students learn and provide an opportunity to reach children with different learning styles. Studies have shown that interdisciplinary programs that emphasize movement bridge the gap between abstract concepts and the hands-on, real world. The primary concern about interdisciplinary learning is the fear that as you move away from a discipline-based curriculum, you will lose important content. The time commitment needed to complete the collaborative process can be discouraging, and issues such as teaching style or restructuring schedules must be addressed.

Interdisciplinary efforts in physical education have evolved as the discipline has defined and redefined its content and its place in the educational enterprise. As the 21st century approaches, the concept of interdisciplinary learning has increasingly taken a place in the redesign and reform of curriculum at the state and national levels. National standards documents in physical education, dance, and teacher preparation describe what students and teachers should know and be able to do in a comprehensive physical education program. These documents serve as the future framework for curricular design and assessment.

A variety of models that follow an integrative approach have been proposed over time; no one model describes all the ways that interdisciplinary learning can be delivered. These models begin with a relatively simple intradisciplinary approach and move to progressively more complex models of interdisciplinary teaching. Three selected interdisciplinary teaching models—connected, shared, and partnership—are introduced, defined, and illustrated with examples of practical applications. The selection and application of a model should be based on the desired goals for the learning experience and the level of commitment agreed on by the teachers involved. Chapter 2 introduces several strategies for implementing an interdisciplinary learning experience.

2
CHAPTER

Successful
Interdisciplinary
Teaching

Successful interdisciplinary teaching requires careful thought and planning for the skills and knowledge students will learn in a lesson or unit of lessons. This approach to teaching offers an opportunity for teachers to look at the curriculum from a new perspective. As teachers develop an integrated curriculum, they must identify how integration will increase teaching effectiveness and contribute to expanding student learning.

This chapter is written to answer many of the questions you may have about beginning to teach using an interdisciplinary approach. It provides guidance on how to get started, develop ideas, and locate information. We offer strategies for selecting an interdisciplinary teaching model and outline a process that will help you take your first steps toward implementation. You will also find a section on assessment of interdisciplinary learning with practical examples using the three selected interdisciplinary models. The chapter concludes with suggestions on how to develop a successful support network to help you achieve your initial attempts and to provide the support for ongoing efforts.

Accepting the challenge of integrating content from your curriculum with another subject area is a worthwhile task. You will find new and interesting ways to teach, become personally invigorated as a learner, and experience the excitement of collaborating with colleagues. Not all lessons need to be integrated with other subjects; however, you should always recognize the association between what is being taught, how it fits into the broader curricular picture, and how it applies to life experiences.

Getting Started

You will have many questions as you begin your new initiative. Some questions will have fairly easy answers, while others will be answered as you become more engaged in the planning process. Ultimately, these answers will give you the information needed to develop a meaningful lesson or unit. Begin by asking yourself these questions:

- What subjects do I want to integrate?
- Where do I find information to use?
- Whom will I work with?
- What is the best way to create a learning experience?
- What will students learn in each of the subject areas, and how can the learning be assessed?
- How does integrating subjects meet the national standards for each subject area?

Creating an interdisciplinary learning experience can be accomplished on your own using the connected model, or through a collaborative effort, as described in the shared and partnership models. Table 2.1 describes a set of strategies you can use as a guide for developing an interdisciplinary learning experience.

Review Curriculum Guides

A good source of information is the curriculum guides adopted by your school district. These curriculum guides describe the content of various subjects, the scope, the recommended grade level, and the sequence in which the content

Table 2.1

STRATEGIES FOR DEVELOPING AN INTERDISCIPLINARY LEARNING EXPERIENCE
Review curricular guides and scope and sequences
Select content (themes, topics, issues)
Gather content information
Decide on the interdisciplinary teaching model(s)
Create lesson plans, include specific activities
Determine scheduling, materials, equipment, organization, facilities
Decide how to assess student learning

should be taught. Table 2.2 presents a sample scope and sequence of physical education movement concepts and skills taught in elementary schools. Chapters 3 through 7 present scope and sequence summaries for language arts, mathematics, science, social studies, music, theater arts, and visual arts. Reviewing curricular guides lets you see what will be taught during the school year. This process will help you select the skills, content areas, or units of study that will link your program to another in the school.

Table 2.2

SCOPE AND SEQUENCE OF PHYSICAL EDUCATION CONCEPTS AND SKILLS TAUGHT IN ELEMENTARY SCHOOLS

Movement concept	Grade						
	K	1	2	3	4	5	6
Body awareness							
Body-part identification	x	x	x				
Shapes	x	x	x	x			
Action of the whole body and its parts	x	x	x	x			
Space awareness							
Personal space	x	x	x				
General space	x	x	x				
Levels	x	x	x	x			
Directions	x	x	x	x			
Pathways	x	x	x	x	x	x	
Extensions	x	x	x	x	x	x	x
Effort							
Time	x	x	x	x	x		
Force			x	x	x	x	x
Flow					x	x	x
Relationships							
Body parts	x	x	x	x	x	x	x
With other people			x	x	x	x	x

Movement skills	Grade						
	K	1	2	3	4	5	6
Locomotor							
Walking	x	x					
Running	x	x	x	x			
Jumping	x	x	x	x			
Hopping	x	x	x	x			
Galloping	x	x	x	x			
Skipping		x	x	x			
Leaping			x	x	x		
Sliding		x	x	x			
Rolling	x	x	x	x	x		
Nonlocomotor							
Turning	x	x	x	x			
Twisting	x	x	x	x			

(continued)

Table 2.2 *(continued)*

Movement skills	Grade						
	K	1	2	3	4	5	6
Swinging	X	X	X	X			
Stretching/bending	X	X	X	X			
Pushing/pulling	X	X	X	X	X		
Falling/rising					X	X	X
Starting/stopping	X	X	X	X			
Balancing	X	X	X	X	X	X	X
Jumping and landing	X	X	X	X	X	X	X
Transferring weight	X	X	X	X	X	X	X
Manipulative							
Throwing, underhand	X	X	X	X			
Throwing, overhand		X	X	X	X	X	X
Catching	X	X	X	X	X	X	X
Bouncing	X	X	X	X	X		
Rolling			X	X	X		
Kicking	X	X	X	X	X		
Trapping			X	X	X	X	X
Volleying			X	X	X	X	X
Striking, with racquets and paddles		X	X	X	X	X	X
Striking with long-handled implements			X	X	X	X	X
Fitness concepts							
Effects of exercise on pulse rate			X	X	X		
Strength				X	X	X	X
Flexibility				X	X	X	X
Cardiovascular endurance				X	X	X	X
Muscular endurance					X	X	X
Body composition					X	X	X
Health-related fitness tests			X	X	X	X	X

Select Content

Once you have reviewed the curriculum guides, you are ready to select the content of the interdisciplinary learning experience. Choose the knowledge and skills you want to teach, rather than falling into the trap of using activities that may, at best, result in a superficial or contrived connection. Begin with one lesson or a part of a lesson focused on a specific topic or single idea. Set reasonable objectives for the learning experience, and move to the next step of gathering content information and materials. Try to develop an awareness of natural relationships between subjects. When the ideas flow and they make sense, use them—this is a powerful way to teach. When there is no natural match, don't try to force the issue. Forcing connections makes for poor teaching of both subject areas.

Gather Content Information

It is essential to research information and gather materials before teaching an integrated learning experience. Your success is largely based on accurate information that is relevant, current, and age appropriate. You can more effectively integrate multiple subject areas when you are familiar with the concepts and skills taught in the subject areas you have chosen to integrate.

The school library is a valuable place to search for information. You may find books on a specific topic or reference books that lead to additional sources. Your colleagues will have access to additional information in files, classroom texts, or possibly in their personal collection of books, materials, or computer programs. You can also access information regarding specific subject areas, themes, or topics in a variety of sources described in table 2.3.

You can place a call for materials in a district or professional association newsletter, make an announcement at a professional meeting, or contact parents through a flyer. As you begin to ask for information, you will also have the opportunity to inform others of your plans to integrate your curriculum with other subject areas. The reward for your efforts will be increased dialogue with colleagues or interested individuals seeking opportunities to collaborate, as well as a wealth of information and materials.

Plan the Delivery

Collaboration with colleagues frequently occurs as a result of a school or district planning session or simply from informal conversations during lunch. Be proactive and let others know you are interested in working on an interdisciplinary learning experience. You should start small, select a class or group of students where you think success is possible, and keep planning and implementation manageable.

Select a Model

Chapter 1 describes three interdisciplinary teaching models that can help you decide the extent to which you will pursue an interdisciplinary learning experience. Your decision will determine the type of collaboration and amount of planning time needed to successfully implement an interdisciplinary learning experience. The connected model provides a place to begin interdisciplinary teaching. This model allows you to plan independently, select content from another subject area—one you may find personally interesting or have experience in, and integrate it at a time that fits your plans. You can also consult with another person for resources on a topic. For example, if you are teaching a dance lesson focused on changing levels, you can use the scientific concept of evaporation as an image of water rising from the earth to the sky. In preparation for teach-

Table 2.3

ACCESSING INFORMATION SOURCES

Read broadly in journals, text, or newsletters of other disciplines.

Visit a bookstore.

Use key words on an Internet search engine, such as interdisciplinary, curriculum standards, or integrated curricula.

Draw on your own experiences, e.g., travel.

Build a resource library of books, posters, or videos.

Enroll in a class for your professional growth and to increase your knowledge and awareness.

Attend a poetry reading.

Visit museums.

Observe a theater, dance, or music performance.

Visit classrooms and learning centers.

Participate in a music, art, or math lesson.

Interview students about what they are learning.

View hallway displays or exhibits.

Observe the strategies used in the classroom to teach other disciplines.

Reach out to the community to find experts, places, or sources for thematic activities.

ing this lesson, review the process of evaporation to ensure accuracy in your lesson.

As you gain confidence, you can expand the depth of content integration in your program by using the shared model or the partnership model. Take the initiative and schedule a meeting with another teacher (see figure 2.1). Review the two subject areas and the respective standards; give some thought to the area(s) of content you would like to pursue. Remember to consider your colleague's teaching approach. Again, begin small and allow your collaboration efforts to grow.

As you can see, the effort needed for success requires creativity, commitment, and flexibility on the part of each teacher. Once you have taken the initial, small step with one colleague, you may decide to pursue a more inclusive effort to increase the number of opportunities to integrate the curriculum. This can lead to a conversation with a group of teachers or participation in a thematic event involving the entire school. Working with a group calls for teamwork and an understanding of group processes. Respect the group process—learn to negotiate and be sensitive to interpersonal issues. After all, the process will involve professionals with different teaching styles, viewpoints, perspectives, and approaches to solving problems.

Create Lesson Plans and Address Logistics

You are now ready to get down to specifics. If you are working with a colleague, this is a good time to take a moment to brainstorm many activities you can use in meeting the lesson's objectives. As you design the lesson, keep in mind that the students should feel that the activities are fun and exciting and see meaningful links between the subject areas.

You will need to determine whether the activities can fit into your current schedule, whether an adjustment can take place between colleagues, or whether a change is needed schoolwide. Identify the materials and equipment you will need, and discuss the type of space you will need for a successful experience. Finally, plan how you will organize students to work (individually or in groups), how you will attend to individual needs and learning styles, and how you will ensure that everyone is actively involved.

Assessment of Interdisciplinary Learning

The integrated curriculum is dynamic, interactive, situational, and creative. There is no single model, thus there cannot be a single model for evaluating success. Assessment of interdisciplinary learning experiences requires us to move beyond the conventional approaches to assessment. Planning for assessment is an integral part of planning for instruction. Objectives, learning activities, and assessment procedures are closely interrelated and cannot be designed independently. Select those most relevant to your students' learning.

Link Assessment to Learning

Past attempts at evaluation and assessment have largely been linked to grading. Too often discrete tasks alone (such as multiple-choice or true-false paper-and-pencil tests and product scores in physical education, or a time for the 50-meter dash or distance in feet and inches for a throw) have been used for the purpose of determining a student grade. In physical education, standardized tests for assessing physical fitness, sport skills, knowledge, and psychosocial characteristics have often been used as norm- or criterion-referenced measures to compare students to national standards. From a practitioner's point of view, these types of tests tend to be impractical and often fail to measure the instructional objectives of interest to teachers (National Association for Sport and Physical Education, 1995a). These factors have contributed to inappropriate assessment practices and poor instruction in general. As a result, reform in education has refocused the goal of assessment on the enhancement of learning, rather than simply on the documentation of learning. When seen in this view, assessment becomes more formative in nature. It focuses on the process of learning. It becomes more informal, authentic, practical, and expedient.

Alternative Assessment Strategies

A number of alternative assessment strategies have emerged from the educational reform movement. They are particularly appropriate

because they emphasize outcomes-based education, integrated learning, and critical thinking skills, each of which is focal to reform in education. Examples of alternative assessment include student portfolios, projects, logs, journals, interviews, debates, observation, self-assessment, role playing, event tasks, anecdotal records, checklists, rating scales, and video analysis. Most of these types of alternative assessment techniques use defined criteria to judge student performance. Rubrics describe the range of possible student performances or responses based on a defined set of criteria. The criteria should be written by teachers before instruction begins and are shared with students as a unit of work is explained. When students are aware of the criteria for performance, they understand the quality their work should exhibit. Clearly defined criteria allow you and your students to provide meaningful feedback during instruction.

You are encouraged to develop your own assessment instruments to document student learning in an interdisciplinary lesson. Consider the following concepts when developing assessment instruments:

- The assessment instrument must be consistent with the objectives.
- Assessments must enable students to demonstrate learning.
- Assessments must be reliable and consistent over time.
- Assessments must be understood by students, parents, and administrators.

There are a wide variety of alternative assessment options; choose an assessment instrument that is most relevant.

Examples of Assessment Instruments

This section presents three examples of assessment instruments for the three interdisciplinary teaching models introduced in chapter 1. The examples include the content areas, suggested grade level, description of activity, and assessment instruments.

Physical Education and Science Using the Connected Model

Content Areas: Physical education—overhand throw for distance; science—third-class levers

Suggested Grade Level: 2-3

Description: In this learning experience the teacher has instructed the students on how to perform a mature overhand throw for distance. The instruction includes an explanation of how an overhand throw uses the principles of a third-class lever system. The science principle is included to illustrate the biomechanical operation of the arm in a throw. The student can see how a science principle is used in a practical situation. The instruction is followed by time for the students to practice the overhand throw. The teacher emphasizes the following performance criteria during instruction: side to target, step with opposite foot, elbow out and back, and follow-through.

Assessment Instruments: The teacher uses a performance checklist to score how well students use mature form when performing the overhand throw for distance. The assessment will show the teacher how many students have mastered the skill and how many need more practice and instruction.

To assess the students' understanding of the connection between the physical skill of the overhand throw and the science principle of third-class levers, the students write in their physical education journal about how an overhand throw uses the principles of a third-class lever. The teacher reads the journal entries and comments to each student about his or her description.

Physical Education and Mathematics Using the Shared Model

Content Areas: Two teachers are both teaching about the concepts of symmetry and asymmetry during the same time period. In the physical education program the concepts are taught using shapes and balances in gymnastics, and in the mathematics program they are taught in a geometry lesson focused on dividing the space of triangles, squares, and rectangles.

Suggested Grade Level: 4-6

Description: In the physical education class, partners create a gymnastics routine using three different static balances that demonstrate symmetrical and asymmetrical shapes. Together they explore making various symmetrical and asymmetrical balanced shapes with their bodies at low, medium, and high levels and then select three shapes for the routine. In the geometry lesson the mathematics teacher asks students to find different ways to symmetrically then asymmetrically divide the space of a triangle, square, and rectangle.

Assessment Instruments: The gymnastics lesson is completed using a peer assessment. Each pair of students observe another set of partners performing their gymnastics routine and score the routine based on a set of criteria and a scoring rubric that has been developed by the teacher and students at the beginning of the lesson. An example of the rubric is as follows:

Excellent: Partners include symmetrical and asymmetrical shapes in their routine. They can hold all three balances for a count of three and move smoothly from one balance to another.

Good: Partners include symmetrical and asymmetrical shapes in their routine. They hold two balances for a count of three or hesitate when moving from one balance to another.

Needs Improvement: Partners do not include both symmetrical and asymmetrical shapes in their routine or hold only one balance for a count of three.

Assessment of the geometry lesson includes each student drawing his or her solutions demonstrating how each shape can be divided into three symmetrical and three asymmetrical shapes. The scoring rubric describes the number of accurate drawings needed for each level of achievement, for example, Outstanding, 16-18 accurate drawings; Very Good, 13-15 accurate drawings; Satisfactory, 10-12 accurate drawings; Needs Extra Help, 9 or fewer accurate drawings.

After each lesson is assessed, the scores for each child from the gymnastics lesson and the geometry lesson are collated to evaluate the student's understanding of the concept of symmetry and asymmetry in different situations.

Physical Education, Language Arts, and Music Using the Partnership Model

Content Areas: The physical education teacher, the music teacher, and the language arts teacher plan and team-teach a learning experience to meet the objective that students will develop collaborative skills that contribute to successful friendships.

Suggested Grade Level: 4-6

Description: All three teachers present activities that result in the students writing poetry on the theme of collaboration in friendship and then using the poems as inspiration for creating instrumental music and dances. Collaboration is the focus for all activities during the creative process as well as when presenting the final products. The learning experience concludes with a performance that includes a choral reading of the poems, an instrumental music piece composed and played by a small group of students, and a dance performed to the music piece.

Assessment Instruments: The teachers have developed several instruments for evaluating the students' understanding of the concept of collaboration that include student self-assessment, teacher assessment, and peer assessment.

Self-Assessment: Before the learning experience, students complete a set of questions about their understanding of the meaning of collaboration and when it appears in their daily life. At the end of the learning experience, they complete a similar set of questions that asks them to describe how collaboration was used in the activities and to comment on their personal feelings about collaboration during the learning experience. The teachers review the responses with each student in a personal conference.

Teacher Assessment: The teachers identify the collaborative behaviors they want to see exhibited by the students during the creation of the music composition and the dance choreography. They develop a checklist and record which behaviors they observe and how many times they appear. Each teacher takes a turn to observe and assess a student group while the other two teachers work with the students.

Peer Assessment: Students view a videotape of the performance and write or draw a picture to describe a part of the performance where collaboration is used.

Develop a Successful Support Network

The development and success of an interdisciplinary curriculum are often determined by the support you receive from school administrators, parents, students, and colleagues. It is important to include these individuals in the early planning stages and keep them informed as the process unfolds.

Administrators

Gaining your administrator's support for interdisciplinary teaching is an important step toward achieving success. The administrator can be an advocate with the school board and parents. He or she can be an ally when you want to expand the interdisciplinary program to include more students and teachers or to continue it for extended periods of time. Your administrator will also be helpful when scheduling changes are necessary, when coordinated planning time is needed, or when materials and equipment require school funds. "Enlightened administrators will have established a school culture that supports innovation and risk taking. As you plan your curriculum, seek the participation of the administrator. He or she need not be part of the team meetings but should receive progress reports on the planning. His or her ideas for support or reallocation of resources can enhance implementation. If you feel the administrator will not support the integrated unit outright, discuss among yourselves ways of introducing him or her to your more general goals and beliefs. Copying an article on integrated curriculum to share with the administrator may start the support process. Another method is to find a colleague in another school who is active in implementing integrated curricula. Ask if that school's administrator can call your own administrator to discuss the advantages of the integrated approach" (Maurer, 1994, pp. 31-32).

Parents

Parents can play a key role in supporting interdisciplinary learning experiences. For many parents, the concept of integrating subjects may be unfamiliar and they will welcome information on the objectives and activities so they can reinforce your efforts at home. "A letter home or an attractive flyer announcing the unit would also alert them that some new activity is about to start. It is hoped that the child's enthusiasm will also reinforce your message. If there is a culminating activity at the end of the unit, such as a presentation, skit, or simulation, invite the parents" (Maurer, 1994, p. 29).

Students

Success in any interdisciplinary learning experience depends on the enthusiasm with which your students participate in the activities. Selecting and planning lessons that are interesting and relevant is certainly necessary; however, you may need to explain to your students the purpose for integrating one or more subjects and the benefits that will result from the lesson. Students may at first be skeptical and ask, "Why are we doing math in physical education?" You can help them make the transfer of skills and knowledge from one subject to another through planning meaningful activities that invite inquiry, challenge, and ultimately success for the student.

Colleagues

Once you have completed an initial collaborative effort with a colleague, look for ways to maintain the relationship that lead to additional opportunities for integration. Here are ways you can develop collaborative efforts with colleagues:

• Pursue long-term goals for a project by planning in collaboration with other teachers. As the units are designed you can plan yours to complement, lead into, or follow the unit in the classroom.

• Initiate brief exchanges about what area the students are studying. When a teacher drops off a class for physical education, ask what books they are reading or what they are currently studying in science.

• Provide colleagues with information about what you are currently teaching. They may be able to use the topic in a writing lesson or as the focus in a mathematical problem-solving situation or use the words you have emphasized in your class as spelling words.

• Attend curriculum meetings in other content areas to stay current with content and practices. These meetings may take place in your school or may be held on a district-wide basis.

• Attend grade-level meetings to gain an understanding of specific issues and program direction.

• Invite other teachers to observe a part of your class to see how you have integrated an idea. Ask them for additional suggestions or assistance. Teachers will be pleased to see you have an interest in their discipline or grade level.

- Invite teachers to participate in the physical education class. Even if it is not feasible for them to attend the entire class, they will appreciate the invitation and may be able to observe or listen to a portion of the class.

- Set up a weekly or monthly meeting time with colleagues to maintain the interest and continue to informally share ideas. Having someone with whom to brainstorm ideas is a huge help.

- Ask teachers to place a note in your mailbox about upcoming units of study. Leave them a note to keep them up to date with what you are doing.

Summary

Interdisciplinary teaching offers an opportunity to deliver knowledge and skills from a new perspective. It maintains the integrity of the subject areas and benefits from clearly defined objectives and performance expectations. This approach to teaching is initiated through a review of the scope and sequence in current curriculum guides before a specific content area is selected for integration. The next step is to gather information from a variety of sources. Begin the journey by reflecting on your own experiences, seek out your colleagues, review texts from other subjects, or visit classrooms. Select the interdisciplinary teaching model that is appropriate for meeting the lesson or unit objective. The connected model can be used individually as you link one subject with another, the shared model expands the depth of content integration with another teacher, and the partnership model requires meeting with colleagues to plan and team-teach. During the planning process, consider the logistics of implementation, including schedule changes, facilities, materials and equipment, and the organization of students. Start with a topic or skill you feel comfortable with, be sure to keep it small and manageable, and build on those accomplishments.

Planning for and implementation of an interdisciplinary learning experience should always include a means of assessing the objectives of the lesson. Various forms of assessment can be used, including a self-assessment, peer assessment, teacher assessment, portfolios, journals, video analysis, checklists, and written responses to questions.

Efforts to integrate subject areas are more likely to succeed when you communicate your plans and gain support from administrators, parents, and students, in addition to developing relationships with your colleagues. Don't underestimate the value of an administrative advocate, one who can speak knowledgeably about your program and who can provide support in the decision-making process.

Practical Applications of Interdisciplinary Programs

You must be the change you wish to see in the world.
—Mahatma Gandhi

The second part of the book includes five chapters dedicated to how you can integrate the content of language arts, mathematics, science, social studies, music, theater arts, and visual arts with the content of physical education in an active learning experience.

The purpose of these chapters is to provide both classroom and physical education teachers with many practical ideas on how to use experiences based in human movement to enhance the presentation of content from other subjects to children in elementary school. Chapter 3 focuses on the language arts abilities of reading, writing, speaking, listening, and viewing. Chapter 4 addresses the mathematical concepts and skills of numbers, measuring and graphing, geometry, patterns and functions, probability and statistics, logic, and algebra. Chapter 5 contains information on science concepts from the biological and life sciences, earth and space sciences, and physical sciences. Chapter 6 presents the areas of product skills, process skills, and human relations skills in the social studies discipline. The final chapter addresses music, theater arts, and visual arts. In addition, each chapter contains an introduction describing the impact the discipline has on a child's education and the value that is gained when reinforcing the skills and concepts using movement. You will also find a sample scope and sequence of discipline content for each chapter that provides an overview of the skills, concepts, or processes that teachers use to develop curricula and lessons.

Twenty examples of complete learning experiences, four in each chapter, are presented to offer a practical approach to interdisciplinary teaching. You can use each learning experience as written as a teaching model, or the examples may be an inspiration for you to develop your own learning experiences. They provide actual language to be used with the students when presenting the tasks. Each of the learning experiences illustrates one of the interdisciplinary teaching models described in chapter 1 and provides an example of real-life implementation. These learning experiences can also serve as the basis for a conversation with a colleague about how two or more disciplines can be linked together to provide an enriched lesson or unit of study for your students. You will also find over 150 additional ideas for developing active learning experiences that may provide the stimulus for creating your own interdisciplinary endeavors.

Explore, experiment, and enjoy using the learning experiences. They are for you, your colleagues, and your students to share as you discover new ways of using an interdisciplinary approach to teaching.

Active Learning Involving Language Arts

"The language arts are an integral part of education at the elementary level. They are the abilities that enable one to think logically and creatively; express ideas; understand and participate meaningfully in spoken, written, and nonverbal communications; formulate and answer questions; and search for, organize, evaluate, and apply information" (New Jersey Department of Education, 1996). A comprehensive language arts program is characterized by an integration of the skills and concepts in reading, writing, speaking, listening, and viewing (see figure 3.1). These skills and concepts are essential for communication and learning in all disciplines.

The descriptions in the scope and sequence section of this chapter are a summary of information gathered from various state standards documents, the *National Standards for the English Language Arts* (National Council of Teachers of English and the International Reading Association, 1996), curriculum guides, and program activities. You may find a slightly different version in your state or school district, one that has been designed to consider local perspectives and needs.

You can provide opportunities in the physical education class that support learning language arts skills and concepts and that incorporate the physical education experiences as part of the learning experience in the classroom. Connor-Kuntz and Dummer (1996) reported that students who were taught language skills during physical education activities showed improvement in language abilities. The study also found that language skills can be easily implemented in physical education classes without sacrificing the physical skills being taught or requiring additional time. Remember as you develop interdisciplinary experiences that the activities should enhance children's educational experience in both disciplines.

When children make the shapes of letters using their bodies in an alphabet dance, they reinforce the development of letter formation gained through a handwriting exercise. They may also use an action of the body to increase understanding of word meanings, such as *around the corner, bend over backward,* or *climb to the top.* The content found in a physical education program offers experiences that can be used as inspiration for writing stories, reflective pieces, news articles, poems, or reports. Students also find enjoyment in reading novels, stories, and poems that highlight a physical activity they may have experienced. These readings may also inspire students to create dances, games, and movements that represent the ideas, events, and characters portrayed in the literature. Speaking and listening skills are reinforced when students give or receive directions for an activity, explain and discuss a game strategy, or share feedback with a classmate. As part of all learning experiences, students gain valuable information by viewing presentations by the teacher, observing others as they perform skills, or learning from videos or visual displays.

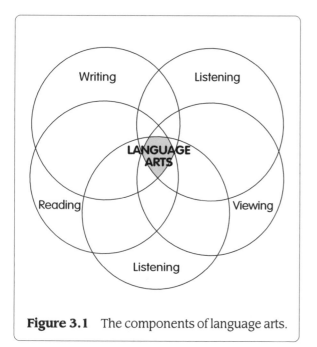

Figure 3.1 The components of language arts.

Scope and Sequence for Language Arts

The language arts curriculum content is composed of five basic academic competencies. The following section defines the areas of reading, writing, speaking, listening, and viewing. The matrix in table 3.1 indicates the grade in which specific language arts skills and concepts are presented. Some skills and concepts introduced during the primary grades are continued during the intermediate grades at higher levels and with more complexity.

Table 3.1

SCOPE AND SEQUENCE OF LANGUAGE ARTS CONCEPTS TAUGHT IN ELEMENTARY SCHOOLS							
Concept	**Grade**						
Reading	K	1	2	3	4	5	6
Reading for different purposes	X	X	X	X	X	X	X
Literature study	X	X	X	X	X	X	X
Conventions of language	X	X	X	X	X	X	X
Vocabulary	X	X	X	X	X	X	X
Comprehension	X	X	X	X	X	X	X
Reading strategies	X	X	X	X	X	X	X
Story Structures	X	X	X	X	X	X	X
Writing							
Writing for a variety of purposes	X	X	X	X	X	X	X
Composition	X	X	X	X	X	X	X
Handwriting	X	X	X	X	X	X	X
Spelling	X	X	X	X	X	X	X
Mechanics	X	X	X	X	X	X	X
Speaking							
Speaking for different purposes and audiences	X	X	X	X	X	X	X
Questions and answers	X	X	X	X	X	X	X
Oral presentations					X	X	X
Group discussions	X	X	X	X	X	X	X
Directions or instructions	X	X	X	X	X	X	X
Listening							
Listening for a variety of purposes	X	X	X	X	X	X	X
Oral directions	X	X	X	X	X	X	X
Questions and answers	X	X	X	X	X	X	X
Note taking					X	X	X
Music and sounds	X	X	X	X	X	X	X
Critical listening			X	X	X	X	X
Viewing							
Viewing for a variety of purposes	X	X	X	X	X	X	X
Personal interactions, live performances	X	X	X	X	X	X	X
Visual arts involving oral or written language	X	X	X	X	X	X	X
Print media	X	X	X	X	X	X	X
Electronic media	X	X	X	X	X	X	X
Factual and fictional representations	X	X	X	X	X	X	X

Primary-Grade Language Arts Skills and Concepts

Most children experience many rich and valuable life experiences before their arrival at school. Experiences such as watching television, listening to music, drawing pictures, communicating through speaking, and an introduction to books provide a readiness that will enhance the formal learning process that begins in kindergarten. In kindergarten and first grade, students learn about letters, listen to stories and poems, and develop a sight vocabulary. They are encouraged to speak about their experiences and describe them through drawings, words, or simple sentences. At this level, children are introduced to different types of literature and enjoy sharing stories and their writing with peers and adults.

The language arts program in the second and third grades continues to focus on the development of a solid foundation of the basic skills and concepts. These skills and concepts are needed to acquire information, communicate ideas, and ultimately provide the means for the student to enjoy success. Students learn to apply reading strategies for decoding and comprehension, expand their vocabulary, organize thoughts, and write for a variety of purposes. Their speaking abilities are enhanced through giving brief oral presentations, participating in group discussions, learning to summarize information, and practicing giving clear directions. Listening skills are developed through activities that use a hands-on approach to interpret information from a variety of sources. Children become better at following a series of oral directions, asking relevant questions, listening critically, and restating what others say. Students develop strategies to gain meaning from visual experience and become skilled at using visual media to support their reading, writing, and speaking.

Intermediate-Grade Language Arts Skills and Concepts

The intermediate grade level is characterized by a refining of the language arts skills and concepts and the further integration of these skills and concepts with learning in the other disciplines. Students read novels and stories that directly relate to social studies and science units. Research and note-taking skills are introduced, and the editing process becomes common practice in their writing. Students have internalized the skills and strategies necessary to read text, make the connections between what is read and their own experiences, and understand the components of a story. The study of literature at this level includes nonfiction, fiction, poetry, and dramatic works representing a diversity of cultures and authors.

Students increase proficiency in speaking by delivering oral presentations based on research, learning to use body language, effectively using the voice, increasing eye contact, and participating in collaborative speaking activities. Through active listening, students increase comprehension of oral reports, discussions, interviews, and lectures and are able to restate, interpret, respond to, and evaluate increasingly complex information. Students use viewing to respond thoughtfully and critically to both print and nonprint visual messages. Intermediate students view and use simple charts, graphs, and diagrams to report data and respond to and evaluate the use of illustrations to support text. They learn about different media forms and how these forms contribute to communication.

When students learn to read, write, speak, listen, and view critically, strategically, and creatively and when they learn to use these arts individually and in groups, they have the literacy skills they need to discover personal and shared meaning throughout their lives. The language arts are valuable not only in and of themselves but also as supporting skills for students' learning in all other subjects. Students can best develop language competencies, like other competencies, through meaningful activities and settings.

Learning Experiences

Each of the four learning experiences (see table 3.2) demonstrates one of the interdisciplinary teaching models presented in chapter 1. The learning experiences have been designed to include skills and concepts from physical education and language arts. Each learning experience includes a name, suggested grade level, interdisciplinary teaching model, objectives, equipment, organization, complete description of the lesson, and assessment suggestions. In addition, tips on what to look for in student responses, how teachers can change or modify the lesson, and ideas for teachable moments are offered to provide further insights into each learning experience.

Table 3.2

LANGUAGE ARTS LEARNING EXPERIENCE INDEX			
Skills and concepts	**Name**	**Suggested grade level**	**Interdisciplinary teaching model**
Language arts: Listening and responding to a story through movement; comprehension of word meaning Physical education: Traveling movements, level, and tempo; creating a dance; observing a dance	The Rumpus Dance	K-3	Connected
Language arts: Letter recognition and reproduction Physical education: Traveling movements and balances	Alphabet Gymnastics	K-1	Shared
Language arts: Writing descriptive information and speaking before a group Physical education: Using throwing and catching skills in a game	Create-a-Game	4-6	Partnership
Language arts: Effective speaking using body language, inflection, enunciation, eye contact, and intonation Physical education: Creating a conversation dance using the call and response form	A Moving Conversation	4-6	Shared

The Rumpus Dance

SUGGESTED GRADE LEVEL

Primary (K-3)

INTERDISCIPLINARY TEACHING MODEL

Connected
Children listen to a reading of Maurice Sendak's *Where the Wild Things Are* as part of an author-of-the-month program and create a dance expressing the feeling of being at the wild rumpus.

Language Arts
Listening and responding to a story through movement; demonstrating comprehension of word meaning

Physical Education
Performing traveling movements using change of direction, level, and tempo that express the meaning of a word; creating a dance that has three movements; observing and responding to a dance performed by another student

OBJECTIVES

As a result of participating in this learning experience, children will

- verbally discuss and create a written list of words to define the word rumpus from Maurice Sendak's book *Where the Wild Things Are*,
- explore different movements that express the list of descriptive words for rumpus, and
- create a rumpus dance using changes of level, direction, and tempo.

EQUIPMENT

Where the Wild Things Are by Maurice Sendak, fast-tempo music, chalkboard or chart paper, chalk or markers

ORGANIZATION

Students create and perform movements individually and then work with partners to observe each other's dances.

DESCRIPTION

"You have just heard the story *Where the Wild Things Are*. This is an exciting story about the adventure of Max as he visits a strange land where the Wild Things live. Now you are going to create a dance about the wild rumpus that happened in the story."

WRITE the word rumpus on the top or in the center of the chalkboard or chart.

"Do you remember when the rumpus happened in the story? Let's look at the pages in the book and see how the Wild Things and Max are moving during the rumpus."

SHOW students the pages in the book.

"What kinds of movements are they doing at the rumpus?" Students respond, for example, "hopping, jumping, skipping, turning, hanging, swinging, stretching, marching."

WRITE the words on the chalkboard or chart paper (see figure 3.2).

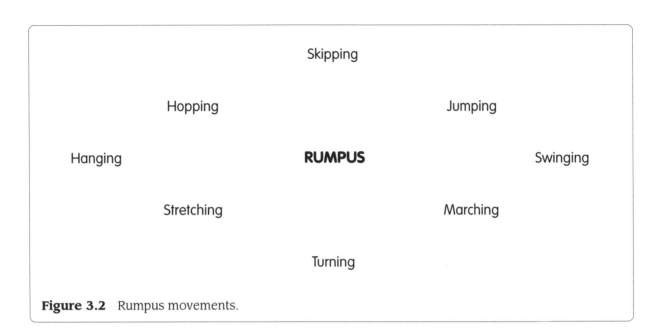

Skipping

Hopping   Jumping

Hanging   **RUMPUS**   Swinging

Stretching   Marching

Turning

Figure 3.2 Rumpus movements.

TELL the students that they will try these movements as part of their warm-up today.

FIRST, have each student find his or her own space and begin hopping in forward, backward, and sideways directions. Remind students to give each foot a turn. Ask them if they can hop four times on one foot in one direction and four times on the other foot in another direction.

NEXT, encourage them to try big skips that lift them up off the floor. Ask them to find a way to add a turn while they are skipping.

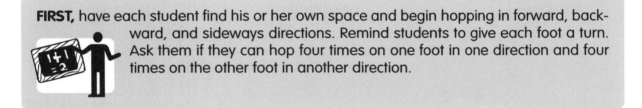

NOW have them combine jumping and stretching together. Jump and stretch to the right, then jump and stretch to the left. Repeat the movement to the right and left several times.

TELL them that they will not be using swinging today, but they will use swinging the next time they use the gymnastic apparatus.

"Now we are going to create our own rumpus movements. Tell me some words that describe a rumpus." Students answer, "wild party, going crazy, being very excited." "What movements can you do to express the meaning of the word rumpus that we did not do in the warm-up?" Students answer, "roll on the floor, spin around fast, shake your body, kick your legs up."

ADD these words to the rumpus words already on the chalkboard or chart paper (see figure 3.3).

"Each person, choose one movement from the list of words on the chalkboard. Andrew, what word did you choose?" Andrew responds, "marching." "Now find a space and practice your movement using a forward, backward, and sideways direction. I will play the music while you are practicing."

Wild party	**Going crazy**	**Being excited**

Skipping

Rolling

Hopping   Jumping

RUMPUS   **Kicking**

Spinning

Shaking

Hanging   Swinging

Stretching   Marching

Turning

Figure 3.3 Student-suggested rumpus movements.

MOVE through the class and ask students to identify their movement and demonstrate it in the three directions.

"Everyone stop and return to the chalkboard. Now choose a second movement from the list, find a space, and practice doing this movement changing from low to high and high to low. Again, I will play the music while you practice."

AFTER a brief practice time, have the students stop, then ask them to put the two movements together in a sequence.

"Be sure to move smoothly from one movement to the other. See if you can find a way to blend the end of one movement into the beginning of the second movement."

THE TEACHER moves through the class and observes how children are moving from the first movement to the second.

"Now stop, return to the chalkboard, and choose a third different movement from the list. Practice the movement using strong and fast energy that becomes slower and slower until you stop in a still shape. Can someone demonstrate how they can make a movement start strong and fast and let it become slower and slower until the movement stops in a still shape? I see Meredith would like to demonstrate. What movement are you going to use?" Meredith responds, "I'm going to spin around and wave my arms up and down to show how I go crazy and then get tired at my rumpus." "That sounds great. Let's watch Meredith to see how the tempo of her spinning movement becomes slower and slower until she stops in a still shape."

MEREDITH demonstrates for the class.

"Thank you, Meredith."

 **WRITE** the sequence on the chalkboard or chart paper (see figure 3.4).

"Now practice putting all three movements you have chosen from the chalkboard in a sequence. Remember, the first one uses three different directions, the second one changes levels and the third one starts fast and strong and ends in a still shape. The music will be playing while you practice."

Rumpus movements sequence

First	+	Second	+	Third
Forward—backward—sideways		High—low—high		Strong and fast, slower, then still

Figure 3.4 Sequence of rumpus movements.

WHILE all the students are practicing, approach individual students and ask them to explain their sequence and to demonstrate the movements.

"Now let's show each other the rumpus dance you have created. I would like half the class to sit and observe while the other half demonstrates their rumpus dance. Perform your dance once, then hold your still shape until everyone in the group has finished. I will play the music while you are performing."

EACH group performs their rumpus dance while the music is playing. Lower the music volume as the students begin to stop in their still shapes.

"The second time you perform I will assign a person to observe your rumpus dance. When you are finished your observer will tell you what movements he or she observed. Then you will switch places." (See figure 3.5.)

Figure 3.5 Assign observers to comment on each other's movements.

ASSESSMENT SUGGESTION

- Use the partner conversation at the end of the learning experience as one type of peer assessment.
- The form in figure 3.6 can be completed as a self-assessment. The student writes the first, second, and third movements of his or her rumpus dance on each line. Children can also add a drawing or comments about their feelings as they performed the dance.
- The teacher can videotape small groups of students performing their rumpus dance and have the students observe their performance and match the words they have written describing the dance to the movements they perform in their dance.

LOOK FOR

- Clear changes of direction, level, and tempo and ending the dance in a still shape.
- Smooth transitions from one movement to another. Do the children blend the end of one movement with the beginning of the next?

HOW CAN I CHANGE THIS?

- Emphasize other elements of movement such as size (big or small) or pathways, or develop a specific rhythm for each movement.
- Perform three movements using a pattern, such as first movement, fast and strong; second movement, slow and strong; third movement, fast and strong.
- Use other words or phrases from the story.
- Have students work in pairs or groups of three to select the words and develop the three movements of the dance. They can practice and perform in unison.

TEACHABLE MOMENTS

- Emphasize proper technique for performing movements, such as safe landings from a jump, using balance and strength to make smooth transitions from one movement to another, or using the correct rhythm for a skip.
- Encourage experimentation with the sequence of movements in the dance.

Alphabet Gymnastics

SUGGESTED GRADE LEVEL

Primary (K-1)

INTERDISCIPLINARY TEACHING MODEL

Shared
The students learn to identify and form letters through a variety of hands-on activities.

Language Arts
Letter recognition and reproduction

Physical Education
Traveling movements and balances

shake spin Jump

SPIN ON 1 foot   my Jump

I liked the spin
best.

Figure 3.6 Sample assessment of rumpus dance.

OBJECTIVES

As a result of participating in this lesson, the student will

- identify different letters of the alphabet,
- use his or her body to make the shapes of letters,
- practice writing the letters,
- practice balances using different body parts,
- travel in different directions (forward, backward, sideways), and
- create a sequence of movements using three letters.

EQUIPMENT

Mats, chalkboard or chart paper, chalk or markers, 8 1/2 × 11-inch paper, crayons

ORGANIZATION

Partners or small groups share a mat.

DESCRIPTION

"Today's lesson is called Alphabet Gymnastics. You are going to make your body into the shape of different letters and find a way to hold it still in a balanced position. Then you will find different ways to make the letter travel in the space."

AFTER a brief, running warm-up, the teacher assigns students to a mat.

"We are going to continue to warm up our bodies using stretching letters. Everyone sit on your mat, legs straight and in front, sit up tall, and stretch your arms to the ceiling. What letter did you make?" Students respond, "a capital *L*." "Now slowly reach forward, curving your arms, head, and back to make the letter *C*. Slowly stretch back into the *L* shape. Let's try slowly moving a couple times from the *L* to the *C* so we can warm up our bodies."

THE TEACHER can do the movements with the students.

"Next, stand up on your mat with your feet together and arms stretched out to the side. What letter does this shape look like?" Students respond, "a small *t*." "Slowly twist your arms to the right then slowly to the left. Let's try this movement a couple more times."

STUDENTS can follow the teacher or try the stretch on their own time.

"We are going to do one more stretch using the letter *t* shape. Standing on the mat or the floor, slowly raise your heels, stretching your ankles, and then slowly lower your heels. Remember to keep your ankles straight so you are not leaning on the outside of your feet. Rise up and down five times slowly keeping your stomach muscles tight to help you balance."

TEACHER and students assemble near the chalkboard for the next section of the lesson.

"I would like someone to write a letter from their name on the chalkboard. I see Timothy has his hand up. Timothy, choose a letter from your name and write it on the board."

TIMOTHY writes an uppercase *Y*.

"That's great Timothy. Class, what letter did he write?"

A STUDENT recognizes the letter and tells the class.

"How can you make a *Y* with your body? Lisa, can you show us your idea? I see Lisa is making a standing *Y*. Is there another way to make a *Y*? Yes, Raquib is lying on his back. I want you to return to your mat and try the ways Lisa and Raquib used to make a *Y*. Then try to make a *Y* using your own idea." (See figure 3.7.)

STUDENTS return to their mats and begin to practice.

Figure 3.7   Students using shapes to form letters.

"Everyone stop now and think of the letters in your name. Choose a letter and make your letter using a high, medium, and low level. Ask the other students at your mat to guess what letter you are making."

STUDENTS take turns making letters and guessing the letters formed by the other students on the mat.

NEXT, the teacher writes a letter on the chalkboard or chart and prompts the students for each new letter with the following directions.

"Now, you are going to make letters using a still balance. Make the letter *P* while balancing on one foot. Can you balance and say the alphabet until you come to the letter *P*?

"Make the letter *V* with your legs in the air as you lie on your back. Can you make your letter *V* a little wider?"

"Make the letter *K* as you balance on your right foot. Make a *K* while balancing on your left foot.

"Choose another letter and find a way to make it balance. Hold your body still while you are balancing. What body part are you balancing on? Ask someone on your mat to guess what letter you are using for your balance.

"Now, two or three people get together and make a letter. What body parts are you using to balance on? Let's stop and look at some of the letters people made and see if we can guess the letter and name of the body parts they are using to balance on."

TEACHER calls on each group of students to demonstrate their letters and has a student from another group write the letter on the chalkboard or chart.

"Next, we are going to make traveling letters. You will find different ways to take a trip around the mat with your body in the shape of a letter. Let's start with everyone in a standing position making the shape of the letter *X*."

THE TEACHER draws a large *X* on the chalkboard or chart.

"Great *X*s! I see your arms are apart and reaching up to make the top of the *X* and your feet are apart to form the bottom of the *X*. Using your letter *X*, begin to walk forward around the mat. Keep the spaces between your arms and legs. Try making the *X* walk backward. Tilt the *X* onto one foot and balance for a moment.

"Now try a jumping *i*. Can someone tell the class what an *i* looks like? Ishmael has his hand up and responds, "It looks like this. You make a straight line and put a dot on the top."

ISHMAEL draws the letter in the air using his hand as he verbally describes the letter.

"That's a good way to describe the letter *i*."

ASK another student to draw a lowercase *i* on the chalkboard or chart.

"Everyone draw the letter *i* in the air. Now draw a very big *i* so you have to jump up in the air to put the dot on the top. Make sure you land on your feet at the end of the big jump."

STUDENTS practice making the letter. The teacher encourages the students to reach as high and low as they can to make the long, vertical portion of the *i*. Then have them jump as high as they can to dot the *i* with their hand.

"Now before you draw your letter *i*, I want you to take three little jumps moving forward. The order is jump, jump, jump, draw the straight part of the *i*, and take another big jump to make the dot. Practice the jumping *i* a couple more times.

"Choose a letter and find a way to make the letter travel in the space. You can use your feet or other parts of your body, and try moving forward, backward, and sideways."

AS the students practice different letters traveling in the space, the teacher or other students guess the letter. The teacher can ask students to demonstrate their letter for others.

"Next, you are going to choose three letters and write them on a piece of paper using a crayon. You may choose which letter will be first, second, and third. Your first letter will be a still balance, your second letter will travel in the space, and your third letter will be a still balance. Now choose your letters, write them down, and practice. I will be walking around to see how you are doing."

THE STUDENTS practice, and the teacher observes the letters the students have printed and how they are using their bodies to make the shape. The teacher asks the students to demonstrate for others who are sharing the mat.

ASSESSMENT SUGGESTION

- Students are in pairs or groups of three. One student makes a letter with his or her body in a still, balanced position. The other students in the group write down the letter they see the student make. The students then discuss whether the letters written down on paper correspond to the letter the student made with his or her body.

- Students identify the parts of the body that are used to make the different parts of the letter.

LOOK FOR

- Slow stretching without straining or bouncing.
- Straight ankles during the toe rises, with the body weight distributed evenly on all toes.

- Controlled movement in and out of balances. Students should not fall out of the balances.
- The different ways students use their body and its parts to make letters. Some students may use their whole body, while others may emphasize the shape of the letter with only their arms or legs.
- Accuracy with which students draw the letter on paper.

HOW CAN I CHANGE THIS?

- Create balances from the letters that make up the word balance.
- Use the letters in a word that describes a traveling movement, such as hop, jump, or run (e.g., a running letter r, then u, and finally n).
- Use letters that have only straight or curved lines.
- Use only uppercase or lowercase letters.
- Use the entire class to form a letter.

TEACHABLE MOMENT

- Students can trade their three-letter gymnastic sequence with other students and try to reproduce the letters selected by the other students.

Create-a-Game

SUGGESTED GRADE LEVEL

Intermediate (4-6)

INTERDISCIPLINARY TEACHING MODEL

Partnership
Two teachers present a learning experience covering the process of developing and recording a game. In this learning experience, students create a game based on throwing and catching skills and write a description of the game followed by an oral presentation of the game to their classmates.

Language Arts
Writing descriptive information and speaking before a group

Physical Education
Using throwing and catching skills in a game

OBJECTIVES

As result of participating in this lesson, students will

- practice throwing and catching skills while stationary;
- practice throwing and catching skills while moving;

- work collaboratively to create a game emphasizing throwing and catching;
- compose a description of their game listing the skills, directions, roles of the players, and rules and draw a diagram of the space; and
- teach their game to another group of students through an oral presentation.

EQUIPMENT

Bases or floor markers, balls of various sizes, empty boxes of various sizes, wall targets (12 × 17-inch colored construction paper), tape for wall targets

ORGANIZATION

Students work in pairs or small groups.

DESCRIPTION

"In the past several lessons you have learned and practiced the techniques for the overhand throw, underhand throw, and catch. You practiced these skills from stationary and moving positions, individually and with others. Today you are going to apply these skills in a game that you create. Before you begin your game, you will have a chance to practice throwing and catching using the task cards I will give you (see figure 3.8). I have assigned students to work together. Please look at the chart on the wall to see whom you will be working with. Find your partner, choose a ball, take a card, and begin to practice."

TEACHER observes students and provides feedback.

"Stop and please join me by the poster. As you can see, I have listed the parts of a game you will need to include as you design your game (see figure 3.9).

Throwing and Catching Practice Task Card

You may practice the tasks in any order.

- **Underhand throws.** Throw the ball high to your partner so he or she can catch the ball above the head. Decide how many successful throws and catches you and your partner will accomplish before moving to another task. You need to complete a minimum of 5.

- **Overhand throws.** The catcher makes a target with his or her hands either high or low, or right or left. Decide how many successful catches you and your partner will accomplish before moving to another task. You need to complete a minimum of 5.

- Toss and catch to your partner using either the underhand or overhand throw as you move through the space. Decide how many successful catches you and your partner will accomplish before moving to another task. You need to complete a minimum of 5.

Figure 3.8 Throwing and catching practice task card.

Parts of a Game

Name of the game: _____

Skills: _____

Equipment: _____

Number of players: _____

How is the game played? _____

_____

Rules: _____

_____

Draw a diagram of the space:

Figure 3.9   Parts of a game.

"As you begin your planning, I want you to use the guidelines for the game I have listed on the chalkboard" (see figure 3.10).

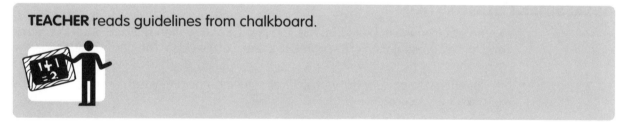

TEACHER reads guidelines from chalkboard.

Guidelines for Creating a Game

- All players must be involved in the game. No one is eliminated.
- Throwing and catching skills must be used.
- Players cannot be targets. Use a piece of equipment, the wall, the floor, or a piece of paper if you decide to use a target.
- You may use a point system or you may decide not to keep score.
- Share the space and equipment with others. You can select from the available balls, boxes, paper wall targets, bases, and floor markers.

Figure 3.10   Guidelines for creating a game.

"Creating a game is similar to the writing process. You gather your ideas, compose a draft, revise it, edit, and then share and publish your final piece. Your game may change several times as you try out different ideas. Once you have completed your game, write a description that includes all the parts listed on the poster. You may begin your planning."

 **STUDENTS** begin to work on their ideas. The teacher circulates among the groups and offers suggestions if needed.

"Pat, have you considered rotating the players to all positions? Do you want to have some type of time limit for the game?

"Take your descriptions with you so you can continue to work on them in the classroom. The next time we get together, please bring your game description so you can make adjustments and changes to your game. Once you have finished creating and recording your game, you will have the chance to teach it to the rest of the class."

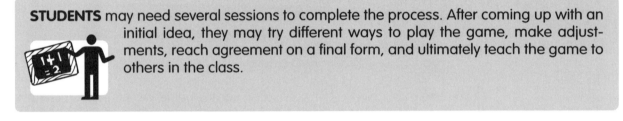 **STUDENTS** may need several sessions to complete the process. After coming up with an initial idea, they may try different ways to play the game, make adjustments, reach agreement on a final form, and ultimately teach the game to others in the class.

ASSESSMENT SUGGESTION

- The assessment is based on the completion of a written description of the game and an oral presentation of the game to the rest of the class. The game must follow the guidelines.
- Students write about what worked well in their game and what changes they made to make it a success.

LOOK FOR

- How throwing and catching skills are used in the game.
- Games that include all players.
- Games that are challenging, yet enjoyable.
- Partners who are having difficulty generating an idea or working cooperatively in the planning and implementation of the game. Provide the partners with strategies to help them work together and solve problems.

HOW CAN I CHANGE THIS?

- Include a different manipulative skill, such as kicking, volleying, or striking with an implement.
- Have all students use the same quantity and type of equipment.
- Assign partners or groups a specific space, such as a corner of the gym; a large square, circle, triangle, or a rectangle taped on the floor; or a space that includes a wall.

TEACHABLE MOMENTS

- Discuss the skills needed to work cooperatively with others.
- Have a student or one of the teachers talk about a personal experience of writing a story. Draw the parallels between the process of writing and the process of designing a game.

A Moving Conversation

SUGGESTED GRADE LEVEL

Intermediate (4-6)

INTERDISCIPLINARY TEACHING MODEL

Shared
The students are currently learning to effectively convey a message. During a dance lesson, students create a conversation with another student using movement.

Language Arts
Effective speaking using body language, inflection, enunciation, eye contact, and intonation

Physical Education
Creating a conversation dance using the call-and-response form

OBJECTIVES

As result of participating in this lesson, students will

- understand the similarity between how movement is used to communicate feelings and ideas and how body language, inflection, enunciation, eye contact, and intonation are used in speaking; and
- understand how the call-and-response form is used as a way of relating to a partner through movement.

EQUIPMENT

Chalkboard

ORGANIZATION

Students work in pairs or groups of three.

DESCRIPTION

"Today we are going to have a conversation with a partner using movements to express our thoughts instead of words. Let's begin to warm up our bodies so we will be ready to move in many different ways. Follow me for all the warm-up movements."

THE TEACHER performs a series of warm-up movements that includes moving the head, shoulders, arms, back, legs, ankles, and feet using bending, stretching, twisting, and rotating body parts.

"Now, you will create movements using a body part to express a thought. Instead of using words to tell someone your thoughts, you will use a movement. Let me demonstrate with a partner."

THE TEACHER and a student stand facing each other for the demonstration.

"I will begin moving my arms and hands in a shaking motion. Andrew, I want you to watch me, and after I stop, you should respond to me by moving your hands in a different way. That's great. What we have just done is use the call-and-response form as a way for two people to move together. The call means that one person starts the conversation, and the other person responds to the call. Then the first person continues with another statement and waits for a response. This pattern continues, just as when you have a conversation with a friend. All right, now let's use different body parts and movements each time we want to say something to each other, just like using different words in a conversation."

THE TEACHER and Andrew continue to converse with each other through movements of their head, shoulders, feet, and back.

"You can see our movements are not exact representations of our thoughts. They are a mixture of gestures and many different movements that may or may not have any specific meaning. When I shake my hands like this, I'm saying hello or 'watch out, you shouldn't do that.' Now I'll assign partners, and you will choose who will begin the movement conversation. Be sure to wait until the person moving has stopped before you move and respond to them. It's like a conversation where one person speaks and when they are finished the other person responds. Do not interrupt each other in the middle of speaking with movements. Watch to see what movements your partner is using; they may determine how you will respond to your partner."

THE CONVERSATIONS begin, and the teacher circulates among the students reinforcing the behavior of waiting until the first partner stops moving before the second partner begins his or her movement response.

"Can someone demonstrate how they might ask a question using movement? Okay, Jim, give it a try!"

JIM creates a short movement sequence and demonstrates it to the class.

"That's great! Eileen, can you answer that question with a movement?"

EILEEN answers Jim by spinning around three times.

"What about a question that uses only one word, such as why? How would you express that thought in movement?"

ANOTHER student demonstrates a short, quick movement of the hands and shoulders.

"Now let's add some long and short questions to the movement conversations—questions that can be expressed using a sequence of movements or maybe using only one movement. Try to respond with another question or an answer that may be one word, or try one answer with a long sentence."

STUDENTS continue to create movements that reflect questions and answers using long and short sentences.

"Next, you will change the intensity of your movement conversations. You can make the movements small and light to express a whisper or talking softly to someone. You can make the movement big and strong to express yelling or shouting to get your message across. Also, consider how fast or slow you want to speak to someone. Are you a fast talker, or do you want to say it slowly? Your personality still plays a role."

THE STUDENTS continue their movement conversations with an emphasis on the amount of force they use in their movements.

"The last part of this lesson will allow you to have different movement conversations with other people in the class. Use long and short statements, ask questions, use soft and loud or fast and slow statements, and carefully watch the other person to see how you will choose to respond. Sometimes use just a body part and sometimes use your whole body. Now find a different partner and begin your movement conversation. I will signal you when to stop and find another partner."

THE STUDENTS find new partners and use the call-and-response relationship in a variety of different ways, similar to improvised dance.

ASSESSMENT SUGGESTION

- Students can write a list of several movements they used in their conversation and describe how they were performed. Were they fast, slow, big, small, strong, or light? What did the movements communicate? For example, a student may write, "I waved my hands very fast using a lot of strong movements. It was like I was trying to tell someone to get away from me."

- Students can describe a movement their partner made and how they chose to respond.

- Students can describe what type of movements dominated their conversations.

LOOK FOR

- Students who may need ideas for movement. They may feel uncomfortable expressing themselves through creating movements. Have these students begin with frequently used hand gestures—those they normally use when talking—and have them make the gestures bigger, smaller, faster, or slower.

- Students in groups of three may need to decide whether they will take part in the conversation in a predetermined order or whether the conversation will be random.

HOW CAN I CHANGE THIS?

- Add different types of music, and have the students relate their conversation to the tempo, style, and volume of the music.

TEACHABLE MOMENT

- The students can write a conversation and recreate the conversation using only movement.

Additional Ideas for Developing Learning Experiences

This section offers additional learning experiences to develop the language arts abilities identified in table 3.1: reading, writing, speaking, listening, and viewing. Curricular areas, suggested grade level, and a brief description are provided for each activity. These activities are intended to inspire additional ideas for interdisciplinary work between classroom and physical education teachers. Teachers are encouraged to develop these ideas more completely. Sometimes the connected model will be most appropriate, while other times the shared or partnership model may be used. Your main concern should be to meet the developmental levels and needs of your students; you can adapt activities to accommodate your teaching schedule, equipment, and available space.

Reading

Alphabet in the Air

Language Arts
Letter recognition and formation

Physical Education
Body-part identification

Grade Level
K-1
Students draw the shapes of the alphabet in the air using different body parts. They can imagine a body part is covered with paint. The students paint the letter above their head or behind their body, reaching high and low, as slow or as fast as they can, from small to big, using different locomotor movements, making a letter with their right and left hands at the same time, or using two different body parts at the same time.

The Alphabet Children

Language Arts
Letter recognition and formation

Physical Education
Locomotor and nonlocomotor movements

Grade Level

K-1

Students move in the following sequence with their bodies in the shape of a letter. All the letters are sleeping on the floor. They slowly begin to wake up by stretching and slowly rise to their feet. The letters go out to play and skip, run, jump, or use other traveling movements. The letters also try to twist, bend, swing, or use other nonlocomotor movements. Then they become very tired and slowly sink to the floor and go back to sleep.

Alphabet Freeze Tag

Language Arts

Letter recognition and formation

Physical Education

Running, dodging, and matching shapes

Grade Level

2-3

The game is similar to the traditional freeze tag. However, in this game students freeze in the shape of a letter when tagged. To become unfrozen another runner mirrors the same letter shape of the frozen player.

Letter Targets

Language Arts

Letter recognition and formation

Physical Education

Throwing underhand or overhand for accuracy

Grade Level

K-3

Using large letters printed on 8 1/2 × 11 inch or 11 × 17 inch paper as wall or floor targets, children practice throwing beanbags or balls underhand or overhand at a letter. They identify the letter they are aiming at, identify the letter they hit, and write the letter on paper or the chalkboard.

Alphabet Activities

Language Arts

Letter recognition and beginning letter of a word

Physical Education

Identifying physical activities and sports that are part of an active lifestyle

Grade Level
K-3
Create a bulletin board using the letters of the alphabet. Place words or pictures (or both) of physical activities, sports, or skills that begin with the corresponding letter.

Sports News

Language Arts
Increasing vocabulary; word meaning and use

Physical Education
Identifying sport movements and skills

Grade Level
4-6
The teacher and students clip movement phrases used by sportswriters from articles on the sports pages. Discuss the phrases and demonstrate their meaning through movement.

Bounce-a-Word

Language Arts
Spelling

Physical Education
Bouncing a ball

Grade Level
2-6
The students bounce a ball and spell a word, one bounce for each letter of the word.

Rhyming Movements

Language Arts
Rhyming words

Physical Education
Locomotor and nonlocomotor movements

Grade Level
2-4
Create movement sequences or dances that reflect a series of rhymed words. For example, use the words *ball*, *small*, *fall*, and *tall.*

Opposite Pairs

Language Arts
Antonyms

Physical Education
Locomotor and nonlocomotor movements; shapes

Grade Level
2-6
The teacher or students develop a list of antonyms, such as high and low, big and small, fast and slow, over and under, open and close, or push and pull. The students work individually or with a partner. They choose a set of antonyms and create a movement or still shape to express each word.

Dancing Books

Language Arts
Understanding story sequences and characters

Physical Education
Creating movements and shapes

Grade Level
K-6
The teacher or the student chooses a story or a character from a story. The student then creates movements that reflect a sequence of events and demonstrate the way the character moves.

Poetry in Motion

Language Arts
Expressing meaning through movement

Physical Education
Creating movements and shapes

Grade Level
4-6
Students in small groups create a dance using a poem. Each student is assigned one line of the poem and creates movements that reflect the meaning of the words.

Weather Report Gymnastics

Language Arts
Reading

Physical Education
Making shapes; rocking and jumping

Grade Level
2-4
Students read a weather report printed in the newspaper and create movements that represent the weather words, for example, *sunny*—make the shape of the sun by stretching the whole body or stretch the arms up toward the sun; *windy*—rock forward, backward, and sideways on different parts of the body; rain—jump into and over puddles; *ice storm*—freeze in different shapes; *cloudy*—make the shapes of clouds with the body and travel in the space.

Moving Adverbs

Language Arts
Action verbs and adverbs

Physical Education
Throwing, kicking, striking; locomotor and nonlocomotor movements

Grade Level
3-6
Develop a list of adverbs currently being used or studied by the students. The students change the way they throw, kick, strike, or use locomotor and nonlocomotor movements as they apply an adverb to the action, for example, throw softly, kick quickly, or strike smoothly.

Direction Words

Language Arts
Reading and identifying words

Physical Education
Traveling over, under, and between pieces of apparatus using locomotor movements

Grade Level
2-4
Attach movement and directional words to different pieces of apparatus for students to follow. Words such as *jump over, crawl under, walk between, step over*, or *roll under sideways* can be used.

Letter Lineup

Language Arts
Letter recognition

Physical Education
Organization for lines, teams, or issuing equipment

Grade Level
K-4
Students form groups or lines based on the letters in their first or last name. Students can be organized using the first letter, the last letter, or any other letter of their name.

Toss-a-Word

Language Arts
Spelling

Physical Education
Tossing a ball

Grade Level
2-6
A single student tosses a ball into the air. With each toss, he or she calls out a letter and completes the spelling of the word with additional tosses. Partners can toss a ball to each other and spell a word with each successive toss.

Action Pictures

Language Arts
Nouns, verbs, and adjectives

Physical Education
Identifying activities that demonstrate and promote active lifestyles

Grade Level
3-6
Children cut out pictures from magazines of people participating in active lifestyles. Ask children to study the pictures and list nouns, verbs, and adjectives that their pictures suggest.

Writing

Body Spell

Language Arts
Letter formation and spelling

Physical Education
Making shapes

Grade Level
K-6
Each student can individually spell words by making each letter with his or her body in sequence as it appears in a word. A group of students can spell words by each forming a letter using his or her body and then arranging the letters to spell a word.

Gymnastic Sentences

Language Arts
Writing sentences

Physical Education
Rolling, turning, and balance

Grade Level
2-6
Students create a gymnastic sequence using rolling, turning, and balances. They record the sequence by writing a sentence that describes the movement.

The Jump-Rope Rhyme

Language Arts
Writing rhymes

Physical Education
Jumping rope

Grade Level
3-6
The students create a rhyme to be used when jumping rope.

Name It

Language Arts
Writing words and identifying them with objects

Physical Education
Identifying the names of pieces of equipment

Grade Level
2-4
Students write labels for the equipment used in the gym, such as playground balls, jump ropes, softballs, Frisbees, vaulting horses, and scooters. The labels can be used at stations or to mark places for storage.

Drawing Pathways

Language Arts
Writing and spelling

Physical Education
Pathways; locomotor and nonlocomotor movements

Grade Level

2-6

Students draw a pathway on a piece of paper using straight and curved lines and create movements to perform while traveling on the pathway. The names of the movements are written on the path.

Writing a Warm-Up

Language Arts

Writing

Physical Education

Games, sports, gymnastics, or dance

Grade Level

4-6

Students write a list of warm-up exercises that can be used in a gymnastics, dance, game, or sport lesson. They can describe how to do the exercise through writing, drawing pictures, or speaking.

Speaking, Listening, and Viewing

Scooter Maze

Language Arts

Speaking and giving directions

Physical Education

Demonstrating understanding of directions, such as right, left, around, backward, forward, or stop and go

Grade Level

2-4

Students work in pairs; one partner moves on a scooter while the other partner gives directions to move through a scooter maze. The person on the scooter can move only when he or she receives a verbal direction.

Word Hopscotch

Language Arts

Reading, writing, speaking, and identifying vocabulary words currently used in the classroom or physical education lesson

Physical Education

Hopping and jumping patterns

Grade Level

2-4

Using chalk, students draw a hopscotch pattern on the sidewalk. Instead of numbers, they write words and call out the words as they hop or jump. Rhyming words or other categories—such as nouns, verbs, adverbs, prepositions, or contractions—can also be used.

Listen Before You Speak

Language Arts
Speaking and listening

Physical Education
Teaching a skill

Grade Level
3-6
The teacher makes an oral presentation describing how to perform a skill such as the badminton forehand overhead stroke. During the same class or in the next session, a student restates the information to the class. In pairs, each student can restate the information to a partner.

Seeing Is Knowing

Language Arts
Viewing to gain information

Physical Education
Teaching a skill

Grade Level
3-6
The teacher presents a video or charts describing a skill, such as a technique for jumping rope. The students view the visual information then perform the skill. The teacher relies on the video or chart to provide the information instead of using oral directions.

Summary

The integration of five basic academic abilities—reading, writing, speaking, listening, and viewing—forms the K through 6 language arts curriculum. It is through language arts that students acquire knowledge, shape experience, and respond to their own particular needs and goals. The language arts are valuable not only in and of themselves but also as supporting skills for students' learning in all other subjects. Students can best develop language competencies through meaningful activities and settings. It is through the physical education program that students gain the essential kinesthetic learning experiences that will enhance their ability to communicate effectively through both movement and the language arts.

The learning experiences describe how a favorite children's book becomes the inspiration for a dance, how the letters of the alphabet come alive in a gymnastics sequence, how the use of throwing and catching skills in a game provides the opportunity to refine students' writing and speaking skills, and how movement and language share similarities when communicating feelings or ideas. The additional ideas can be used as a springboard to develop your own learning experiences in the language arts and physical education.

Active Learning Involving Mathematics

The film *The Mirror Has Two Faces,* starring Barbara Streisand and Jeff Bridges, depicts a modern love story. The main characters are both Columbia University professors, she in literature and he in mathematics. A wonderful subplot woven into the story is that she is an incredibly successful teacher who ties to everyday life themes from the classics that could be boring and outdated. Students flock to her classes, often staying after asking questions. He is a brilliant mathematician who has published books and is in demand on a European lecture circuit. The courses he teaches, however, are stale. Students rarely ask questions, often fall asleep in class, and are ready to leave before class time is over. At one point in the story, he asks her for some help on becoming a better teacher. She teaches him to use practical applications from everyday life to bring his subject alive. He finally catches on and uses a baseball game to help illustrate calculating ball velocity and distance a hit ball will travel. Students become excited. They ask a lot of questions. They stay after class to continue discussions. This is a powerful example of the relevance of interdisciplinary integration and tying theory into practice.

In much the same manner play experiences and game situations are often used in mathematics textbooks to enhance the presentation of mathematical concepts and problems to children in the elementary school. In fact, instructional practices call for mathematics teachers to develop concepts concretely then abstractly, to develop problem situations from other content areas and from everyday experiences, and to give attention to connections between mathematics and other content areas.

Whitin and Wilde (1992), two of the leading authors of elementary mathematics education textbooks, have documented how children's literature provides a meaningful context for mathematics. Their book cites numerous children's stories that serve as a springboard for mathematical investigations. Selected books are described to illustrate how children learn about classification, place value and numeration systems, counting, arithmetic operations, fractions, estimations, big numbers, geometry, and measurement. Whitin, Mills, and O'Keefe (1991) use children's interests in dinosaurs, eggs, losing teeth, bicycles, pancakes, animals, and speed to further illustrate how mathematics develops out of human experience and re-

store an aesthetic and affective dimension to mathematical learning. Classroom teachers also often use physical education activities and play experiences such as team scores, practice attempts, and batting averages to teach mathematics more effectively to their children.

A number of studies have been conducted to determine the effectiveness of the integration of mathematics with physical education. Ashlock and Humphrey (1976), Cratty (1985) Gilbert (1977), Humphrey (1974), and Werner and Burton (1979) have published books concerning research and practical implementation ideas for integrating physical education activities with mathematical content ranging from the simple mathematics concepts such as whole numbers (figure 4.1) and counting to mathematics set theory. Other studies advocating integration of mathematics concepts with physical education evolved in a series of lessons combining the two subjects. Memmel (1953) illustrated lessons in which rope jumping, team games, throwing, kicking, marching, rhythms, and shooting baskets were integrated with mathematics concepts. Jensen (1971) offered the use of jump ropes for solving simple arithmetic problems and designing geometrical patterns through physical education. More recently, Werner, Bowling, and Simmons (1989) designed physical education experiences to enhance children's understanding of geometric shapes, angles, numbers, and addition and subtraction. Lessons for the teaching of number concepts, addition, subtraction, multiplication, division, averages, linear measures, time, geometric forms, and the metric system have also been presented by various other authors. All authors indicated a positive response by the children to the active learning experiences.

Scope and Sequence for Mathematics

If children are to be taught mathematical concepts in physical education, teachers should be aware of the mathematical concepts that are taught at the various grade levels. Review of several mathematics textbook series and mathematics projects such as the School Mathematics Study Group, Stanford Project, and Minnesota Mathematics and Science Project indicate that the following mathematics concepts are

Figure 4.1 Simple mathematical concepts such as whole numbers can be taught through movement activities.

taught at the elementary school level: numbers, measurement, geometry, patterns and functions, probability and statistics, logic, and algebra (table 4.1).

Primary-Grade Mathematical Skills and Concepts

During the primary grades, concepts taught within the major category of numbers are the meaning of numbers through 100,000; computation using addition and subtraction; modeling fractions of 1/2, 1/4, 1/3, 1/10, and 1/16; recognizing money and making change; and comparing numbers using less than (<) and greater than (>) symbols. Measurement topics at the primary level include comparing nonstandard and standard units of measure; identifying time in terms of days, weeks, months, yesterday, today, tomorrow; telling time; sequencing sea-

sons; measuring temperature; using customary and metric measures; and finding areas of simple geometric figures. While studying geometry in the primary years, children learn to model, recognize, and name simple geometric figures; to understand terminology regarding position and spatial orientation such as *over, under, around,* and *through;* to recognize symmetrical patterns; to find and compare sides and angles of polygons; to recognize and find right angles in everyday life; and to show congruency by flipping, sliding, and turning figures. While studying about patterns and functions at the primary level, children learn to find patterns in everyday life; to identify missing objects in a pattern; to identify objects that do not fit a pattern; to translate and describe patterns from one medium to another; to order objects into a specific pattern such as large to small; to recognize regularities in events,

Table 4.1

SCOPE AND SEQUENCE OF MATHEMATICAL CONCEPTS TAUGHT IN ELEMENTARY SCHOOLS							
Concept	**Grade**						
	K	1	2	3	4	5	6
Numbers	x	x	x	x	x	x	x
Meaning of numbers 1-12	x						
Meaning of numbers through 99		x					
Meaning of numbers through 999			x				
Meaning of addition and subtraction		x					
Addition and subtraction computation			x				
Meaning of numbers through 100,000				x			
Meaning of multiplication and division				x			
Meaning of numbers through 1,000,000					x		
Multiplication and division computation					x		
Meaning of decimals through hundredths					x		
Meaning of decimals through thousandths						x	
Meaning of addition and subtraction of fractions and decimals						x	
Number theory						x	
Meaning of multiplication and division of fractions and decimals							x
Integers and ratios							x
Percents							x
Measuring and graphing	x	x	x	x	x	x	x
Geometry	x	x	x	x	x	x	x
Patterns and functions	x	x	x	x	x	x	x
Probability and statistics	x	x	x	x	x	x	x
Logic		x	x	x	x	x	x
Algebra			x	x	x	x	x

shapes, designs, and sets of numbers; to skip-count forward and backward; to classify numbers as odd and even; and to identify rules of a given pattern. Judging everyday events as certain, possible, or impossible; reading and summarizing pictographs and bar graphs to describe concepts of *more, fewer,* and *same;* predicting outcomes of events using terms such as *more, all, none, most likely, probably,* and *definitely* are all concepts that are learned by primary-grade children while studying about probability and statistics. With respect to logic, primary-grade children learn to sort objects by attributes such as color, shape, or size; to place items in logical sequences; and to speculate and draw conclusions about everyday situations using terminology such as *all, and, every, some, none, or, many,* and *not.*

Intermediate-Grade Mathematical Skills and Concepts

At the intermediate level children learn more complex concepts in each of the mathematics categories. With respect to numbers, children learn to read and write numbers through 1,000,000; to demonstrate a working knowledge of multiplication and division problems based on everyday life; to compare, order, and sequence decimals and fractions; to model and explain exponents; and to write and solve percentage problems based on everyday life. Measurement concepts at the intermediate level include learning to find elapsed time based on problems of everyday life; learning to solve and explain problems involving time; using linear measurement to the nearest fraction and in metric units; modeling standard and metric units of measure; and converting measurements between the metric and customary systems when given conversion charts. Modeling more complex geometric figures; classifying triangles based on their properties; identifying, drawing, and defining acute, right, and obtuse angles; using compasses and protractors to draw and measure geometric figures; and drawing front, side, and top views of concrete objects are topics about geometry that are taught to children at the intermediate level. Concepts regarding patterns and functions that are taught at the intermediate level include classifying patterns as repeating patterns or growing patterns; using a constant function on a calculator to create a pattern; translating numbers in a function table to a graph; and using powers of 10 to create patterns. Probability and statistics concepts included at the intermediate level involve finding means; interpreting and summarizing graphs; conducting experi-

ments of dependent and independent events; comparing predictions of results with actual results; and using sampling to predict the composition of the whole population. Children learn to construct flowcharts to show steps that are used to complete a task; use the process of elimination to justify conclusions; use inductive and deductive reasoning to justify conclusions; and demonstrate *if and only if* statements using examples from everyday life while studying about logic during the intermediate grades. Demonstrating the field properties of commutation, association, identity, and zero with multiplication and division; using and explaining formulas for the area of simple geometric figures; and graphing number sentences are topics in algebra that children study at the intermediate level.

Learning Experiences

Each of the four learning experiences (see table 4.2) demonstrate one of the interdisciplinary teaching models presented in chapter 1. The learning experiences have been designed to include skills and concepts from physical

Table 4.2

MATHEMATICS LEARNING EXPERIENCES INDEX			
Skills and concepts	Name	Suggested grade level	Interdisciplinary teaching model
Mathematics: Whole numbers, counting, addition, subtraction Physical Education: Balancing, steplike weight transfer	I'm Counting on You	K-2	Connected
Mathematics: Repeating and growing patterns Physical Education: Axial gestures (clap, snap, tap) and locomotor patterns (hop, jump, step)	Pete and Repeat	1-3	Shared
Mathematics: Geometric shapes, commutative and associative properties Physical Education: Balance, locomotor patterns (walk, hop, jump)	Playing the Field	4-6	Connected
Mathematics: Measuring and graphing Physical Education: Locomotor patterns (hop, jump, leap)	Measuring Sticks	3-5	Partnership

education and mathematics. Each learning experience includes a name, suggested grade level, interdisciplinary teaching model, objectives, equipment, organization, complete description of the lesson, and assessment suggestions. In addition, tips on what to look for in student responses, how teachers can change or modify the lesson, and ideas for teachable moments are offered to provide further insights into each learning experience.

I'm Counting on You

SUGGESTED GRADE LEVEL

Primary (K-2)

INTERDISCIPLINARY TEACHING MODEL

Connected
Children learn to recognize and count whole numbers and to perform simple operations such as adding and subtracting in mathematics during the early elementary years. As part of this learning experience, the teacher can refer to counting books such as *Moja Means One* (Feelings, 1971) and *Count and See* (Hoban, 1972) to connect number concepts to physical education experiences with a focus on balancing and traveling actions.

Mathematics
Whole numbers, counting, addition, subtraction

Physical Education
Balancing, steplike weight transfer

OBJECTIVES

As a result of participating in this learning experience, children will improve their ability to
- balance on different numbers of body parts with a focus on stillness and good principles of stability,
- travel in different pathways and directions using a variety of locomotor patterns,
- count using whole numbers to 100 and solve simple addition and subtraction problems,
- count and perform simple mathematical operations using selected foreign languages, and
- use another number system, such as Roman numerals, to represent the same number concepts

EQUIPMENT

Mats spread out in scattered formation. In the absence of mats the children could safely attempt their balances on the floor.

ORGANIZATION

Throughout this lesson the children will work by themselves spread out in general space.

DESCRIPTION

"Hello, girls and boys. Have a seat. See these two books I have today? They are about counting, and I know from talking to Mr./Ms _____ that you are learning about counting [or adding or subtracting] in your math classes. Well, today we are going to use some ideas from counting, adding, or subtracting to help us move today. Let's look at a few pictures first. See, here there is one what? (Fire hydrant). Yes, one fire hydrant. Here's what? (Two friends). Now what? (Three school buses). What about here? (Eight windows). How many on the bottom? (Five). Top? (Three). Right. Well, 5 + 3 = 8. This next book is about counting in a different language called Swahili. [It could just as easily be French, Spanish, or German.] Let's see how to count in Swahili. See this picture? It is of one mountain—the highest one in Africa. It is called Kilimanjaro. One in Swahili is *moja* (mo' • jah). So we see *moja* mountain and *moja* what else? *Moja* sun. Right, one sun. Here we see two friends playing a game. Two in Swahili is *mbili* (m • bee' • lee). So we see *mbili* friends. Here we see *tatu* (ta' • too) or three coffee trees. Coffee is grown in Africa. Here are *nane* (nah' • nay) or eight market stalls. How many on one page? *Tano* (tah' • no) or five. How many on the other page? *Tatu* (ta' • too) or three. Guess what? *Tano* plus *tatu* equals *nane*.

"With those ideas in mind, let's start to move. While you are still sitting there, use just your fingers, hands, or arms and show me how you can make the shape of a one, or *moja*. How about a three, *tatu*? A four, *nne* (n' • nay)? Okay, get up and let's spread out into an open space. Show me with your whole body how you can make a six, *sita* (see' • tah); an eight, *nane* (nah' • nay); a nine, *tisa* (tee' • sah); a seven, *saba* (sab' • bah); and a five, *tano* (tah' • no). Can you make a ten, *kumi* (koo' • mee)? Perhaps make a one followed by a zero.

"Now let's make the task a little harder. I will say a number, and I want you to balance like a gymnast on that number of body parts. Are you ready? Two. Oh, that's too easy. I see a lot of people standing on two feet. Do two again, but this time use other body parts. Great, Susie, a foot and a hand, belly to the sky. Nice, Demetria, an elbow and a knee. Way to go, Saudah, a seat and a hand. Now you're thinking. I'm seeing a good variety of balances each with two body parts touching the floor. One more point. Remember that when we are trying to be gymnasts, for each balance we choose we want to hold very still for five seconds. You could even count to yourself silently. Stay with two body parts, but change your level. Low, medium, high. Can you balance on two body parts and be wide? Narrow? Symmetrical? Asymmetrical? Let's try balancing on *nne* (four) body parts. [Repeat the preceding variations.] How about *moja?* [See figure 4.2.] *Tatu?*

"Next we will do some locomotor actions while we use our counting skills. For starters, let's count together to ten as we jump in place. Ready, 1, 2, 3 . . . Let's do the same but count in Swahili. We'll jump slowly so you have time to think of what number comes next. Ready? Moja, mbili, tatu . . . Let's count backward from ten while we take backward steps. Ready? Ten, nine, eight . . . Backward in Swahili while taking backward steps. Ready? Kumi, tisa, nane . . . Rather than staying in one place, begin to travel somewhere with your locomotor actions. Try hopping forward three times. Slide sideways eight times. Take four big jumps forward, then two tiny jumps backward. Do tisa gallops with one foot forward and then saba gallops with the other foot forward."

TEACHERS, it is up to you to create additional tasks according to your children's ability levels. Combine simple locomotor actions with a focus on a specific number of steps in a specific direction or pathway. If your children are ready for it, try simple addition or subtraction problems. For example, two hops plus three hops equals how many hops? Nine jumps minus five jumps equals how many jumps?

Figure 4.2   Balance on moja body part.

ASSESSMENT SUGGESTIONS

- Have children call out, match corresponding foreign numbers, or solve simple addition or subtraction problems as they perform movement experiences in physical education. For example, balance on *ein* body part; jump *dos* times; skip *dix* times. Observe children's responses for correctness.

- Simple paper-and-pencil quizzes can check students' knowledge.

LOOK FOR

- Good quality balances are important to this experience. The children should be able to keep their center of gravity over their base of support and hold their chosen balances for five seconds without falling or wobbling all over the place. In addition, good lines and angles without sagging body parts are important.

- Locomotor actions should be done with mature patterns in mind. For jumping, a two-footed takeoff and two-footed landing are important. A good arm swing and body lean are also important to initiating a good jump. Hopping actions should be done on one foot to the same foot under control. The arms should be used for balance and to help attain some elevation. The free foot should be held up behind the hopping leg. Skipping should be done on alternating sides: step, hop, step, hop.

- Watch the children's responses very carefully to notice whether they understand the number concepts. When *three* is the correct answer, are they balancing on three body parts? When *five* is the correct answer, are they jumping five times and stopping?

HOW CAN I CHANGE THIS?

- Include counting in other foreign languages such as Spanish, French, or German (table 4.3).

- Combine static balances and locomotor actions into a sequence, for example, jump three times, then balance on four body parts.

- Increase the level of mathematics to include two, three, or four operations in one problem. For example, balance on the number of body parts that is the solution to this problem: $4 + 3 - 5 + 2 =$ ___.

Table 4.3

NUMBERS FROM ONE TO TEN IN SELECTED FOREIGN LANGUAGES				
English	**French**	**Spanish**	**German**	**Swahili**
One	Un	Uno	Eins	Moja
Two	Deux	Dos	Zwei	Mbili
Three	Trois	Tres	Drei	Tatu
Four	Quatre	Cuatro	Vier	Nne
Five	Cinq	Cinco	Fünf	Tano
Six	Six	Seis	Sechs	Sita
Seven	Sept	Siete	Seiben	Saba
Eight	Huit	Ocho	Acht	Nane
Nine	Neuf	Nueve	Neun	Tisa
Ten	Dix	Diez	Zehn	Kumi

TEACHABLE MOMENTS

- Use task cards placed at stations around the floor that require children to read a math problem, figure out the solution, and perform the corresponding number of balances or locomotor actions. This will enable children to see interrelationships among reading, mathematics, and movement.

- Introduce another number system, such as the Roman numeral system, to teach the same lesson. Children profit from learning multiple ways to represent the same concepts.

Pete and Repeat

SUGGESTED GRADE LEVEL

Primary (1-3)

INTERDISCIPLINARY TEACHING MODEL

Shared
As children learn about repeating (•,#,•,#) and growing (•; •,#; +) patterns in mathematics, repeating themes (ABAB, ABAC, etc.) in music, and repeating lines and patterns in art, they can simultaneously learn these concepts in physical education through a coordinated effort with the classroom teacher. In this example lesson the ideas for movement will focus on axial and nonlocomotor gestures, such as snap, clap, tap, bend, stretch, twist, and on locomotor actions such as step, hop, and jump.

Mathematics
Repeating and growing patterns

Physical Education
Axial gestures (clap, snap, tap) and locomotor patterns (hop, jump, step)

OBJECTIVES

As a result of participating in this learning experience, children will improve their ability to

- perform simple axial gestures such as bending, stretching, tapping, snapping, and clapping in sequence;
- perform simple locomotor actions such as stepping, hopping, and jumping in sequence;
- copy repeated and growing patterns through axial and locomotor actions after observing and listening to patterns established by the teacher; and
- develop their own repeated and growing patterns through axial and locomotor actions with and without musical accompaniment.

Suggested references: Clap, Snap, Tap (Brazelton, 1975), Only Just Begun (Brazelton, 1977), Modern Rhythm Band Tunes (Palmer, 1969), Simplified Lummi Stick Activities PK-2 (Johnson, 1976), Rhythmically Moving (Weikart, 1989), (Silver Burdett, 1974).

EQUIPMENT

A record player and one or more of the suggested records will be used during the lesson. In addition, children may use small percussive instruments such as drums, sandpaper blocks, maracas, wooden (lummi) sticks, or triangles to develop and play their own repeated patterns. Children will write patterns on 3 × 5-inch index cards.

ORGANIZATION

During the first part of the lesson, the children will work individually, spread out through the work space, listening to, observing, and copying patterns established by the teacher. For the second half of the lesson, the children will work in pairs or small groups to design their own repeating and growing patterns. The pairs or groups are spread out through the work space as well.

DESCRIPTION

"As you come in today, watch what I'm doing, and as soon as you figure it out, begin to join me."

PERFORM a repeating pattern of groups of four sounds or actions, for example, clap, clap, clap, clap, snap, snap, snap, snap, or touch one hand to head four times then one hand to knee four times. You may choose to have music in 4/4 time as an accompaniment. To begin, keep the pattern simple, ABAB.

"Well, I'm impressed. You sure picked that up in a hurry! Who can tell me what we were doing? Any guesses? Tana?" Tana answers, "Warming up." "Yes, that's part of what we are doing. Kelly?" Kelly responds, "Doing things in groups of four." "You're right, too. As a matter of fact, not only were we doing things in groups of four, but we were repeating the patterns over and over: four claps, four snaps, four claps, four snaps, and so on [or four heads, four knees, four heads, four knees, and so on]. We could call that an ABAB pattern. Are you learning about patterns in any of your other classes? Jenny?" Jenny answers, "When we had music last week, we learned about repeating melodies in songs." "You're quite right. Peter?" Peter says, "Ms. Bauer is teaching us about repeating patterns in math." "Great. It may be a surprise to you, but I've been talking to your teachers, and we all planned together that we would teach you about recurring patterns that happen in all subjects and in everyday life. So what we are going to do in physical education today is first copy some patterns that I will do with you. Then I will give you a chance to invent some of your own patterns and share your patterns with a partner.

"When I say go, I want you to get up and spread out so that you have your own personal space to work in. Our boundaries today are the four cones you see set up. Remember to stay inside them so we can stay away from the walls and be safe. As you find your space, I want you to stop and look at me so I know you are paying attention. Go. . . . Freeze. First, we want to work on different types of repeating patterns. A repeating pattern is set up and then is done over and over again. When you came in, we were doing repeating patterns. Let's do some more, but think of types of patterns we can do. One pattern is called unilateral, when we do something on one side of our body. Let's all do bend, stretch, bend, stretch with one arm. Ready, go. . . . Stop. Can you think of another body part we can bend and stretch? Barclay?" Barclay says, "Leg." "Let's try it. This is a 1, 2, 1, 2 repeating pattern because it counts the number of axial gestures. Let's do some more. With one hand, touch your ear, shoulder, hip, knee, and foot on the same side. Keep repeating the pattern. This is a 1, 2, 3, 4, 5 pattern because it does five actions. It is also a unilateral pattern because all actions are on the same side of the body. Another pattern might be called bilateral. Like a bicycle, it means two sides. Let's use both sides of our body to clap, clap, clap, tap [on thighs], tap, tap. Ready, go. . . . Stop. Some more bilateral patterns might be bend, stretch, bend, stretch with both arms or both legs or use both hands at the same time to touch both ears, shoulders, hips, knees, feet."

TEACHERS are encouraged to invent their own additional bilateral patterns.

"Another pattern is called alternating. For example, we could do something right, left, right, left. Ready, tap right hand to right thigh, left hand to left thigh, right, left. . . . Stop. Now snap right fingers, left fingers, right, left. . . . Stop.

"I'm getting tired of just sitting or standing and doing these patterns. How about you? We could do some of the unilateral, bilateral, and alternating patterns by using our traveling actions. First, let's hop four times on one foot, then four times on our other foot. Ready, go: One, one, one, one, other, other, other, other. . . . Stop. We could jump with our feet close together, then wide apart. What kind of pattern is it when we use two sides at the same time? Remember the "bi" word? Alden?" "Bilateral." "Very good. You have a good memory. Ready, follow me. Close, close, wide, close, close, wide. . . . Stop. Let's change that a little and jump short, short, short, long. Ready, follow me. Short, short, short, long, short, short, short, long. . . . Stop. What about some alternating patterns? The easiest is walking. Everyone with me, ready, go. Step, step, step, step, step. . . . Stop. What about step, hop, step, hop, step, hop, step, hop? Does anyone know what that is called? Tim?" "Skipping." "Way to go! Let's all do it. Ready, go: Step, hop, step, hop. . . . Stop. I can see that almost everyone is a good skipper, but a few are not. We'll work on getting better at that pattern another time.

"Next we'll try to mix up some of the patterns a little. We don't have to do only nonlocomotor actions (clapping, snapping, touching body parts) or locomotor actions (walking, hopping, jumping, skipping) in separate patterns. We could put them together. These are some examples. How about clap, clap, clap, step, clap, clap, clap, step; clap, step, snap, step, clap, step, snap, step ; hop, hop, touch tummy, hop, hop, touch; step, step, step, tap thigh, step, step, step, tap. We could even change the size, time, or force of our patterns. For example, while jumping, we could go short, short, short, long. While hopping, we could go slow, quick, quick. While stepping, we could go light, heavy, heavy, light, heavy."

YOU are encouraged to develop additional repeated mixed patterns of your own. At this time you are encouraged to use one or more of the suggested records. Each of the records contains a variety of activities that include repeated patterns. Examples include using lummi sticks, simple percussive instruments, axial gestures such as clapping and snapping, and locomotor actions to both double and triple time. Each of the records comes with a simple teacher's guide and has both a narrative and an instrumental side to allow teachers and children the option of following a scripted pattern or inventing their own to the music.

"So far we have been working on repeated patterns that you have been working on in your classes in mathematics, music, and art. There is another kind of pattern that we can create. Does anyone remember the name of that pattern? No one? Well, that's okay. It is a hard one to remember. It is called a growing pattern. I'll give you an example to help you remember. If I snap my fingers [snap], then clap my hands [clap], snap, clap, clap, snap, clap, clap, clap, snap, . . . , what do you think comes next? Jawan." "Four claps." "Awesome! You paid attention to the fact that first there was one clap, then two, then three. That is an example of a growing pattern. Let's do some more. What about hop, hop, jump, hop, hop, jump, jump, hop, hop, jump, jump, jump, . . . ; tap thighs, clap hands, jump, tap, tap, clap, clap, jump, jump, . . . ; step, hop, step, step, hop, step, step, step, hop, . . . ; touch head, touch shoulders, quick jump, slow walk, head, shoulders, jump, jump, walk, head, shoulders, jump, jump, jump, walk. . . . You really catch on quickly to all of my patterns.

"You're so good, in fact, that I'm going to challenge you to make up some of your very own patterns. First, you need some time to experiment with your ideas. Remember the types of patterns that we have already tried. You don't have to invent a pattern that no one has ever done before. However, I am asking that you combine some of the nonlocomotor gestures and locomotor actions in ways that we haven't tried yet. Think of all of the types of patterns we have tried [unilateral; bilateral; alternating; 1212; 123123; 12341234; patterns that include changes in size, time, or force; growing patterns. I'm going to give each of you three index cards and a pencil. After you experiment with a pattern and develop one you like, I want you to write it down using one-word cues so that you can remember it. I'll give you an example. If I did touch nose, touch elbow, slap bottom, long jump, hop, hop, I might write, 'nose, elbow, slap, jump, hop, hop.' Get the idea?" A student responds, "Yes, but why do we get three cards?" "I'm giving you three cards because I want you to make up three different patterns. All right, then. Everyone get started. Raise your hand if you need some help, and I'll listen to your ideas."

ALLOW several minutes for the children to develop their ideas and write them down.

"Okay, stop. On the count of three, find a partner and sit down beside him or her. One, two, three. What I want you to do now is to share with your partner. You can use one of your cards at a time to help you remember, but I want one partner to perform one of their patterns. The observing partner will watch. Then as soon as possible I want the observer to verbally say what he or she thinks the pattern is and get up and do the pattern alongside his or her partner. How about an example? Anyone want to show us one of their patterns? All right, Gabrielle. [Open mouth, close mouth, arms out to side, arms down, hop, hop, long jump.] Good work. That pattern includes both gestures and locomotion and was a 1, 2, 3, 4, 5, 5, 6 repetition. Everyone share your patterns with your partners now. . . . Stop.

"Get a new partner. One, two, three. The last thing that I want you to do is share one of your written cards with your new partner. See if you can read the pattern on the card and, with no demonstration, try to see if you can do the pattern. Then talk with your partner to see if you got it right. If not, let your partner show you, and then do it together. Finally, talk with your partner and see if you can describe in words the type of pattern it is."

ASSESSMENT SUGGESTIONS

- As children develop different repeating and growing patterns in movements, have them record their patterns in writing as journal entries.

- Assign partners after children create a pattern, and have the observing child verbalize or write out the pattern he or she sees the moving partner perform. Also encourage children to compare their responses to other patterns in art and music.

LOOK FOR

- Some children have trouble with transitions from one movement to another. Try to help these children move smoothly during transitions in whatever pattern they are having trouble with.

- Sequential memory is an essential skill for performing repeating or growing patterns well. This includes both auditory and visual sequential memory. Make sure you start with simple patterns, and move to more difficult patterns only when the children are successful with the easy ones. Pair those who have trouble remembering the patterns with a buddy who catches on readily.

- When the children work on developing their own patterns, a few may lack the confidence to think up their own or may not feel that they can work independently. Work closely with these children: Use their ideas to develop a pattern, and say "See, you can do that. I'll bet you have more ideas just like that." Or allow them to work with a friend to get started.

HOW CAN I CHANGE THIS?

- Include other activities using equipment such as bouncing balls, streamers, jump ropes, and so on to develop patterns, for example, bounce, catch, toss, catch (with a ball) or four clockwise circles overhead, four figure eights in front of body, four clockwise circles to the right side, four clockwise circles to the left side (with a streamer).

- Use simple aerobic dance or step aerobics actions to develop patterns with the children. Include music in the background to enhance the experience, and perform the pattern to a steady beat.

- Make music patterns an integral part of the experience by using the concepts of measures; whole, half, quarter, and eighth notes; tempo; pitch; and dynamics. The children can perform nonlocomotor gestures and locomotor actions to music that they create.

TEACHABLE MOMENTS

- Help children become aware of the patterns in their everyday lives. Even a routine of getting up, eating breakfast, and going to school is a pattern. Days of the week, months of the year, seasons, and so on are patterns as well. How many other life patterns can you and the children think of?
- Listen to music or sing familiar songs (e.g., "Old MacDonald," "The Hokey Pokey," "The 12 Days of Christmas"), and analyze the types of patterns they contain.
- Bring in some famous paintings, and look for repeating lines or patterns.
- Help children recognize patterns in fence posts, bridge designs, windows in buildings, basketry, clothes, and other everyday objects and places.

Playing the Field

SUGGESTED GRADE LEVEL

Primary (2-3)

INTERDISCIPLINARY TEACHING MODEL

Connected
As children travel from marker to marker and create balance shapes, they can understand in a practical sense the relationships among body shapes and angles and geometric shapes and angles, and the commutative and associative rules of mathematics.

Mathematics
Geometric shapes, commutative and associative properties

Physical Education
Balance, locomotor patterns (walk, hop, jump)

OBJECTIVES

As a result of participating in this learning experience, children will improve their abilities to

- make body shapes,
- balance on a variety of large and small body parts, using characteristics of good form,
- balance in a variety of selected symmetrical and asymmetrical shapes,
- use their feet to travel by exploring each of the five basic steplike actions,
- relate body shapes to basic geometric shapes and angles, and
- understand the commutative field property of addition in mathematics.

EQUIPMENT

A half sheet of newspaper for each student

ORGANIZATION

A large, open space is needed for this activity. A hard surface or gym floor is preferred. Students work individually in scattered formation.

DESCRIPTION

"Hello, girls and boys. As you come into the gym today, you will see that I have several stacks of half sheets of newspaper spread about the space. When I say 'go,' you are to get a piece of newspaper, take it to a personal space, lay it down on the floor, and sit on top of it. I'll know you are ready when everyone is sitting, looking at me. Go. . . . Thanks. You sure did that quickly, and you selected good personal spaces. Everyone is spread out nicely. That will be important for today's lesson because we are going to do a lot of traveling (running, hopping, jumping, skipping, and sliding) and balancing. While we are moving and balancing, we will also relate what we are doing to some concepts you are learning about in math.

"As we begin, I want you to imagine that the newspapers you are sitting on are houses or buildings and that you are all superpeople—superwomen and supermen. You have the power to leap over a building in a single bound. Let's start with your own home. Stand up and step outside. Have the front of your body face the front of your house. Now jump over your house: a two-footed takeoff and a two-footed landing. Do that several times. Remember to swing your arms and reach for the sky as you jump. Also crouch and explode with your legs. Then land softly—squash. Good, Kim. That was a powerful jump and a soft landing. Can you jump backward over your house as well? Sideways? Backward and sideways are harder, so remember to keep a two-footed takeoff and a powerful, explosive leg action. Still try to swing your arms to help you get lift. Can you try a hop over your house: from one foot to the same foot? What about a leap: one foot to the other? One foot to two? Two feet to one? Great, Rodney, Juaquin, Jolene. You can jump over your house in a variety of ways. Stop. Sit down in your home.

"You're getting good at bounding (hopping, jumping, leaping) over your own building, so now we are going to take a trip. First, look where you are right now. That is your home and neighborhood. To help you remember, look all around. Where is your home in this gym? What lines or walls is your home near? Who are your neighbors to your front? side? back? We'll take a short trip first. When I say go, travel (run, hop, jump) to another house and jump over it, then return to your own home by traveling in a different way, and balance in it on three body parts. Watch. [Demonstrate as you explain.] I'm going to leave my home and hop. As I get to Susan's home, I'll jump over it, then return to my own home by skipping, and end by balancing on three body parts in a shape that I choose. I'll know everyone is finished when I see everyone balancing very still with three body parts touching the floor. Who can tell me what you are supposed to do? Shandria . . . Yes, good. Go. . . . Whoops. One or two people got a little lost. Remember to go to only one house, then return home. If you are not sure, don't travel too far before returning home. If you are confident, you might want to travel way across the gym, and then find your way home. Let's try that again. Go. . . . Much better that time. Everyone found their way back without getting lost.

"Now we're going to make the task even more difficult. This time when I say 'go,' I want you to keep traveling, and when you get to a house, jump over it. Keep traveling to another house and another, each time jumping over the house in a different way. When you hear my signal of a drumbeat, go to your home as quickly as you can, and balance on four body parts in a shape of your choice. Who can tell me what they are going to do? . . . Good remembering, Johnny. Travel, jump, travel, jump, and so on, drum, return home, and balance on four body parts. Go. . . . Way to go. I see some people skipping, others sliding, others jogging while traveling. Good jumps, too. Some frontward, some sideways, some from one foot to two feet, some from two feet to two feet. Good variety. [Drum.] Wow. Everyone still remembered where their home was. [Repeat several times.] Stop. Gather in front of me. Sit down and listen.

"What we are going to do next is a little bit complicated, but I know you can do it. We are going to travel and visit some other homes. While you are at those homes, you will balance inside them for five seconds. To help you remember, our balances will concentrate on the idea of shapes. Think of the geometric shapes you have learned about in math. Round or curved body shapes are like circles, spheres, or curved lines. Pointed body shapes with bends at the elbows, knees, hips, and the like can remind us of the corners or joints in triangles, squares, rectangles, and so on. Straight shapes can remind us of long extended lines."

BALANCES can also focus on symmetry or asymmetry or acute, right, and obtuse angles.

"Your first balance in the first house you visit will be round or curved. Watch me. I'll start at my house and travel any way I like to the house of anyone I choose—let's say Peter's house (Peter won't be there because he will be busy visiting someone else's home). When I arrive at this house, I will balance in it for how many seconds? Five. Good listening, Sam. It will be important for you to remember the house you visit, so while you are balancing, take a look around at where you are. What lines or walls are close? Also remember the balance you do in that house: round or curved. After balancing for five seconds, I will return to my own home and sit down. So the task is to travel, round or curved balance, travel home, sit down. Ready, go. . . . Can you remember where you went and the balance you did? Try it again. Go to the same place and do the same balance. Go. . . . Excellent. Everyone is seated, which tells me that you are back home. Now comes the tricky part. We are going to add a second house. You will start from your home and travel to your first house. What type of balance do you do there? Round or curved, right! Then you will go on to a second house and balance with a shape that has a lot of points (elbows, knees, hips, and so on bent at angles). Hold that balance for five seconds, look where you are, then travel home, and sit down. Watch Lauren demonstrate. Let's tell her what to do as she is doing it. Travel, round or curved balance, travel, pointed-shape balance, travel home, sit down. Thanks, Lauren. Everyone try it. Go. . . . I'm noticing that almost everyone is doing their balances while on their feet. I'm going to give you one chance to change your balances, and I ask that you try to balance on different body parts and still be rounded or have pointed shapes. Still remember the houses you are balancing in. Go. Travel, balance, travel, balance, home, sit down. Very good. I saw some excellent rounded or curved and pointed balances on different body parts that time. Do you think you could remember your travel route if you did it backward? What I mean is go to your second house first and do your pointed balance, then go to your first house and do your round or curved balance. Let's try. Go. . . . Stop. A couple of people got confused, but most did real well. Let's try again. Travel, pointed balance, travel, round or curved balance, travel home, sit down. That's it, much better. While you are sitting, I would like to talk about what you are learning in mathematics for a minute. When you are adding numbers—say 1 and 2—does it make any difference what order you add them? No. 1 + 2 = 2 + 1. That is called the commutative property of math. Well, we just did that in our balances. We reversed the process. The order changed, but we still did the same two balances. Pretty tricky, right!

"Let's see if we can make our sequence even harder. Let's add a third balance. The third balance will be straight or stretched. I want to see good extensions, arms and legs straight. You can do these straight or stretched shapes while balancing on different body parts. Let's rehearse. Travel, rounded or curved balance, travel, pointed balance, travel, straight or stretched balance [see figure 4.3], travel home, sit down. Go. . . . Good work. Do it again. . . . You seem to have mastered it. Now do it in reverse. I'll talk you through it. Travel, straight or stretched balance, travel, pointed balance, travel, rounded or curved balance, travel home, sit down. Well done. Do it on your own. Go. . . . Stop. Gather in here. Remember when we talked about the commutative property of math? Well, you just did another property. You have been learning that if you add 1 + 2 + 3, you get the same sum as if you add 3 + 2 + 1. That is also called the commutative property of mathematics. It works in physical education too. Even if we reverse the sequence of our balances (round, pointed, straight = straight, pointed, round), we balance the same number of times (three). Can you think of any other situations that you might use the commutative or associative properties of math? Very good. Yes, we could take turns in a different order. We could listen to the tunes on a CD in a different order. There are a lot of ways we could use these properties. It's time to leave class now. Good-bye for now."

ASSESSMENT SUGGESTION

- As children travel to different "homes," check for the correctness of their responses. Are the shapes round, pointed, or straight when they are supposed to be? Can the children name objects in the real world that are round, pointed with lots of angles, or straight? Can they reverse their balance sequences? To assess their knowledge of the commutative and associative properties of mathematics, have them write a simple mathematics or movement problem to illustrate their understanding.

Figure 4.3   Travel, then create a straight or stretched body shape.

LOOK FOR

- Children should focus on quality traveling actions. This is not a race. Look for a change in their method of traveling after visiting each "house." Also encourage variety in their choices of direction, pathway, and speed: They should not always travel forward, straight, and fast.

- Quality in the children's balances is also important. Stillness while holding shapes, well-defined lines and angles of body parts and joints, and a concentrated focus of intent are key to producing definitive work.

- Some children may get lost after visiting another "home" and returning to their own "home." Suggest that these children don't travel as far away (e.g., go next door and return) or that they travel to easily located houses (e.g., one in the center circle of the basketball court) to help them remember. Or they could travel with a friend.

HOW CAN I CHANGE THIS?

- For more advanced students, add a fourth and fifth balance to further develop sequential memory skills.

- Include mapping as a skill in this lesson. Children could draw a map of their route, including their pathway to each stop on the route, their method of travel, and the type of balance at each house visited. This process may be compared to an itinerary or a travel plan.

- Do the same lesson, but focus the balance shapes on symmetry and asymmetry or on acute, right, and obtuse angles.

- Use a map and compass, and turn this into an orienteering experience. From their own "home," children could move five paces at 30 degrees, for example.

TEACHABLE MOMENTS

- Use this lesson to reinforce spatial awareness and body awareness concepts such as front, back, side, inside, outside, over, and so on.

- Teach compass directions north, south, east, and west.

- Talk about finding your way. Concepts such as street signs, familiar landmarks, travel routes, and using maps are topics that can be used to enhance this lesson.

- The topic of neighborhoods from social studies can also be included. The amount of space people need to live; what a neighborhood consists of, such as close friends, stores, churches, open spaces for play, and so on; and urban, suburban, and rural communities could be included.

- The concept of motorways—interstate highways, city streets, and back roads or blue highways—provides a model that children can associate with this physical education lesson. Sometimes they can travel fast and go mostly straight ahead. At other times they have more traffic, smaller roads, and regulated speeds. On the back roads they must travel slowly, make many sharp turns, and change gears often.

Measuring Sticks

SUGGESTED GRADE LEVEL

Intermediate (3-5)

INTERDISCIPLINARY TEACHING MODEL

Partnership

The classroom teacher and physical education teacher can work as a team during this learning experience. As children learn how to measure using different units in mathematics, they can use this learning experience for practical application of this information in physical education by measuring and graphing the distances of their traveling actions.

Mathematics

Measuring and graphing

Physical Education

Locomotor patterns (hop, jump, leap)

OBJECTIVES

As a result of participating in this learning experience, children will improve their abilities to
- use good body mechanics to hop, jump, and leap;
- combine basic locomotor actions into a sequence (e.g., hop, step, jump);
- measure and record their performances on scoring sheets; and
- diagram their performances on charts and make decisions about which efforts produce the best results.

EQUIPMENT

A ruler, yardstick, newspaper wand, bat, or stick with which to measure; a score sheet or histogram chart and pencil to record results; markers to mark jump length (popsicle sticks, tape, pencil line, etc.)

ORGANIZATION

Students will work in pairs in an indoor or outdoor space.

DESCRIPTION

"Good morning, boys and girls! Are you ready to do some exciting jumping today? What I have in mind for us is to do different styles of jumping and to see which ones allow us to jump the farthest. In addition to jumping today, the most important thing we are going to learn is how to measure our jumps, record our scores, and graph our performances.

"First get a partner and stand back to back. Go. . . . If you don't have a partner yet, raise your hand, and I'll help you find one. Good. Now let's warm up. Play follow the leader with your partner, trying to stay close to each other. Vary the way you travel: sometimes jogging, hopping, jumping, skipping, and so on. Remember to change directions, pathways, and speeds. Perhaps take long and short steps, heavy and light steps. Stop. . . . Change leaders. Repeat. . . . Stop. Now let's do a few stretching exercises especially for our legs because we are going to use them a lot today."

PERFORM exercises of your choice, but remember to stretch hamstring, quadriceps, and calf muscles.

"Stop. Quickly come here in front of me. Sit down. I'm going to hand out some score sheets, graphs, measuring sticks, and pencils to each of you. [Distribute materials.] When I say 'go,' you and your partner will find or make a [chalk] line within our space. This will be your jumping line. Each time you jump, you will start with your toes on, but not over, the line. [Demonstrate.] That is important because you will use that line for measuring every jump. After placing your toes on the line, you will make your jump. Your partner will mark your jump by putting a marker where your heels land or, if you fall backward, the part of your body that touches nearest the takeoff line." [Demonstrate.]

NOTE that children's abilities to measure accurately differ. Depending on the level of the child, crude measurements may be used, such as the number of lengths of a shoe, folded newspaper, book, or forearm (see figure 4.4). Children who have more advanced measuring abilities may use more accurate measures, such as the nearest yard, foot, inch, or centimeter. Work with the classroom teacher on measurement skills.

"Each time you make a jump, measure it with your partner and record it on your score sheet. [Demonstrate.] Spread out and find a good jumping space with your partner. Go. . . . Stop. Good, I see that you are spread out and that your jumps will not interfere with each other. You have also chosen or made good lines from which to jump. For your first jump, I want you to place your toes on the line and jump. Use a two-footed

Figure 4.4   Measure your jumps with a bat, book, shoe, or another object.

takeoff. Don't swing your arms much or bend your legs. Just an easy jump. [Demonstrate.] Measure and record it on your score sheet. Take turns with your partner. Go. . . . Stop. On your next jump, try swinging your arms back and then forward and up (reach for the sky). [Demonstrate.]

"Make three jumps, and record your best jump. Go. . . . Yes, way to go, Lauren. Good arm swing. I like the way Tom and Tyron are cooperating by taking turns jumping then measuring. Remember to measure accurately, then record the score on your sheet. Stop. Now, let's try crouching and exploding in addition to the arm swing [Demonstrate.] Swing, crouch, explode. Try three more jumps each, and record your best score. Remember to take turns, and help each other mark the jump and measure. Go. . . . Wow! What an explosive jump, Daniel. Super, Sharon and Devon, I see that you are recording your scores in the right places on your sheets. Does anyone need any help with the score sheets or with their measuring? Okay, Sharon and Devon, would you go and help Amy and Liz for a little while? Answer the questions they have about measuring or scoring. Thanks. . . . Stop. Do you think it makes any difference if we lean forward (45 degrees) as we jump? [Demonstrate.] Swing, crouch, lean, explode! Try three more jumps, and record your best score. Go. . . . Stop.

"Let's graph what we have so far [see figure 4.5]. On the horizontal graph line (X axis), indicate the type of jump. On the vertical line (Y axis), mark the distance of your jump. [Demonstrate.]

"Everyone, graph each of your best jumps. Use the scores from your score sheets. Work with your partner, and help each other. Make sure you get each jump recorded correctly. Raise your hand if you need any help. . . . Okay, look at your graph. What type of jump gave you the best results? Yes. As you added body parts (arm swing, leg explosion, trunk lean), you were able to jump farther. In science this is called using a summation of forces to get better results. Can you think of any other type of physical activity where you use a summation of forces to get better results? Yes, when we throw or kick, we use our whole body in our effort to throw or kick a far distance.

"Now let's try some other types of locomotor skills and see how far we travel through the air. What about a hop (one-footed takeoff, same-foot landing)? Try three hops and record your best score. Go. . . . Stop. Now try a leap (one foot to the other). Try three leaps, and record your best score. Now graph those performances and compare them

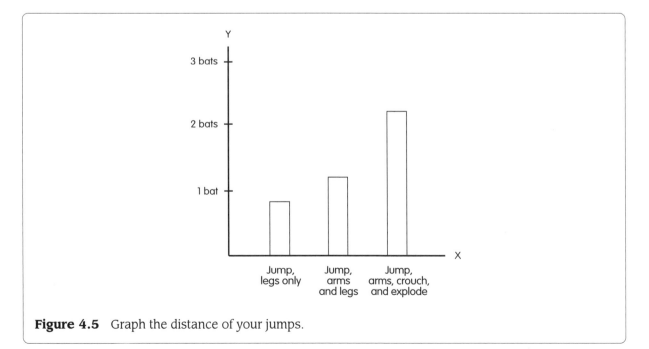

Figure 4.5 Graph the distance of your jumps.

with your jumping performances. Were you able to travel farther with a jump, hop, or leap?

"Finally, move back from the takeoff line. What I want you to do now is to take several steps before you jump so that you have forward momentum as you go into your jump. It will be important to plant your takeoff foot or feet on, but not over, your measuring line. [Demonstrate.] As in the rules for track and field, any takeoffs that go over the line do not count. Make several tries at jumping with a walking approach. Work out your steps to get them just right. Try a one-footed takeoff (hurdle step) and a two-footed takeoff. [Demonstrate.] Always land on two feet. Remember to still swing your arms and explode with your legs at takeoff. As you land, rock forward from heels to balls of your feet and lean forward. Go. . . . Your toes went a few inches over the takeoff line that time, Leigh. Correct the error by starting back about six inches from your present mark. Then you will plant your toes right on the line at takeoff. Yes! That's it. Very good that time. Stop. Now that you have your steps down, choose your best way of jumping and make three tries. Measure each attempt. Record your best score. Place the score for your moving jump on the graph. Go. I can see that you have learned to measure accurately, Brent and Riley. You measure from the takeoff line to the point of impact nearest the line each time. Each score is to the nearest inch [or foot, book, stick]. Your graphs are giving you an accurate picture of your results. Stop. Everyone come in here and sit down. Let's talk about jumping and what your scores and graphs are telling you. Were you able to jump as far or farther using a moving jump? What does this tell us about momentum and the sum of forces? Thanks. You worked hard today. You are learning a lot, not only about how to jump better, but also about how mathematics and science can help us understand how our bodies move."

ASSESSMENT SUGGESTION

- In addition to the graph in figure 4.5, have the children graph the distances of other traveling actions, such as a hop, leap, and moving long jump. Also give them an oral or written test on their understanding of the concepts of momentum and summation of forces.

LOOK FOR

- Children need to use good mechanics to get optimal results. A good arm swing, explosive leg action, and leaning at a 45-degree angle are the key to successful results. Timing is also a key. Some children will swing their arms, then stop and jump. Others will crouch, then stand up straight and jump up. Placing a barrier (a towel or small hurdle to jump over) sometimes helps.

- Children are often confused about measuring. Be clear about the unit of measurement. Start with crude measurements. It is easier to understand "five books" or "five sticks" than inches as a fraction of a foot or yard. Also be clear about where to start the measurement and how far to measure.

- Converting scores to graphs is not an easy task. Work with the classroom teacher on this task and on helping the children understand the meaning of the results. Analysis and interpretation require higher-level thinking skills.

HOW CAN I CHANGE THIS?

- Combine locomotor skills into a sequence. How far can children jump using a step or leap (from one foot to the other) then a hop (from one foot to the same foot)? three jumps in a row (two feet to two feet)? a hop, then jump? a hop, step, jump?

- Measure and graph high-jumping skills.

- Measure and graph throwing or kicking efforts.

- Measure and graph heart rate after different types of exercise of different durations and levels of intensity.

TEACHABLE MOMENTS

- Although this lesson is about learning to jump better, it is also about learning in a very practical way how to use mathematics and science. Rather than measuring lines in a book to the nearest fraction of an inch or centimeter, the children are actually doing an experiment in human performance. They are learning to measure and graph real attempts and can see which attempts produce better results. They can also readily see that by using certain scientific principles, such as summing body forces and using momentum, their performances will improve.

Additional Ideas for Developing Learning Experiences

This section offers additional learning experiences to develop children's understanding of the mathematics concepts identified in table 4.1: numbers, measuring and graphing, geometry, patterns and functions, probability and statistics, logic, and algebra. Curricular areas, suggested grade level, and a brief description are provided for each activity. These activities are intended to inspire additional ideas for interdisciplinary work between classroom and physical education teachers. Teachers are encouraged to develop these ideas more completely. Sometimes the connected model will be most appropriate, while other times the shared or partnership model may be used. Your main concern should be to meet the developmental levels and needs of your students; you can adapt activities to accommodate your teaching schedule, equipment, and available space.

Numbers

Whole Number Designs

Mathematics
Number recognition and formation

Physical Education
Body shapes, use of air and floor pathways

Grade Level
K-1

- Written numbers are made of straight, curved, or diagonal lines. Categorize each of the numbers by discussing the composition of each number. Categories may vary, depending on how you teach the children to form the numbers.

    Straight line 1, 3, 4, 9

    Curved line 0, 2, 3, 6, 8, 9

    Diagonal line 4, 7

    Straight and curved 2, 3, 5, 9

    Straight and diagonal 4, 7

Have children make the shape of each of the numbers using different body parts or the whole body.

• Can you make the shape of a number from 0 to 9 using your whole body? What other numbers can you make using your whole body? Can you make number shapes using different body parts? Can you make the same number shapes while changing your body level? Can you stand, kneel, or lie on the floor to make your body shapes? What numbers can you make with a partner or small group? Can people in a partnership or small group combine to make one number, or each make a separate digit of a bigger number (0-9999) (see figure 4.6)?

• Use air or floor pathways to trace number patterns. Can you hop or skip and make a 3 or 7? Can you use your elbow, knee, or head to trace an 8 in the air? Use two or three different body parts to trace the same number simultaneously.

• As a teacher make a line grid on the floor or pavement, as in figure 4.7, or have the students draw the grid. Then have the children jump, hop, walk, slide, or skip along the lines on the grid to make the numbers from 0 to 9. Move forward, backward, or sideways to make the numbers. Move fast or slowly while making the numbers.

• I am going to call out a number. When I do, put that same number of body parts on the floor and create a balance. When I say 'three,' you should touch three body parts to the floor. Can you use your hands, wrists, elbows, shoulders, tummy, seat, side, shins, thighs, knees, feet? Ready? Four. That's it. I see two knees and two elbows. Four again, but use four different body parts."

• As a teacher, construct beanbags into the shapes of numbers or, have a parent support group stitch the beanbags. Then, while playing catch with a partner, have the children identify the number of the beanbag you are about to catch while it is still in the air.

• Make the shape of a number with a jump rope on the floor. Walk, hop, slide, or jump as you trace the number along the floor. Jump or hop from side to side or into and out of the empty spaces of the number you chose. Move backward or sideways to trace along the number.

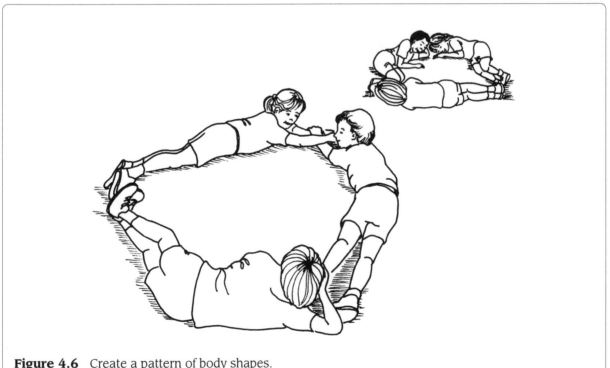

Figure 4.6   Create a pattern of body shapes.

Figure 4.7 Travel along the lines on the grid to trace each whole number.

Count on Me

Mathematics
Counting

Physical Education
A variety of locomotor, balancing, and manipulative experiences and exercises

Grade Level
1-3

• "As I call out a number, I want you to take that many steps in one direction or pathway. Ready? Five steps forward. Eight steps backward. Six slides sideways. Ten skips in a curved pathway. Seven hops in a straight pathway."

• "As I clap my hands, silently count the number of claps to yourself. Then make the shape of the number you counted with your body." Do additional counting problems by snapping fingers, tapping thighs, clucking tongues, and stamping feet. Each time children make a body shape of the number counted.

• While doing exercises, count the number you perform. Count from 1 up, or count down to zero.

• Count exercises in sets. For example, count four repetitions of a two-count exercise, such as a toe touch or sit-up, as 1, 2; 2, 2; 3, 2; 4, 2, or count a four-count exercise by fours (1, 2, 3, 4; 2, 2, 3, 4; 3, 2, 3, 4; 4, 2, 3, 4). Count the measures in a piece of music using the same procedure. Then make up an aerobic dance routine or dance sequence to represent actions for each of the measures.

- Use your counting abilities to keep score in games such as hopscotch or shuffleboard. Or use your counting abilities to keep score in a game that you make up.

- Count the number of throws and catches you and your partner can make without dropping the ball. Count the number of consecutive forearm passes you can make to yourself in volleyball without making a mistake. Count the number of consecutive forehand strokes you can make against a wall from a distance of 20 feet without losing control of the ball.

- Play a game starting with a certain number of points and count down to zero by 1s, 2s, 3s, and so on.

- Count the number of times you can jump a rope in a minute. Count by 1s, 2s, 3s, and so on.

- Count the number of times you can bounce a ball or throw a ball in 10 seconds. Use different time trials, and use addition or subtraction to compare the sums or differences between trials.

- In certain types of games, such as line games in which a certain number of children are caught, count the number of children caught. The number of children not caught and the total number of children in the class can be used in addition and subtraction problems.

- Using a children's counting book (e.g., Feelings, 1971; Hoban, 1972), hold up a picture with a number of objects in it. Have the children form the shape of the number they counted with their bodies.

- Hold up a number card (1-20) or point to a number on a chart. Have the children bounce a ball, twirl a hoop, or jump rope that number of times.

- While working with partners, children hop, jump, skip, or slide a self-chosen number of times. The observing partner should count the number of tries and then verbally express the total, for example, "I saw you skip five times."

- Create number lines from 1 to 100 across the floor. Ask the children to move and count the numbers by 2s, 3s, 4s, 5s. Have them jump to 10 counting by 2s or skip to 50 counting by 5s. For each of the sums or products, have them shape the answer with their bodies.

You're a Real Operator

Mathematics
Addition, subtraction, multiplication, division, fractions

Physical Education
Body shape, locomotor actions

Grade Level
2-4

- As a teacher construct a 5 × 5 or 6 × 6 number grid of all the single-digit numbers from (0-9) (figure 4.8) on the floor or pavement. Then, have the children jump or hop into each of the sequential numbers from 0 to 9. Hop into the odd numbers. Jump into the even numbers.

- Using the same number grid as in the preceding lesson, perform simple addition and subtraction problems from your math class (e.g., 1 + 4 = 5) as you jump or hop into the appropriate numbers.

Figure 4.8 Jump or hop into the odd and even numbers.

• Using the same number grid as in the preceding lesson, perform more complex math problems of multiplication and division. For example, for 4 × 6 = 24, hop from the 4 to the 6 and finish by jumping and landing with one foot in a 2 and the other in a 4. Try 35 ÷ 5 = 7. What other math problems can you solve?

• Let's use our bodies to calculate some math problems. First, we'll use body shapes. Someone choose a shape. Oh, that's good—balancing on two knees and one hand. Now, if we had three more people copy that shape, how many total people would be balancing in that shape? That's right, four. So let's do that by making a math sentence: 1 + 3 = 4. We'll need one person each to make the + and = signs, and enough people to do the balances for each number. Now, we'll do some more problems: 2 + 4 = 6, 5 − 2 = 3, 4 − 4 = 0. Can you think of other balances for each of the problems?

• This time we'll do body-number computation. Who can make his or her body into the shape of a 3? We'll need someone to be a plus sign. Lauren, can you make a 4? Brian, be the equal sign. Who can form the answer? That's right. It is a 7. 3 + 4 = 7. Get into small groups of five and calculate several math problems. (Students can also do multiplication or division problems if they are capable.)

• Using nonlocomotor actions do the following in sequence. One twist, two punches, three swings, four stretches, five presses, six bends, seven turns, eight shakes, nine pulls. Can you think of a way to do a locomotor sequence?

• Try doing a sequence of activities in one order. Then, reverse the order of the sequence. For example, one hop, two jumps, three slides, four ball bounces, then four ball bounces, three slides, and so on.

• As the teacher, set up a sequence of stations (see figure 4.9). Each station should have an ordinal number of objects. Give each child a task card with a list of tasks to accomplish. To avoid children waiting in line, vary the station and ordinal position of equipment each child uses. For example, while one child skips around the fourth hoop, then jumps over the fifth wand, another might bounce the second ball 10 times, then do a forward roll on the first mat.

• Think about how you could divide your body in half. You could have a top half and bottom half or a right half and a left half. Can you bend your body parts on the right half and stretch your body parts on your left half? What about twisting the top half of your body while leaving the bottom half straight? How else can you divide your body in halves?

• Let's divide the room into fourths. Can you run through one-fourth the distance of the room fast, then walk slowly across the remaining three-fourths? What about skipping the first half of the distance, then walking the next fourth, then again skipping the last fourth? Using walking, skipping, leaping, hopping, jumping, sliding, and crawling, what other fractions can you illustrate while moving across the floor?

• In groups of six to eight, make a geometric shape while lying on the floor. Then divide that shape into halves, thirds, or fourths using your bodies to create lines to make the correct fractions.

• Answer the following questions about fractions by jumping, hopping, skipping, or leaping the correct number of times. What is 1/5 of 15? What is 1/4 of 16? What is 3/4 of 8? What is 1/2 of 10? What is 2/3 of 24?

• Throw or kick a ball at a target 10, 15, or 20 times. Count the number of successful tries. Then, calculate the percentage of successful tries. For example, 7 out of 10 tries is .70 or 70 percent.

• Let's see if we can remember the rules for whether number computations result in odd or even numbers when adding, subtracting, multiplying, and dividing. If the answer is even, make an E shape with your body, or balance on an even number of body

Figure 4.9   Set up an ordinal or sequential obstacle course.

parts. If the answer is odd, make an *O* shape with your body, or balance on an odd number of body parts. Ready? Even + Even = Even, Even + Odd = Odd, Odd + Odd = Even. Get the idea? Now you do the rest. Even – Even, Odd – Even, Odd – Odd, Even × Even, Even × Odd, Odd × Odd, Even – Even, Odd – Even, Odd – Odd.

Measuring and Graphing

I'm This Many

Mathematics
Measuring using nonstandard units

Physical Education
Balancing, locomotor activities

Grade Level
K-2

Measuring starts by teaching children quantitative concepts using nonstandard units. Even in prekindergarten children should learn concepts such as big/little, long/short, tall/short, high/low, wide/narrow, many/few, and all/none and positional concepts such as in front, behind, over, under, below, around, between, on, off, and through. The following examples show how children can learn these concepts in physical education and dance:

• Make a big body shape. Can you hold it still? Can you stay in that big shape and move around the room? Make a small shape. Hold it still. Move your small shape around the room (figure 4.10).

• Take short, baby steps to move across the room. Take long, giant steps back the other way. Which way did you take many more steps? Which way took fewer steps? Try jumping and hopping using long and short steps.

• Create a balance position. Can you put your hips higher than your head? Can you put your elbows lower than your knees?

Figure 4.10 Make big and small, tall and short body shapes.

• Balance your body at a high, medium, or low level. Create different shapes at each level.

• Can you stretch your arms or legs out sideways and make a wide shape at a high or low level? While in that wide shape, can you move across the room? Now pull your arms and legs in to your sides and make a narrow shape. Can you make a narrow shape at a high, medium, low level? Can you move your narrow shape across the floor? Can you make part of your body narrow and another part of your body wide at the same time? Can you move across the floor in that position?

• Hold up a few fingers [one or more, but less than five]. Now hold up many fingers [five or more]. Let's see if we can experiment with many and few. Hop a few steps. Skip taking many steps. Many children stay standing, while a few sit down. Many children crawl, while a few jump. [Experiment with other ideas focusing on group awareness and cooperation with the children.]

• Place your hand above your head. Now put your elbow in front of your tummy. Get a partner. One move around the other. Create a balance, one over the other. One partner make a bridgelike shape, while the other partner goes over and under the bridge like an airplane or ship.

• Find ways to move on, off, over, under, through, into, out of, and around a piece of equipment such as a hula hoop, jump rope, wand, box, or bench. Balance in front of, beside, and in back of the equipment.

• Create situations in physical education in which children are asked to make comparative measurements such as longer than, heavier than, cooler than, and so on. For example, a stamp is heavier than a step. A pressing action is more forceful than a dab. Have children make two different shapes, one longer than the other.

It's Getting Loud in Here

Mathematics
Volume, pitch, tempo

Physical Education
Responding to music qualities

Grade Level
1-3
Volume, pitch, and tempo are quantitative mathematical concepts. Experiment with volume, pitch, and tempo concepts using music and dance. Focus on concepts such as loud or soft, high or low, and fast or slow.

• Make loud sounds on a drum, triangle, or another percussion instrument, and have the children respond with big, powerful movements. Make soft sounds, and have the children respond with small, light movements. Develop patterns of loud and soft sounds.

• Can the children move against the music? Have them move with big, powerful actions when the sound is soft and with small, light actions when the sound is loud.

• "Now we'll play some notes on the piano. When the pitch is high, make a high shape or travel at a high level. When the pitch is low, make a low shape or travel at a low level. What about a medium note?"

• Change the tempo of the music being played. Have the children move quickly when it is fast and move slowly when the tempo slows. Create patterns of fast and slow tempos.

- Find several short pieces of music that contrast the concepts of volume, pitch, and tempo (Boorman, *Pompous Potatoes*). Use pieces with high pitch, fast tempo, and loud volume; low pitch and slow tempo; fast tempo and soft volume; and so on. Have the children respond accordingly.

How Long Will It Take to Get There?

Mathematics
Time awareness

Physical Education
A variety of games and dance and gymnastics experiences

Grade Level
1-4

- Awareness of time sequences starts with focusing on before, now, and after. A good way to demonstrate these concepts is out on the playground at the slide: Stand at the bottom (before); sit at the top (now); slide down to the bottom (after). Create a sequence of setting a ball up on a batting tee, hitting it off, and having partner retrieve it and throw it back. Have the children create interpretive movements for "yesterday it rained" (splash in the puddles), "today it is sunny" (play catch, go fishing, jump rope).

- Use days of the week, seasons of the year, and months of the year as a way to designate positions in a circle on the floor. Then use the positions to group children, or sequence the days, seasons, or months (see figure 4.11).

- Use the seasons of the year to develop a movement sequence, for example, spring—ice melting, flowers blooming; summer—swimming, playing ball, going on a trip; fall—leaves falling, raking leaves, playing football; winter—cold, snow falling, ice skating.

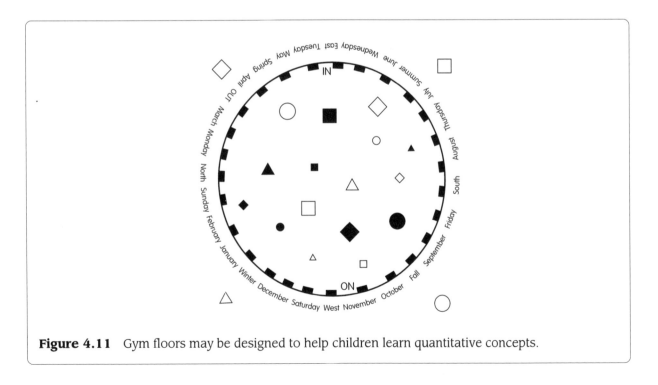

Figure 4.11 Gym floors may be designed to help children learn quantitative concepts.

• Make number shapes representing the month you were born, important holidays (day and month), and important days in history (day, month, and year).

• In a small group of three, draw a clock face on the floor. Then, by lying on the floor show three o'clock, seven o'clock, and so on.

• Using the same clock face, stand with your feet at six o'clock. Then place your hands in the center of the clock, kick both feet into the air, and bring them down together softly at five o'clock, seven o'clock, three o'clock, nine o'clock. Can you start at six o'clock and finish at 12 o'clock? That is a cartwheel.

• Divide the children into small groups of three. One child each represents seconds, minutes, and hours. Use a piece of 4/4 time music. Have the child representing seconds perform a movement (tap, punch, step, jump, bend, etc.) for every quarter note. The child representing minutes should move to every other beat—half as fast, or on beats 1 and 3 or on beats 2 and 4 of each measure—using a different movement. The child representing hours should move to only the first or last beat of the measure using a different movement. If the children have good musical awareness, "seconds" should make one move for every quarter note, "minutes" every half note, and "hours" every whole note. Ask children to identify who moves fast, medium, and slow.

• Time sequence work in gymnastics or dance from beginning to end. How many seconds does it take to perform?

• Using a stopwatch, keep track of how long you can jump rope, dribble a ball, pass and catch with a partner, hit forehands continuously against a wall. How many seconds? How many minutes? Record and graph your performances.

• Run, hop, skip, slide, or gallop various distances. How long does it take you to go 10, 20, 50 yards doing each? Time, record, and graph your results. Which type of traveling action is your fastest way to travel (which requires least time to cover a given distance)?

• Have students record elapsed time in minutes and seconds for various track events, such as 200-meter, 400-meter, 800-meter, and mile runs. For more sophisticated students, include tenths and hundredths of a second, especially for shorter distances of 10, 20, and 50 yards. Over trials or between days, have students record and graph performances to show improvement.

• When working with students on any task, indicate a starting and ending time. Then have them figure out elapsed time. For example, "If you started at 10:12 and ended at 10:27, how much time did you spend practicing? How many practice trials did you make? How many trials per minute does that make? Let's see if we can do better next time." Or, "I'll start you jogging at 11:15. See how long you can go before you care to stop. Shandra, you kept going until 11:20.42. How long was that?"

• Teach the children where their carotid artery is. Then have them count their resting pulse for six seconds and multiply by 10. Have them perform various activities for 10 seconds, 30 seconds, or one minute, each time stopping to count pulses, measure, and record each effort. Graph the results (figure 4.12). Work toward the concept of establishing a target heart rate and knowing what types of exercise get the heart working at various levels.

You Weigh a Ton

Mathematics
Weight measurements

Physical Education
Lifting heavy objects

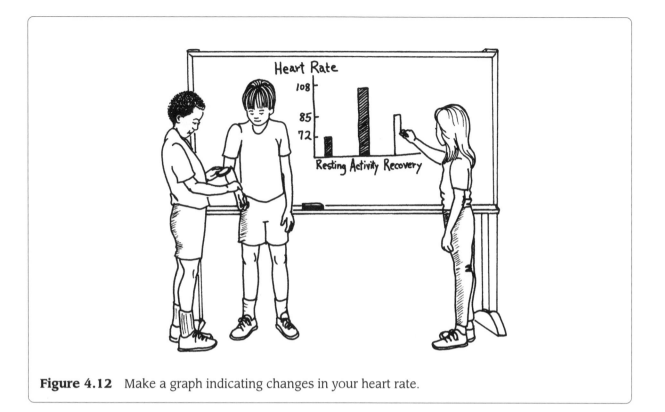

Figure 4.12   Make a graph indicating changes in your heart rate.

Grade Level
2-4

• Show me how you would move if you weighed a ton. Even if you are heavy as an elephant, can you still move fast? Soft? Now you are light as a feather. How will you move now?

• Use small scales to measure play objects. How much does a ball, bat, or racquet weigh? Record and graph all the data.

• Lift small, light dumbbells (one to five pounds or one to five kilograms). Perform several repetitions of several different exercises. If you lift two pounds eight times, how much weight have you lifted altogether?

• Weigh the children using customary or metric scales. Ask them to support their weight on different body parts (feet, seat, hand and knee, etc.) Ask them which ways are easier and why. (Large muscles of the legs, back, and abdomen are stronger and more capable of supporting weight.) Ask what happens if they support their weight in a push-up position or hang from a chin-up position. (Arms tire quickly.) Have them try supporting someone else's weight partially or completely (figure 4.13).

• "Now we are going to play a little game. I want you to solve some problems and create your answers by assuming body shapes. How many ounces in a pound? How many grams in a kilogram? How many feet in a yard? How many yards in a mile? This time use your body to make letter shapes, and show me the abbreviations for gram, centimeter, liter, yard, foot, ounce, pound. Finally, use your body to make the shape of the object indicating the correct answer. Which weighs more, a pound of pencils or 12 ounces of chocolates? Which weighs least, 16 ounces of dog food or a pound of feathers? Which weighs most, a pound of cookies or 400 grams of paper clips?" Have the children get with a partner and create their own brain teasers. One person creates the question. The second forms the answer using a body shape.

Figure 4.13 Can you support someone else's weight partially or completely?

I Went the Farthest

Mathematics
Linear measure

Physical Education
Selected jumping, throwing, and running events

Grade Level
2-5

• Have the children measure the distance of various lines or the results of movement efforts using nonstandard measures. "How many people lying head to toe does it take to go from end to end of the basketball court? volleyball court? Which takes more? less? How many hands high is your friend? Lie on the floor, and have a partner mark where your foot starts and head ends, then count how many forearms tall you are. Take three giant steps. How many strings (one-foot long) did you go? Take three hops, then three jumps. How many strings for each? What way took you the farthest? Everyone stand side by side and be as wide as you can. How many children does it take to get across the room? Bat a ball off a tee. Then measure how many bats the ball traveled."

• Use a foot or yard ruler to measure your walking stride. How far would you go if you took five strides? Hop five times, and measure the distance to the nearest inch, foot, or yard. Jump one to five times, and measure the distance to the nearest inch, foot, or yard. Create a graph showing how far you get using one to five strides, one to five hops, and one to five jumps. Which way do you go the farthest?

• Measure various performances in physical education using whole unit measures of both customary and metric units. Use inches, feet, yards, centimeters, decimeters, and meters. How far can children jump or hop? How far can they throw different types of balls? How high can they jump?

• While learning to high-jump, throw for distance, and so on in a track and field unit, have the children measure and graph their best performances each day. Combine several days' efforts to record improvement in performance.

• As children become more sophisticated, make measurements more precise: to the nearest half unit, quarter unit, eighth of an inch, or even millimeter.

• During jumping or throwing events, have the children perform math conversions within a measurement system. For example, "Sue just jumped four feet, six inches. How many total inches is that? John threw the ball 65 feet. How many yards does that make?"

• During jumping or throwing events, have the children perform math conversions between customary and metric measurement systems. For example, "Amanda threw the softball 70 feet. How many meters does that make?"

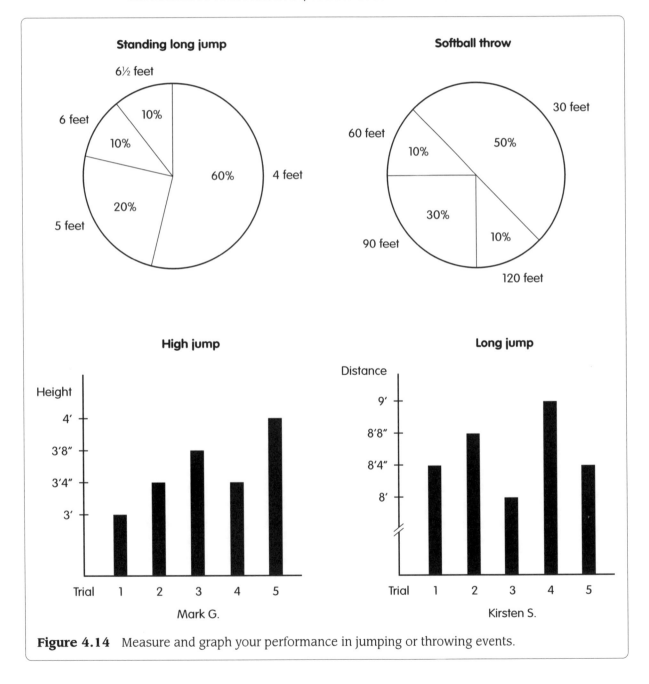

Figure 4.14 Measure and graph your performance in jumping or throwing events.

• After the children jump or throw various distances that are measured and recorded, have them create graphs of their performances (figure 4.14). Use conversion scales to help interpret results, such as 1 inch = 10 feet, 1 centimeter = 1 meter, and so on. Then have them compare performances (e.g., today's with yesterday's, first try with tenth) using the graphs they have created. Do they see improvement in their performances?

• Many physical education activities require boundaries and certain dimensions. Children can measure and lay out the necessary boundaries and field dimensions and make scale models of the playing areas.

Geometry

Shape Up

Mathematics
Simple geometric shapes

Physical Education
Selected locomotor, manipulative, and gymnastics activities

Grade Level
1-3

• Have the children find ways to move over, under, in, out of, on, off, in front of, in back of, and beside objects such as hoops, wands, ropes, boxes, benches, or markers on the floor. For instance, they can jump over a rope forward, backward, or sideways; stand beside a box; and by placing their hands on a bench find ways to move over it. Find other ways to challenge children's awareness of position in space.

• Use commercially purchased geometric shapes or shapes cut out from cardboard and supported by slits in 2 × 4s as an obstacle course. Have the children crawl through a circle, go through a triangle head first, or go feet first, belly up through a square. Continue with similar challenges.

• Have the children throw yarn balls, sponge balls, or beanbags at a target with openings in the shape of circles, squares, triangles, rectangles, and diamonds. They can call out a shape and try to throw the object through that shape.

• Give partners a set of homemade or commercially made beanbags in the shape of circles, squares, triangles, rectangles, and diamonds (figure 4.15). The throwing partner conceals the identity of the shape before the throw. The catching partner calls out the shape of the beanbag in the air as soon as he or she identifies it, before catching it.

• Using a grid on the floor or outdoor playground drawn with chalk by the children or teacher, have the children walk, hop, jump, skip, or slide along the lines that make a circle, triangle, square, rectangle, and other shapes (figure 4.16).

• Use different body parts to make a circle, square, triangle, or other shapes. Make the same shapes with a partner or a group of three or four.

• Make geometric shapes with your body at different levels. Make a square at a low level. A circle at a high level. A triangle at a medium level.

• "I'm going to show you pictures of objects and it is your job to classify them by properties or characteristics. The first set of pictures will be about size. When you see a large shape, make a big body shape. When you see a medium or small shape, make that size body shape. Next, you'll see the same pictures, but I want you to look at the number of corners the shape has. Then balance on that number of body parts. If you

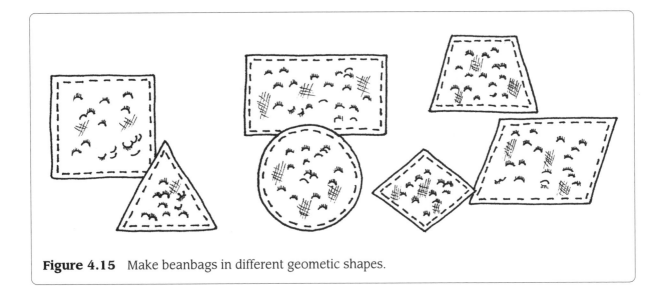

Figure 4.15   Make beanbags in different geometic shapes.

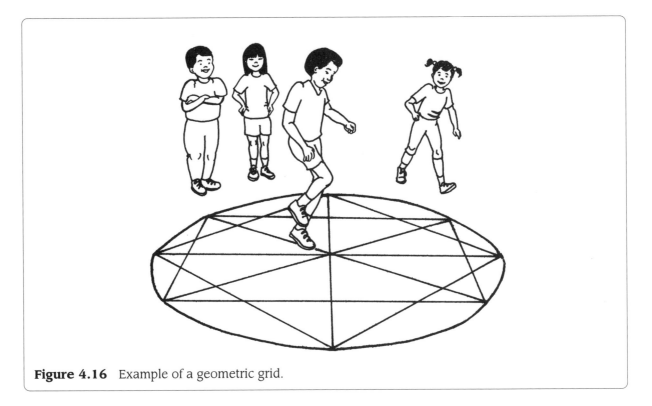

Figure 4.16   Example of a geometric grid.

see a triangle, how many parts will you balance on? That's right—three. What about a circle? None. Next we'll characterize the pictures as to whether they roll or don't roll. If you see a picture of something that rolls (circle, sphere, cylinder, ball, pencil, etc.), do a forward roll. If you see a picture that doesn't roll (triangle, square, rectangle, box, cube, etc.), create a balance shape."

• Use air pathways to draw geometric patterns through space. Try different body parts to trace the patterns in the air.

• "I will briefly hold a picture up for you [1-10 seconds]. After you see it, walk that pattern on the floor [circle, triangle, square, rectangle, diamond]. Try other locomotor actions to trace the shape on the floor."

• "This time I will hold up a picture of two or three shapes. After you see the shapes, choose one form of locomotion to make one shape and a second form of locomotion to make the second shape." This activity helps develop visual sequential memory.

• Have children do the preceding activity but use a locomotor action to make one shape and trace the second shape in the air with a body part.

• While working with a partner, make shapes that are the same; for instance, both make a circle. Keep the same shape, but make one large, one small. Change shapes (triangle, square, rectangle, and so on). Change levels. Make different shapes: One partner makes a circle, the other a triangle. Make different shapes that are different sizes then different levels.

It's Getting Complicated

Mathematics
Complex geometric shapes

Physical Education
Body shapes

Grade Level
3-5

• Under the direction of teacher challenges, have the children make different geometric body shapes. Specifically, have the children assume shapes that create awareness of the concepts of concave and convex. Can they make concave and convex shapes while lying on the floor (figure 4.17)? Can they make concave and convex bridgelike shapes—back bend (belly up) and angry cat (belly down)—at a medium level? By hanging from rings or parallel bars can they make concave and convex shapes? Can they make concave and convex shapes at high levels while standing?

• Have a large group of 10 to 12 children model a given shape and the parts of that shape. For example, a group assigned to create a circle could make the circumfer-

Figure 4.17   Make your body assume concave and convex body shapes.

ence, center, radius, and diameter. Height, length, depth, diagonal, or perimeter could be represented for a triangle, rectangle, or square.

- Create partner shapes that emphasize perpendicular, parallel, and intersecting lines. Create these shapes at low, medium, and high levels.

- While moving with a partner, show pathway lines that are parallel. Show a different way to move so that your pathways intersect.

Twins

Mathematics
Symmetry

Physical Education
Body shapes

Grade Level
2-4

Let's practice making symmetrical shapes (both sides the same). Show me a symmetrical shape at a low, medium, high level. Then make both sides different (asymmetrical). Try these shapes at different levels.

- Work with a partner. One person will make a symmetrical shape. Then the partner will make exactly the same shape. In physical education we might call that mirroring. In mathematics it could be called congruent. Make congruent shapes at different levels.

- While working in groups of three or four, develop ways to make body shapes that show different types of triangles or quadrilaterals. For example, could you make an isosceles, right, obtuse, acute, equiangular, and scalene triangle? Can you make a trapezoid, rhombus, parallelogram, square, and rectangle?

- Can you make the preceding shapes with one or two people and a piece of equipment such as a bench or rope? You may need to use counterbalances to create your shapes.

You Make Me Flip

Mathematics
Transformations

Physical Education
Body shapes

Grade Level
3-5

Make a shape. Then try to transform that shape by using a flip (reflection or mirror), slide (move shape around a flat surface), or turn (rotating around a point). If you kneel down, what would it look like if you were lying on your side or back? What would a tip-up, tripod, or headstand look like right side up? What other shapes can you transform?

Let's Go Angling

Mathematics
Right, acute, and obtuse angles

Physical Education
Body shapes

Grade Level
3-5

Show me a way to make a right angle with your hands. Okay. You can make an *L* by sticking out your thumb from your hand or bending at the knuckles or wrist. Show me a way with your whole body. (Sitting with back straight and legs straight out to the front, standing position with back bent like a table.) We can also bend at other joints to make right angles. What joints can you bend to make right angles? (Shoulder, elbow, hip, knee, neck, ankle.) Can you make your body create a shape with two, three, or four right angles at the same time? Can you move across the floor while you have different body parts bent at right angles?

• In addition to right angles, we can make our joints bend at acute and obtuse angles. Choose a joint and create an acute angle with it. Change and show me an obtuse angle. Change joints and make acute and obtuse angles. Can you bend one joint and make an acute angle and another with an obtuse angle at the same time? Can you create a symmetrical body shape that emphasizes acute angles? Can you jump into the air and make a body shape with acute or obtuse angles while you are in the air?

• While you are moving around the room by walking, hopping, jumping, or skipping, I will make three sounds. When you hear a drum, change your pathway at right angles. A triangle means an acute turn. A maraca means an obtuse-angle turn.

Patterns and Functions

Matching Patterns

Mathematics
Growing and repeating patterns

Physical Education
Beat awareness using nonlocomotor and locomotor activities

Grade Level
1-4

• Using the *Rhythmically Moving* (Weikart, 1989) series of records or any instrumental music with a strong 4/4 beat (marching music), begin developing patterns of unilateral actions to the beat of the music. Initially focus on the macro beat (first beat of a measure), for example, stretch (one arm up high), 2, 3, 4, bend (same arm pulled in), 2, 3, 4, stretch, 2, 3, 4, bend, 2, 3, 4. Continue with other patterns, for instance, tap (thigh), 2, 3, 4, punch (air), 2, 3, 4, tap, 2, 3, 4, punch, 2, 3, 4. Perform bilateral patterns to a macro beat, such as two-arm stretch, 2, 3, 4, two-arm bend, 2, 3, 4, stretch, 2, 3, 4, bend, 2, 3, 4. Perform the preceding patterns to the micro beat of a piece of music in 4/4 time: stretch, bend, stretch, bend. Point out to the children that you are doing a repeated pattern, ABAB.

- Perform the preceding activity but use locomotor actions to establish patterns, for example, step, hop, step, hop (ABAB) and hop, jump, jump, jump, hop, jump, jump, jump (ABBB).

- Show the children a symbolic pattern (•, #, +, -, •, #, +, - or •, #, •, #) and ask them to develop a movement pattern that reproduces the pattern of the symbols. For example, they could punch, twist, stretch, bend, punch, twist, stretch, bend to the first pattern.

- Using small musical instruments such as drums, shakers, triangles, sand blocks, and so on, beat out a rhythmical pattern, for example, half note, quarter note, quarter note or quarter note, quarter note, eighth note, eighth note, quarter note. Have the children beat out the rhythm pattern you create on their instruments. Then have them draw a representation of each pattern using pencil and paper. Have them design their own rhythmical patterns and play them with their instruments. Then, have them perform locomotor or nonlocomotor actions to their rhythmical patterns.

- Perform a specific pattern several times over and have the children observe. Then ask them to use a paper and pencil to create a symbolic code for the pattern. For example, "slow movement, slow movement, quick, quick, quick, repeat" might look like —, —, -, -, -, —, —, -, -, -. Next have them take turns with a partner performing a pattern that their partner codes on a piece of paper.

- Require children to observe a repeating pattern, then have them translate and verbally describe the pattern they saw. For example, tap thigh, clap hands, snap fingers, tap, clap, snap. The children's response would be to say "tap, clap, snap, tap, clap, snap." Next have the children choose partners and verbally translate patterns that their partner develops.

- Tap out a pattern on a drum, such as soft, loud, loud, soft, loud, loud, or play high and low notes on another musical instrument. Have the children respond with appropriate movements, for example, a gentle step, a powerful stamp, stamp, step, stamp, stamp.

- Encourage children to recognize growing patterns, such as •, #; •, #, #; •, #, #, #, by translating them into movement patterns, such as step, hop, step, hop, hop, step, hop, hop, hop or catch, bounce, catch, bounce, bounce, catch, bounce, bounce, bounce. What other growing patterns can you think of?

- Experiment with a variety of repeating and growing patterns, for example, ABAB, ABACAD, ABBA, •#••#•••#. After providing a demonstration, divide the class into pairs, and have them develop nonlocomotor and locomotor sequences in which they recognize, translate into movements, describe, and classify the patterns.

- Have the children create a series of statuelike poses or balance positions. Then order the poses or balances into a pattern from big to small, wide to narrow, tall to short, and so on (figure 4.18). For example, the sequence front support, tip-up, scale, headstand, handstand progresses from a low level to a high level.

- As the teacher, demonstrate a pattern several times using different movements for each repetition, for example, clap, clap, stamp, stamp; or bounce, bounce, strike, strike; or hop, hop, jump, jump. Then have the children describe to you the underlying pattern (AABB). Have the children form partnerships and take turns performing patterns and identifying the rules to the patterns.

- Skip-count forward and backward by 2s, 3s, 5s, or 10s while jumping rope or playing a game. For example, while jumping rope, count out 3, 6, 9, 12, . . . , or strike a balloon up in the air with a body part while counting backward from 100 by 5s.

- Play a game such as basketball or volleyball, and keep score using pattern counting such as even numbers, odd numbers, by 4s, or by 10s.

Figure 4.18   Use body shapes to create a pattern of small, medium, and large shapes.

• Perform a pattern two or three times, Then, perform it again, but intentionally leave out or change one part. Ask the children what part of the pattern was left out or changed. For example, ABAB, ABAB, then ABAA, or step, step, step, hop; step, step, step, hop; then step, step, step. With the children working in pairs, one partner develops a pattern using locomotor, nonlocomotor, or manipulative movements then intentionally leaves out or changes a part. The other partner watches to recognize and describe the missing or altered part of the pattern.

• Organize several pieces of physical education equipment into a group related by a common theme or quality with one object that does not fit the pattern, for example, group a tennis ball, softball, baseball, and scarf. Obviously, the scarf is the object that does not fit the pattern. What about a tennis ball, softball, baseball, and football? The football does not fit the pattern because it is not round and it is not struck with an implement as it is used. Switch to a focus on physical activities. Group a skip, punch, hop, and jump. The punch does not fit because it is not a locomotor action. Put together three balances at a low level and one at a high level, and try other combinations of physical activities. Once the children get the idea, have them work in pairs to create their own groups of actions while the observing partner tries to select the movement that does not fit the pattern.

Probability and Statistics

Take a Guess

Mathematics
Predictions, scientific method, recording data, graphing data

Physical Education
Event records of locomotor and manipulative movement patterns

Grade Level
3-5

• Children should be encouraged early in their physical education experiences to participate in small experiments with one variable. They can use their data to record results, create simple pictographs or bar graphs, describe results, interpret results, and judge events as certain, possible, or impossible. For example, they could step on and off aerobic step benches at heights of four, six, or eight inches as many times as possible in 10 seconds. They could record the number of repetitions for each height. Are they the same or different? They could then create a pictograph or bar graph of their results. They could write a report on their results. Based on their results they could predict how many repetitions they might be able to do in 20 or 30 seconds.

• Later experiments might involve two or three variables: for example, number of bent-knee sit-ups during two trials each in two positions (crossed arms on chest, hands cupped behind head), number of push-ups during two trials each of three positions (regular, hands on bench with feet on floor, feet on bench with hands on the floor), and number of shots made on an 8-inch and a 10-inch basket from two or three distances in two or three trials. Again, children should organize their data, create graphs, and describe their results using words such as *more, less, fewer, same, all, none, most likely, least likely, probably, definitely*.

• In their pictographs or bar graphs of data from the preceding experiments, children can use symbols such as a graphic representation of three sit-up positions with open, slashed, and blocked bars to represent scores for each skill (figure 4.19).

• Using two factors, children should be able to determine possible outcomes of everyday events. What are the possible permutations and combinations of moving at three levels and two speeds?

• Give the children a die or a pair of dice, a deck of cards, or a spinner with 6 to 10 numbers on it. Assign a movement task to each number. Have them roll the die, select a card, or spin the needle. They must then do the movement task assigned to the number the designated number of times. They should record the number of times they do each task. Using probability they should predict the results and compare those with the actual results. For example, using a single die, there is a 1 in 6 chance of selecting a given task on each roll. Over a large number of trials, it is predictable that each number or task will rolled approximately the same number of times.

• Have the children work individually tapping a balloon into the air, dribbling a basketball, passing a soccer ball against a wall, striking a forehand against a wall, or hitting consecutive volleyball forearm passes. They should count the number of successful attempts within a specific time (10-30 seconds) and record the results. Tell the children possible ways to improve their performances. Have them conduct several more trials and record the results. After trials are recorded, have them look at all their data and predict how they think they might do on the next trial. Have another try. How close were they to their prediction? More? Less? Why?

• Have the children throw at a target (hula hoop, taped box on the wall) or shoot at a basket from a specific distance. For example, they might throw at a two-foot square target taped on the wall from a distance of 20 feet. Have them make 10 tries and record the results, then perform 10 more tries and record the results. Next, have them predict their score on the third set of 10 tries. How accurate were they in their predictions? Move them back to 30 feet from the target, or make the target larger or smaller. Have them predict their results. What are the actual results? Record and compare the data.

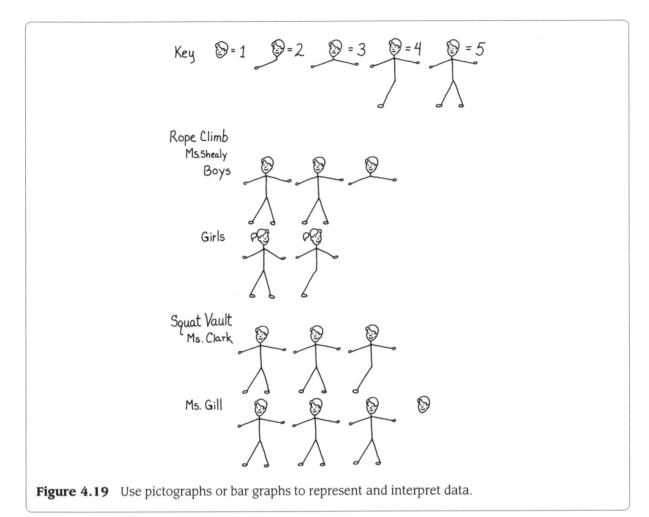

Figure 4.19   Use pictographs or bar graphs to represent and interpret data.

• Use the data from the preceding experiment to create charts or bar graphs. Write up a report describing the results based on an interpretation of the charts, using words such as *more, less, fewer, same, all, none, most likely, least likely, probably, definitely.*

• Over a period of several classes devoted to working on a specific skill (e.g., dribble, pass, shot at target) count the number of successful attempts (3 out of 10) or total successful trials over time (15 successful attempts in 30 seconds). Keep track of results by recording the data each day. After several days have the children create a chart or single line graph. Then, have them describe the results (e.g., get better over time, increase suddenly then plateau).

• Over a period of several classes devoted to working on a specific skill, have each individual keep track of his or her number or successful attempts or total number of successful trials over time. Then have students calculate their own mean, median, mode, and range of scores.

• Collect data on each student's practice trials of a selected skill for over a period of several classes. Have the whole class calculate the mean, median, mode, and range of scores for the whole group.

• While playing 1 versus 1, 2 versus 2, or 3 versus 3 with players of matched abilities on modified courts in modified games of hockey, soccer, basketball, or other team sport, ask the children to predict who will win and state why (e.g., more speed, better passing skills, accurate shots, better defense). After the game compare results with predictions. What factors entered into the game to cause specific results?

Logic

Get Real

Mathematics
Classifying, sequencing, inductive and deductive reasoning

Physical Education
Selected balancing and locomotor sequences

Grade Level
2-5

• Part of logic is related to a precise interpretation of words such as all, every, some, none, both, only, many, either, or, and, and not. Movement tasks can be designed to help children understand these words through a variety of practical or concrete experiences. Here are some examples: "All children balance on three body parts." "Hop or jump in a forward direction." "Many children skip, while some gallop." "Can you balance at a low level and be in a symmetrical shape at the same time?" "While running forward, can you move in either a zigzag pathway or a curved pathway?" "Every child throw five balls at the target using an overhand pattern. None should use an underhand pattern." Teachers and children can develop their own movement tasks using these key words.

• Develop movement sequences that involve a logical order. For example, in dance you might want to portray the passing of a day, a season of growth, or an occurrence such as a rainstorm. As the children, "What comes first, second, third, . . . , last? What is the logical order?" As a movement response, the children can develop appropriate actions to represent getting up, washing, eating, doing daily chores, playing, and finally going to bed at the end of the day. Each piece could be developed separately with appropriate actions and then ordered chronologically.

• Objects are often recognized and sorted by attributes. For example, children can sort blocks by color, shape, size, and so on. Objects can be further sorted (subdivided) by additional attributes. Physical education activities can be sorted by attributes as well. While students are balancing, the teacher asks the class to look around. How many children are balancing on two, three, or four body parts? How many shapes are high, medium, or low? How many children are balancing on three body parts at a low level?

• Have children classify locomotor actions by attributes. While skipping, how many are going fast or slow? How many are going forward or backward? How many are going straight, curved, or zigzag? How many are going fast and forward in a straight line?

• Use a Venn diagram to model the above attributes. See the lesson "Get Set" in the following section on algebra for more information on using Venn diagrams to depict sets, union, and intersection.

• Encourage children to use flowcharts or cues to develop a mental image or schema of how to execute movement patterns. For example, forward roll = squat, tuck, bottoms up, roll, return to feet. Tennis forehand = ready, turn, racquet back, step, swing low to high, home base.

• Use the process of inductive reasoning to help children discover general facts from more simple, specific facts. In a lesson on traveling on the feet, do not tell the children your objectives for the day at the outset. Begin by asking them to walk about the space. Ask them what they are doing with their feet (placing one foot in front of the other, alternating steps). Ask them if they know any other ways to move their feet. Answers might be jump or hop. Ask them what they do with their feet when they jump or hop. Define each. Ask them if there are still other ways to use the feet to move about space. Help them discover the remaining types of steplike weight transfer: "So what did we do today?" "We used our feet to move about space." "How many basic types of steplike weight transfer are there? (Five.) When we move about space with our feet, what is that called? (Traveling or locomotion.) How might we define traveling? (Moving from one place to another.) Are there ways to travel other than using our feet only? (Yes, we can use hands and feet together, rolling, sliding, rocking)."

• Use the process of deductive reasoning to help children discover specific facts based on narrowing ideas from general concepts. For example, have the children throw for distance in any way they choose. In fact, have them experiment with throwing while standing facing the target without using their whole arm (ball up to ear, but elbow down by side) and without taking a step. Gradually introduce them to a more efficient throwing pattern, by allowing them to step. "Which foot is better to step with? (Opposite.) Can you throw better facing the target or starting with your side to the target and turning? (Side to target.) What about your arm? Is it better to throw with your arm in or your arm cocked with your elbow out away from your ear? (Elbow up and out.)" There are many other skills that you can teach using deductive reasoning to help the children to discover the most mechanically efficient way to perform.

• Early experiences in logic include if-then statements. Practice making these types of statements with the children using creative movement. "If the road is bumpy, then the ride will be rough. If the ice is smooth, then skaters will glide across it. If we hurry, then we'll get there faster. If it is really cold outside, then it might snow." Teachers and children are encouraged to develop their own if-then statements and put them into movement sequences.

• Help children to define specific movement skills using "if and only if" statements, for example, "A hop is a hop if and only if the steplike weight transfer is from one foot to the same foot. A skip is a skip if and only if there are steplike weight transfers that alternate between step and hop. A throw is a throw if and only if a held object remains in contact with the body during maximum buildup of momentum (windup) before releasing the object."

Algebra

Less Than, More Than, Equal To

Mathematics
Working with math symbols

Physical Education
Selected exercises and manipulative and locomotor activities

Grade Level
1-3

As children learn the concepts and symbols of less than, more than, and equals ($<$, $>$, and $=$), there are many concrete applications in physical education. For example, for the equation $5 < 7$, one child or a small group of children could do a locomotor pattern five times, make body shape representing the less-than symbol, and finish by doing the same locomotor pattern seven times. Another group could do balances to represent $3 > 1$; a group working with the equation $5 = 5$ could make five throws at a target, a body shape representing an equal sign, then five more throws at the target.

- "We are going to play a game of less than, greater than, or equal to. I want you to choose an action or activity (e.g., jumps, ball bounces, bending actions). Perform that action a specific number of times that you choose. Then I will hold up one of the signs, and you must do that action again a number of times fewer than, equal to, or greater than the previous time."

- Make up a series of task cards placed at various teaching stations around the gymnasium. Several examples follow. You are encouraged to make up your own task cards to fit the ability levels of your students and your teaching situation.

- Exercises
  1. Perform less than (<) 5 push-ups.
  2. Perform more than (>) 10 sit-ups.
  3. Perform < 15 toe touches.
  4. Perform > 5 leg lifts.
  5. Perform a flexed arm hang for greater than or equal to (≥) 10 seconds.
  6. Run in place > 30 seconds but < 2 minutes.

- Gymnastics
  1. Do > 3 forward rolls.
  2. Do < 5 backward rolls.
  3. Do > 4 cartwheels.
  4. Do < 5 different vaults over the horse.
  5. Try > 4 but < 10 different ways to cross the balance beam.

- Ball skills
  1. Bounce the ball < 30 times with your right hand.
  2. Bounce the ball > 40 times with your left hand.
  3. Throw and catch the ball < 25 times against the wall.
  4. Throw and catch the ball with a partner > 15 times without dropping the ball.
  5. Shoot the ball at the basket until you make > 10 but < 20 baskets.

- Rope jumping
  1. Place the rope on the floor and walk along it > 4 different ways.
  2. Place the rope on the floor and jump over it < 5 different ways.
  3. Jump a long rope turned by two other people > 20 times.
  4. Jump a short rope by yourself < 50 times.
  5. Hop a short rope > 15 times but < 25 times before you change to the other foot.

You're out in Left Field

Mathematics
Field properties of math: identity and commutative and associative properties

Physical Education
Selected games and dance activities

Grade Level
2-4

The identity element for addition is the number zero (0). If we add zero to any number, the sum is still the number. The identity element for multiplication is the number one (1). We have identity elements in all human movement in physical education. For example, we recognize certain mechanics of motion as a skill we term running. A skip is a step-hop, one foot in front of the other, alternating flight phase. What are the identity elements/definitions for a bend, stretch, twist, turn, hop, jump, gallop, slide, throw, strike?

The commutative property of addition states that the order of the addends may be changed without changing the sum, that is, $2 + 4 = 4 + 2$, or in general, if a and b are any whole numbers, then $a + b = b + a$. The commutative property of multiplication states that the order of the two factors may be changed without changing the product, that is, $5 \times 7 = 7 \times 5$, or in general, if a and b are any whole numbers, then $a \times b = b \times a$. In physical education we may help children learn this concept by using several practical examples. While sharing a piece of equipment in physical education with a partner, the order in which the partners use the equipment makes no difference, as they will get the same number of tries no matter who goes first. The softball game "Run Around the Bases" (figure 4.20) is another example of the commutative property. When two children run around the bases, regardless of the order or direction they run, they will both return to home plate.

The associative property for addition states than when three or more numbers are being added, the grouping of the numbers may be changed without changing the sum, that is, $(2 + 3) + 5 = 2 + (3 + 5)$, or in general, if a, b, and c are any whole numbers, then $(a + b) + c = a + (b + c)$. The associative property for multiplication states that when three or more factors are multiplied, the grouping of the factors may be changed without changing the product, that is, $(2 \times 3) \times 4 = 2 \times (3 \times 4)$, or in general, if a, b, and c are any whole numbers, then $(a \times b) \times c = a \times (b \times c)$. In physical education we may help children learn this concept by using several practical examples. When groups of three or four children take turns, changing the order in which the children perform results in the same number of performances. For example, when forming groups of 4, have children first pick a partner, then have pairs join with another pair. If partners Arun and Betty join with partners Carlos and Darla, the same group is formed as if partners Arun and Carlos join with Betty and Darla. When performing a Grand Right and Left in square dance, the four male dancers move counterclockwise and the four female dancers move clockwise, but regardless of the direction they move, they finish with their partner and promenade to the home position.

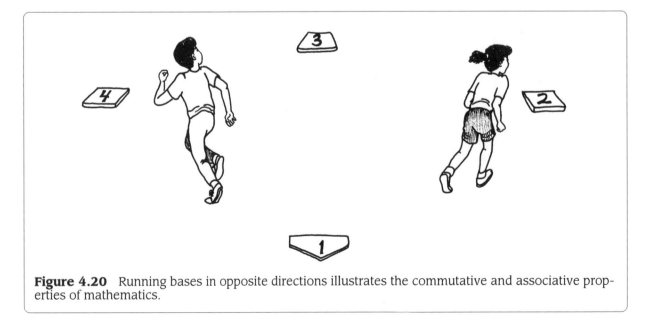

Figure 4.20   Running bases in opposite directions illustrates the commutative and associative properties of mathematics.

Get Set

Mathematics
Math sentences, sets, Venn diagrams, operations on sets

Physical Education
Selected games and dance and gymnastics activities

Grade Level
3-5

Just as children learn to communicate with words and sentences in language arts, they also learn to communicate with symbols in mathematics. Here are some common math symbols:

- Capital letters generally denote sets or members of a group.
- Equal signs (=) denote equality between each side of an equation.
- Braces { } denote enclosure for members of a set or group.
- Symbols or names enclosed in braces are understood to refer to members of sets.
- Commas separate the symbols that represent the members of a set when the members are listed between braces.
- Lowercase letters indicate individual members of sets.
- The symbol $\in$ stands for "is a member or element of."
- A vertical or slanted line through a symbol negates that symbol, for example, $\neq$ means "not equal."
- $A \subset B$ means that A is a subset of B and that B has at least one member that is not a member of A.

  Here are some examples of using math symbols to write sets of physical activities:

1. L = {walk, run, hop, skip, . . . , gallop} can indicate "Locomotion is the set of movement patterns that includes walk, run, . . . , gallop."
2. M = {throw, catch, kick, . . . , strike} can be used to indicate "Manipulation is the set of movement patterns that includes throw, catch, kick, . . . , strike."
3. Throw $\subset$ M can be read as "Throwing is a subset of manipulation."
4. Strike $\notin$ L, which means that striking is not an element of locomotion.
5. Left, right, up, down, forward, backward $\in$ D, which means that left, right, up, down, forward, and backward are elements of direction.
6. F $\notin$ pathway, which can be read as "Moving forward is not an element of pathway."

  Pose movement problems to children, and get them to write their own mathematical sentences to symbolize their solutions. Then have them write a mathematical sentence and perform the solution, for example, {Hop} = transfer of weight from one foot to the same foot. {Walk} = transfer of weight from one foot to the other foot. Skip = {walk, hop, walk, hop, . . . }.

  Sets represent a collection of objects or a group of ideas. A subset is a part of a set. Union and intersection are set operations. Venn diagrams are often used to symbolize operations with sets. In physical education sets can be used to codify movements of the body. They can also be used in conjunction with mathematical sentences to describe movement sequences.

- Use sets to group children. Group children by sex, month of birthday, hair color, color of eyes, age (6, 7, 8, . . . , 25). The set of children 25 years old is a null set because there are no children that old.

- Have the children form a set of body shapes including subsets such as upright, inverted, symmetrical, asymmetrical, low-level, medium-level, and high-level shapes. The concept of shapes while balancing could be thought of as a universal set. Each separate set could be a subset. The union of all possible subsets would include all possible balance positions. An example of the intersection of sets would be symmetrical balances at a low level (e.g., front support, back support) as in figure 4.22.

- Equivalent sets are sets with the same number of elements in them. If you divided a class into small groups or subsets of three, you could have each subset perform a separate locomotor skill. The subsets are equivalent because they have the same number of children doing each skill.

- Have the class begin by performing the set of walking patterns. Practice a variety of ways to walk: fast, slow, long steps, short steps, forward, backward, and so on. Do the same with hopping. Next, do both walking and hopping patterns as a union of sets (figure 4.21). Again practice a variety of combinations of walking and hopping. Walking fast, hopping slow; short walking steps, long hops; walk forward, hop sideways; and eight walks, four hops are examples of solutions, and each could be thought of as a union of different subsets of walking and hopping. Specific subsets you might want the children to try are skipping (step, hop, step, hop, . . .) and schottische dance steps (step, step, step, hop, step, step, step, hop, . . .), which could be thought of as the intersection of walking and hopping.

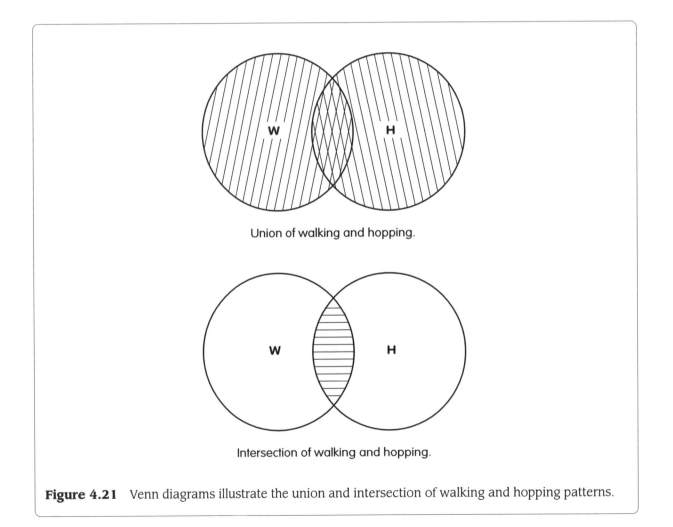

Union of walking and hopping.

Intersection of walking and hopping.

Figure 4.21   Venn diagrams illustrate the union and intersection of walking and hopping patterns.

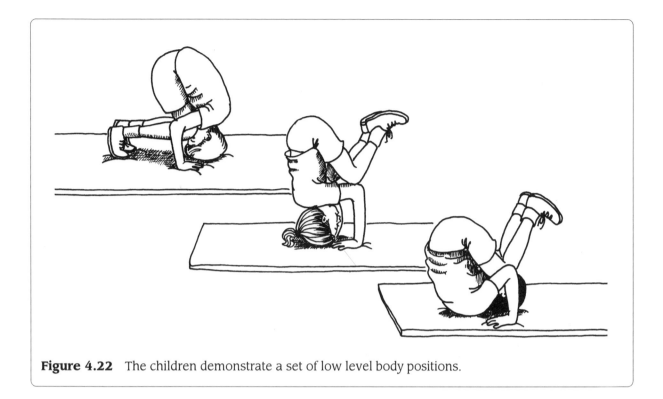

Figure 4.22 The children demonstrate a set of low level body positions.

- Verbally give children directions using mathematical sentences and set terminology. For instance, balance = {high level, symmetrical}. The children should be able to interpret this sentence by practicing many balances at a high level and then many symmetrical balances. Using the intersection of both subsets, they could practice high-level, symmetrical balances. Other examples are skip = {time, direction} or throw = {distance, force}.

- Have the children think of their own sets of locomotor or nonlocomotor movements using appropriate terminology, perform the actions, and then write their movement sets using set notation. For instance, one child as a group leader could direct others in his or her group to "run fast while moving in a forward direction." Another might say, "Balance in a twisted shape at a medium level." Descriptions might be written as {moving fast, using a forward direction} ∈ run or balancing = {twisted shape, medium level}.

Summary

Mathematical concepts taught to children at the elementary level fall into the categories of numbers, measurement, geometry, patterns and functions, probability and statistics, logic, and algebra. We have experimented in our classes with different ways to integrate these concepts in movement settings using different models of interdisciplinary programming. We have always tried to stay true to the principles of maintaining the integrity of each discipline and teaching active lessons. We have shared with you both complete learning experiences and short vignettes of additional learning experiences for you to share with your students.

Try our ideas. Some will work for you. Some may not. Some you may have to modify. Share your ideas with other teachers both in the classroom and in physical education. Try your own new ideas of ways to integrate mathematics with movement concepts. Make mathematics fun and challenging through practical applications in movement.

5
CHAPTER

Active Learning Involving Science

Bill Nye, the "Science Guy," has a TV program on PBS about science each weekday. He lives by two mottoes. One is, "Science rules!" The other is to make science fun. One day he might mix some simple chemicals together (water, glue, and Borax) to make "Sticky Icky." You can stretch it, wad it like a ball and bounce it, or use a drinking straw to blow a bubble with a small portion to make a balloon to tap into the air. Another day the "Science Guy" might get caught in a giant web, like prey caught by a spider. Another TV personality, Slim Goodbody, helps elementary children learn about good nutrition and healthy ways to exercise. Both find very creative ways to capture young children's interest in science. Often it is through active involvement in projects.

Efforts at integrating science with other subject areas, particularly mathematics, are numerous. Research studies as well as practical examples integrating science with other disciplines date back to the 1960s. Werner (1971) conducted a research study integrating selected physical science concepts with physical education in the upper elementary grades. Results indicated a positive learning effect for the experimental group that experienced the integration of science concepts with practical movement experiences. While additional research support concerning the integration of movement with science is scarce, a number of authors (Boorman, 1973; Bucek, 1992; Clements and Osteen, 1995; Gilbert, 1977, 1992; Joyce, 1994; Pica, 1995; Purcell, 1994; Werner and Burton, 1979; Werner, 1996) have continued to pursue efforts at integrating science with physical education and dance in practical settings (figure 5.1). In each instance these attempts at interdisciplinary work with children were pursued because they made the learning environ-

Figure 5.1   Children learn what happens when a little oil is put in a pond, then create an environmental dance about pollution and environmental balance.

ment meaningful and showed positive learning effects in children.

Because of the technological age and culture in which we live, children in the elementary schools must have a variety of meaningful science experiences that lead them to an understanding of the world about them. Leading science educators have constructed a framework for science education (South Carolina Science Framework, 1995) that includes the nature and philosophy, process skills, and knowledge of science.

Students engaged in the nature and philosophy of science develop attitudes and ways of thinking and looking at the world that reflect an appreciation for the nature of science. Attributes of science commonly described include intellectual honesty, continuous inquiry, tolerance of ambiguity, openness to new ideas, curiosity, reflection, ability to make informed decisions, communication and sharing, and being empowered to participate. Because of these attributes it is thought that science should be learned in the following ways: (1) active involvement in hands-on experiments; (2) problem-solving activities designed to facilitate learning as a result of inquiry; (3) relating instructional experiences to everyday life; (4) a sequence of activities proceeding from concrete to abstract; (5) making connections to other disciplines and from grade to grade; (6) working with others; (7) making effective use of technology; and (8) talking, writing, and communicating.

While not all scientists approach their subject in the same way, Gega (1994) and other science educators agree that the following steps or processes are fundamental and are invariably employed by scientists at one time or another: Observing, classifying, measuring, inferring, predicting, communicating, and experimenting are the process skills of science. To help children learn to become scientists and maintain enthusiasm for the scientific process, it is important to engage children in each of these steps through practical, hands-on experiences rather than learning science theory in a textbook.

The knowledge of science is divided into content areas. These areas include life or biological sciences, earth and space sciences, and the physical sciences. Topics in each of the sciences will be more fully developed in later sections of this chapter.

Scope and Sequence for Science

Science experiences through physical education are numerous. The application of science to physical education is almost unlimited. Classroom teachers and physical education specialists often overlook these possibilities. Most classroom teachers are interested in using physical education in every situation where it would help to broaden the pupils' experiences in school life. This desire has been frustrated, however, by the difficulty in obtaining the necessary material or by not having a ready-made source of ideas that integrate science with other disciplines.

If children are to be taught learning experiences that relate science concepts with physical education, teachers should be aware of problems and everyday occurrences that are of real concern to children in their daily lives. While developing materials for this chapter, the main concerns were collecting a variety of ideas for science lessons to include in one source and making these lesson ideas as practical as possible. We reviewed several science textbook series, projects of leading science organizations such as the American Association for the Advancement of Science, and methods textbooks (Gega, 1994) on teaching elementary school science. We found that science concepts were based on and taught through units in the biological and life sciences, earth and space sciences, and physical sciences (table 5.1).

Primary-Grade Science Skills and Concepts

During the primary grades the major concepts taught within the biological or life sciences include the body, the senses, bones and muscles, how living things help people, what plants and animals need, growing seeds, foods, and the ways of plants and animals. Children learn about time, the earth, air and water, weather, the environment, and the moon, sky, and celestial bodies while studying earth and space sciences. While studying the physical sciences at the primary level, children learn to observe things, how things change, where things belong, how things move, forces in action, measuring, exploring matter and changes in matter, and heating changes.

Table 5.1

SCOPE AND SEQUENCE OF SCIENCE CONCEPTS TAUGHT IN ELEMENTARY SCHOOLS							
Concept	**Grade**						
Biological life sciences	K	1	2	3	4	5	6
Your body	x						
How living things help you	x						
What plants and animals need		x					
Your senses		x					
Growing seeds			x				
Foods and you			x				
Your bones and muscles				x			
The ways of plants and animals				x			
Your body and nutrition					x		
The world of animals					x		
Transport systems of the body						x	
The plant kingdom						x	
The world of small living things						x	
Control systems of the body							x
Life cycles and new generations							x
Earth/space sciences							
Explaining time	x						
Our home, the earth		x					
Investigating air and water		x	x				
Weather			x		x		
The environment			x				
Earth, moon, and sky				x			
The changing earth					x		
Conserving the earth's resources						x	
The earth's crust							x
Space: the new frontier							x
Exploring climate							x
Physical sciences							
Observing things	x						
Changing things	x						
Where things belong			x				
Things on the move			x				
Forces in action				x			
Measuring all around you				x			
Exploring matter and changes in matter				x		x	
Heating changes				x		x	
Electricity and magnetism					x		
Energy					x		x
Force, motion, and machines						x	
The structure of matter							x

Intermediate-Grade Science Skills and Concepts

At the intermediate level the major concepts taught within the biological or life sciences include the body and nutrition, the world of animals, transport systems of the body, the plant kingdom, the world of small living things, control systems of the body, and life cycles and new generations. In the earth and space sciences children learn about weather, the changing earth, conserving the earth's resources, the earth's crust, space exploration, and climate. Matter and changes in matter; heating changes; electricity and magnetism; energy; force, motion, and machines; and the structure of matter are topics in the physical sciences at the intermediate grade level.

Learning Experiences

There are four complete learning experiences (table 5.2) in this chapter. They demonstrate two of the interdisciplinary teaching models presented in chapter 1. The learning experiences have been designed to include skills and concepts from physical education and science. Each learning experience includes a name, suggested grade level, interdisciplinary teaching model, objectives, equipment, organization, complete description of the lesson, and assessment suggestions. In addition, tips on what to look for in student responses, how teachers can change or modify the lesson, and ideas for teachable moments are offered to provide further insights into each learning experience.

Table 5.2

SCIENCE LEARNING EXPERIENCES INDEX			
Skills and concepts	Name	Suggested grade level	Interdisciplinary teaching model
Science: Biological sciences—identifying body parts, major muscles, bones Physical education: Balancing	The Hip Bone Is Connected to the Thigh Bone	2-3	Shared
Science: Physical sciences—simple machines Physical education: Lifting, pulling, pushing, rolling, throwing, striking, kicking	The Simple Things in Life	2-3	Shared
Science: Biological sciences—transport systems Physical education: Fitness—cardiovascular running, jumping, skipping	Rainbow Run	3-5	Shared
Science: Earth sciences—weather patterns, cloud formations, wind Physical education: Body shapes; time, force, and space concepts	Weather or Not	4-5	Partnership

The Hip Bone Is Connected to the Thigh Bone

SUGGESTED GRADE LEVEL

Primary (2-3)

INTERDISCIPLINARY TEACHING MODEL

Shared
The purpose of this lesson is to integrate the children's growing awareness of their body when learning about the musculoskeletal systems in science with how their body parts function in a movement setting.

Science
Biological sciences—identifying body parts, major muscles, bones

Physical Education
Balancing

OBJECTIVES

As a result of participating in this learning experience, children will improve their abilities to

- balance on a variety of large and small body parts using good form,
- create balances on the floor and completely or partially on small apparatuses,
- develop a simple balance sequence: balance–weight transfer–balance, and
- name parts of the body on which they balance and the muscle groups, bones, and joints that support them (figure 5.2).

EQUIPMENT

Although this lesson could be taught on the floor, it is best to use gymnastics mats, floor exercise mats, or wrestling mats. Small apparatuses such as benches or cardboard boxes filled with newspaper should be scattered around with enough space between to permit freedom of movement. If this lesson is to be taught outside, a large parachute could be spread out on the grass to protect the children's clothes.

ORGANIZATION

Children work individually in scattered formation or with partners, depending on the number of mats and small apparatuses available.

DESCRIPTION

"Good morning. As you come in, have a seat in front of me on the floor. What body parts are touching the floor as you are seated? Tom? (Seat, bottom, rump). Any other body parts? Theresa? (Hands, feet, thighs, shins). Right. I see many of you in different body positions as you are seated. Well, I've been talking to Mr. LeGrand, and I've found out that in science you're learning about your bodies: your muscles and bones. In our gymnastics lesson today we'll try to use that information by giving scientific names to the body parts we balance on as we build a sequence.

"Can anyone remember the name for your seat or bottom? Lauren? (Gluteus maximus). Well done. And the bones connecting at the hip joint (hip bone) are called the ilium, ischium, pubis, and femur (our long leg bone). We've also said that some of you are seated with your hands (carpal, metacarpal, and phalanges bones), feet (calcaneus, tarsal, and metatarsal bones), thighs (femur bone and quadriceps muscle), or

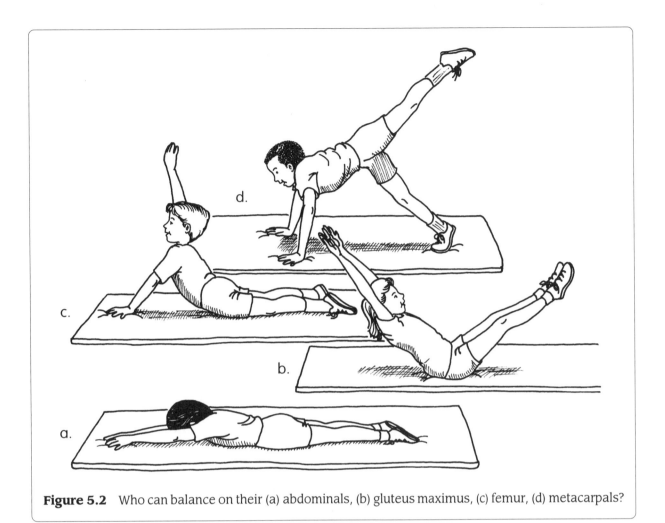

Figure 5.2 Who can balance on their (a) abdominals, (b) gluteus maximus, (c) femur, (d) metacarpals?

shins (tibia and fibula bones) touching the floor. When I say go, we are going to get out of our seated position and spread out on the mats. There is enough space, so I don't want any more than two people to a mat. Go. . . . Stop.

"Everyone sit in a long, seated position with an erect posture. Your seat (gluteus), hamstrings, calves (gastrocnemius), and heels (calcaneus) should be in contact with the floor. Point your toes away from you. Bend over and reach with your arms toward your toes. Hold the position for 15 seconds. Sit up straight again. Straddle your legs, reach first toward your left leg and hold it for 15 seconds, then reach toward your right leg and hold it for 15 seconds. Sit back up straight and bring your legs together. Put your palms (metacarpals) on the floor beside your hips and press up into a back support position. Make your body straight as a board and feel the tightness in your tummy (abdominal muscles) and seat (gluteus). Lean onto one hand with weight also on your feet and rotate your other hand over your head until you are in a front support position (push-up position)."

CONTINUE with more stretching exercises until the children are warmed up. During each exercise mention as many muscles and bones that are being used as you think the children will profit from.

"Good warm-up. You sure are learning the names of many of your bones and muscles. We'll continue class now by balancing in different ways. First we'll try many ways to balance right on the floor. Then we'll try some balances on the equipment. Finally, we'll select three balances and develop a short sequence. When you do your sequence, I'll give you a work sheet so that you can name the body parts (bones and muscles) you balance on for each of the three balances. When I say go, show me one way to balance. Perhaps think of balancing on large or small body parts. Go. That's it, Jamaal. You're balancing on a forearm (radius and ulna bones) and your whole thigh (femur and quadriceps). Great, Keshia. You're balancing on four small body parts. Two hands and two feet, abdomen toward the ceiling, in a back-bend position. Way to go, Carol. An elbow and two knees (patella). Ian, that is an interesting way to balance—on your seat (gluteus) in a *V* shape. That makes you use your abdominal muscles. Each time you hear me give a signal (clap or drumbeat), I want you to change your balance into a new position. [Signal . . . Signal . . .] Stop. You are working hard, but I want to point two things out.

"First, I want you to use good principles of balance when you try things. What that means is that all of your support positions should be strong. If you are balancing on your hands, your elbows or shoulders should be directly above. Use good vertical alignment. Same with your legs: Hips or knees above your feet. I also want to see firm muscles—no sagging bodies. The second thing that I want to see is a real commitment to a chosen shape. What that means is that if a particular body part is straight or stretched, I want to see extension out through the end. If your intent is to create a rounded surface, I want to see a curved shape. Also think of where your head is and where you are looking to make a complete body shape.

"Let's try some more balances. We'll hold each balance for five seconds before you hear the signal to try a new balance. Ready, [signal]. . . . That's it. I see much better quality in your shapes. . . . Stop.

"Next, we'll use the boxes or benches I have placed at each workstation to balance on. I would like to show you two different ways of balancing that I would like you to consider. First, you can balance on the equipment by placing part of your body on the equipment and part on the floor. I'll show you what I mean. I can put my two forearms (radius and ulna) on the floor and my two shin bones (tibia) on the bench or box. [Demonstrate.] Or I could put my two hands (metacarpals) on the floor and my two calf muscles (gastrocnemius) on the box or bench with my body straight and abdomen facing the ceiling. [Demonstrate.]

"The second style of balancing on the equipment that we will work on is to balance with our whole body on the equipment. For example, I can sit in a *V* seat on my gluteus muscles and lean back on my hands. [Demonstrate.] When I say 'go,' I want you to try several ways to balance with your whole body on the equipment. Remember, I want good strong balances, and I want you to hold each balance for five seconds. Go. . . . Stop.

"Next, you can choose either a partial or complete balance on the equipment. I want you to work on your own without a signal and to try at least five different balances. Hold each one for five seconds. Make sure that you do each balance well using the principles we've already talked about. Go. . . . Good work, Ian. I see you balancing completely on the bench in a shoulder stand. You have achieved a good balance by vertically aligning your hips, knees, and ankles over your base. That's it, Suzi. Good partial balance on the box. Your body is straight as a board with your left forearm (radius and ulna) on the box and your left foot (metatarsals) on the floor. Your side is facing the ceiling. . . . Stop.

"Everyone come gather around this mat. For our final activity we are going to develop a short sequence. Your sequence will consist of three balances linked by transition moves such as roll, swivels, steps, or twisting actions. Your sequence may be on the mat only or on the equipment and the mat. As you develop your sequence, I want you to use this special work sheet I have (figure 5.3). [Distribute handout.] I want you to draw a stick figure of each of your three balance positions, label the body parts (bones and muscles) that support your balances, and identify your two transition moves with word cues. Look at my example on the work sheet as I demonstrate, then you can get to work. First, I'm in a *V* seat on the bench. I'm balancing on my gluteus maximus, leaning back on my hands. Then, I use a swivel move to my second balance, which has my stomach (abdomen) on the bench and my hands (metacarpals) on the floor. Finally, I do a forward-roll transition move to two feet (metatarsals and calcaneus bones) and immediately stand in an erect Y position with my arms stretched diagonally toward the ceiling. Does everyone understand how to do the sequence? How many balances are required? (Three.) Do you have to do your sequence on the equipment? (No.) How many transition moves are there? (Two.) What do you have to write on your work sheet? (Draw each of the three balances. Name the body parts, muscles, and bones we balance on for each balance. Describe the transition moves.) You're ready to go then. Work hard. I'll come around and help or make suggestions. Go. [Allow several minutes for students work.] Stop. I can see that you're making progress. Make sure your first balance is held with stillness, as if to say, 'Watch me, I'm going to begin.' Then start your sequence using good, smooth, flowing transitions, and end your sequence with another balance with stillness, as if to say, 'I'm finished now.' Also make sure you begin drawing your three balances and write out the names of the body parts you balance on. Get back to work. . . . Stop.

"What I want you to do now is get with a partner who has not seen your sequence. Take turns sharing your sequence and your work sheet. Observing partners watch the sequence and give help where needed on the work sheet to identify body parts, bones, and muscles used as supports in each balance. Use as many scientific names as you can so we can show Mr. LeGrand how smart you are. If you are not sure of the name of a body part, bone, or muscle, ask me or look at this big musculoskeletal chart I have hung here on the wall. We want to make sure we're scientifically accurate. Go. . . . Stop.

"It is time to leave now. Let me collect your work sheets. I want to share them with Mr. LeGrand so he knows we are learning about how our bodies work in physical education. Good-bye for now."

ASSESSMENT SUGGESTION

Provide the children a chart of the musculoskeletal system. Have them identify or label selected bones or muscles. Or, at the end of class, balance in one to three poses, and have the children identify, name, or label the specific body parts, bones, or muscles on which you are balancing.

LOOK FOR

- Some children may have trouble deciding on balances to perform. You can provide a series of pictures of possible balances (see Werner, 1994a). Other children may want to copy a friend's balances. That is okay at first, but gradually stress and place value on unique balances, using original ideas, and working within one's own abilities.

- Stress quality balances using good principles of support. Children should balance from positions of strength. There should be no weak, sagging bodies.

- During sequence work, watch for three good balances with smooth transition moves.

- Emphasize the quality of written work on the work sheets. Drawing may vary from full-body pictures to stick figures. The key is using accurate names for body parts, bones, and muscles because the focus of the lesson is on integration with life sciences (anatomy).

EXAMPLE:

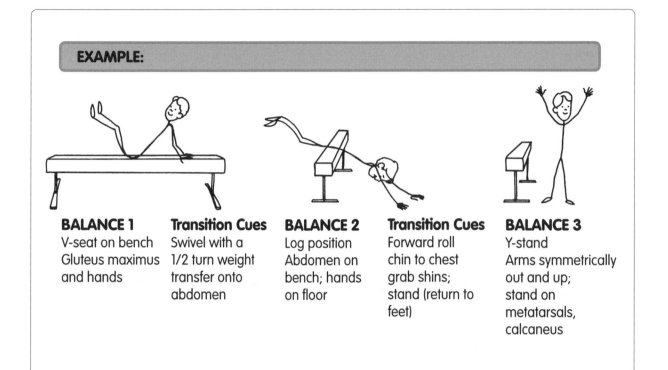

BALANCE 1
V-seat on bench
Gluteus maximus
and hands

Transition Cues
Swivel with a
1/2 turn weight
transfer onto
abdomen

BALANCE 2
Log position
Abdomen on
bench; hands
on floor

Transition Cues
Forward roll
chin to chest
grab shins;
stand (return to
feet)

BALANCE 3
Y-stand
Arms symmetrically
out and up;
stand on
metatarsals,
calcaneus

YOUR SEQUENCE:

Draw 3 pictures of your balances on or off equipment. Identify the body parts on which you balance (bones, muscles).

Use cue words to describe your transition moves (weight transfer).

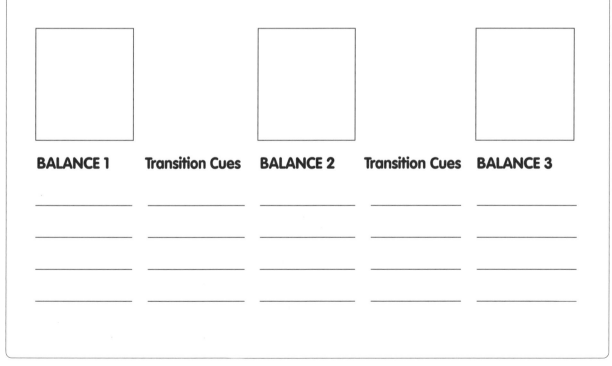

BALANCE 1   **Transition Cues**   **BALANCE 2**   **Transition Cues**   **BALANCE 3**

HOW CAN I CHANGE THIS?

- Develop a partner balance sequence and use the same work sheet to identify the body parts, bones, and muscles used for support.
- Provide a work sheet, and have the children identify muscle groups that are flexed and stretched during warm-up. Have the children identify bones and joints that are moved by the muscles during specific exercises such as jumping jacks, bent-knee sit-ups, or push-ups.
- Have the children identify body parts, bones, muscles, and joints used in various sport actions such as throwing, kicking, catching, and striking.
- Develop a short aerobics routine or set of light weight-lifting exercises that work selected muscle groups. Do the routine or exercises with the children, and identify the muscles, bones, joints, and body parts involved with each.

TEACHABLE MOMENTS

- Collect action pictures of athletes in various sport, game, dance, and gymnastics settings. Have the children analyze selected pictures and attempt to identify the body parts, bones, muscles, and joints used in a given skill.
- Collect action pictures of people at work in everyday life (e.g., truck drivers, computer operators, assembly-line workers, fire fighters). Have children analyze selected pictures and attempt to identify the body parts, bones, muscles, and joints used in a given work task.
- Have children analyze pictures of buildings, bridges, and other structures for strong foundations and principles of balance. Compare the concepts of strong foundations and principles of balance used in construction with those used in building efficient body balances.

The Simple Things in Life

SUGGESTED GRADE LEVEL

Primary (2-3)

INTERDISCIPLINARY TEACHING MODEL

Shared
As children learn about simple machines in science, the classroom teacher and physical education specialist can coordinate their efforts to help children understand how machines assist people to do work and that the human body uses primarily third-class leverage systems to perform most manipulative tasks. Third-class levers offer increased speed and range of motion but require a lot of force production to do work.

Science
Physical sciences—simple machines

Physical Education
Lifting, pulling, pushing, rolling, throwing, striking, kicking

OBJECTIVES

As a result of participating in this learning experience, children will improve their ability to

- lift, push, and pull objects while using the body in an efficient manner;
- throw, strike, kick, and perform other manipulative actions while using the body in an efficient manner;
- use simple machines such as an inclined plane, lever, wedge, screw, and pulley to do work;
- understand the differences among first-class, second-class, and third-class levers; and
- know that the human body uses mainly third-class levers to perform manipulative actions.

EQUIPMENT

A seesaw or teeter-totter (2 inch × 10 inch × 12-foot board and cement block), a slide, a horizontal bar with a single or double pulley system attached, a wheelbarrow or dolly, can openers (electric and church key), a scale, a nutcracker, scissors, a wedge mat (inclined plane), and five balls each for kicking, throwing, and striking

ORGANIZATION

This lesson is designed to be conducted at several different stations outside, on or near the playground. Children work together in small groups and rotate to each station.

DESCRIPTION

"Hello. Today we are going to talk about and do some experiments with machines. We'll also talk about how our body is a machine and performs work. See what I've got here? Yes, it's a can opener. Before we had electric can openers like this one, we opened all of our can lids and even soft drink cans with hand-operated, or manual, can openers. Does anyone know what kind of machine this manual can opener might be? Any guesses? It is a lever. A lever has a resistance arm, a force arm, and a fulcrum. In fact, this is a first-class lever. The resistance is the top of the can. The fulcrum is the edge of the can where the opener hooks around the edge. The force comes from our hand out at the end of the opener (first class = resistance, fulcrum, force). [Demonstrate opening a can with the manual opener.] Did you know that when we cut paper with scissors, we are also using a first-class lever? [Demonstrate cutting paper with scissors, and point out the resistance, fulcrum, and force.]

"Do you know what this is? (It's a nutcracker.) Good, Sara. Watch. I have some nuts here. No matter how hard I squeeze with my hand, I cannot open the shell. And yet if I put a shell in the nutcracker, the force of my hand can easily open the nut. That is another example of a simple machine at work. A nutcracker is an example of another type of lever. It is called a second-class lever. The fulcrum is at the closed end of the cracker. The nut (resistance) is in the middle, and the hand (force) is out at the end of the handle (second class = fulcrum, resistance, force).

"I know you have been studying about machines in science. Can anyone tell me the names of some other simple machines besides a lever? (Wedge.) You're right, Billie. Can anyone think of an example of when a wedge is used? (A knife cutting butter, an ax splitting wood.) What about other machines? (Pulley, screw, inclined plane.) Can anyone think of where pulleys are used? (Sailboat, elevator, auto shop to lift an engine out of a car.) Examples of where screws are used? (Meat grinder, cement mixer.) Inclined planes? (Escalator, ramp in a parking garage, slide on a playground.)

"You already know a lot about machines. Today in physical education we are going to do some experiments about how we use simple machines to do work and how our own bodies work as machines when we do sports activities. What we are going to do is divide our class into five cooperative groups and then rotate to each of five stations that I have set up. While at each station you will perform each of the tasks and answer the questions on the work sheets provided. At the end of class we will all get back together to talk about what we have learned about machines."

ESCORT the children to each station, and briefly explain the activity at each station. Then divide the children into five groups by name—for instance, pulley, lever, wedge and so on—and at a signal have them begin. After five to seven minutes at each station, rotate groups until all the children have visited each station.

Station 1

Equipment: a dolly or wheelbarrow, two to three cases of paper or food from the cafeteria

Activity: Have the children try to lift the heavy boxes in pairs. (Teach them how to lift properly using straight backs and the large muscles of the legs.) Then have them put two or three boxes on the dolly or wheelbarrow and not only lift the boxes but also move them a distance and back as an example of transporting a load (figure 5.4).

Work-sheet questions:

- What type of machine is being used? (Lever, second class.)
- Where is the fulcrum? (Axis of the wheel.)
- Where is the resistance? (Boxes on the dolly.)
- Where is the force? (Lifting out at the end of the handles of the dolly.)
- Is it easier or harder to carry these boxes using the machine?
- Diagram the lever in the space provided.

Figure 5.4   Wheelbarrows or dollies help transport heavy loads.

- Where have you seen this type of machine being used? (Grocery carryout, bellhop in hotel, porter at airport, bricklayer carrying bricks or mortar.)

Station 2

Equipment: a seesaw or board-and-block teeter-totter, two to three cases of food or paper

Activity: Have the children put the heavy load on one end of the seesaw with the fulcrum exactly in the middle. Have them try to lift the load. Because the distance of the resistance to the fulcrum *(RA)* equals that of the force *(FA)*, their lifting force *(F)* equals the weight of the boxes *(R): F × FA = R × RA.* Next, have them shift the fulcrum so that it is only one or two feet from the load. Then have one child show how the heavy load can be lifted by just one person (figure 5.5).

Work-sheet questions:

- What type of machine is being used? (Lever, first class.)
- Where is the fulcrum? (Cement block.)
- Where is the resistance? (Cases of food.)
- Where is the force? (Child lifting at the end of the board.)
- Diagram the lever in the space provided.
- How can you make it possible for just one person to lift a very heavy load? (Shift the location of the fulcrum so that you have a short resistance arm and a long force arm.)

Figure 5.5   The farther away from the fulcrum the force is applied, the easier to lift the box.

- Where have you seen this type of machine being used? (Crowbar, scissors, can opener, tire iron to put tires on rims of wheels, lifting with a shovel.)

Station 3

Equipment: A slide and a gymnastics wedge mat, a case of food or paper, a piece of rope 20 feet long, and a spring scale. If you don't have a wedge mat, a hill or mound on the school playground or an inclined plane made from gymnastics benches would work great.

Activity: Weigh the case of food or paper. Then attach a rope to the box, attach the spring scale to the rope, and place the box at the bottom of the slide. Pull the box up the slide and see how many pounds of force are needed to make the box move. Slide down the slide or roll down (forward, backward, or log rolls) the mat or hill, then do a roll on level ground.

Work-sheet questions:

- How heavy was the box? _____ pounds.
- How much force did it take to make the box move up the inclined plane? _____ pounds.
- Is that force more or less than the weight of the box?
- After doing a roll on level ground and down an inclined plane, in which roll did you move faster or easier? (Inclined plane.)
- Why? (An inclined plane helps to work with gravity to overcome friction and resistance.)
- Would you say that inclined planes help do work

  a. only going uphill (box up slide).

  b. only going downhill (down the slide or hill).

  c. both up and down.

- Name some inclined planes in everyday life. (Escalator, stairs, trough on cement truck, parking ramp, grain elevator.)

Station 4

Equipment: horizontal ladder or chin-up bar, a case of food or paper, a piece of rope 20 feet long, one or two pulleys, and a spring scale

Activity: Weigh the case of canned goods from the cafeteria. Attach a rope to the box through the pulley system. Attach the spring scale to the rope. Pull down on the rope to lift the box. Using the scale see how many pounds of force are needed to lift the box using both a one- and two-pulley system.

Work-sheet questions:

- How heavy was the box? _____ pounds.
- How much force did it take to lift the box with one pulley? _____ pounds. Two pulleys? _____ pounds.
- As you add more pulleys, does it take more or less force to lift an object?
- Name some examples of pulleys being used in everyday life. (Elevator, block and tackle to lift a car engine, boom vang and mainsheet on a sailboat, building crane.)

Station 5

Equipment: balls; bats; batting tees; open area to throw, strike, and kick; tape measure

Activity: Throw five times, and measure the farthest throw. Punt or kick a ball off the ground into the air as far as you can five times. Measure the farthest kick. Bat five balls off a tee, and hit them as far as you can. Measure the farthest batting attempt.

Work-sheet questions:

- What kind of machine is your body when you do these sports skills? (Lever.)
- What class of lever is your body under these conditions? (Third class: fulcrum, force, resistance.)
- Where is the fulcrum? (Body joint—shoulder, hip.)
- Where is the force? (Muscles.)
- Where is the resistance? (Ball out at the end.)
- Diagram the lever in the space provided.
- Rank your skills in order of distance. Shortest _____ , middle _____ , farthest _____
- Why do you suppose you can kick and bat farther than you can throw? (Longer force arm, mechanical advantage, bigger and stronger muscles used.)

"Okay, stop. Everyone come over here by the board and sit down. Who can tell me the names of the machines we used in class today? Yes, Keshia. (Lever, pulley, inclined plane.) Great. Can anyone remember how many classes of levers there are? (Three.) What is a first-class lever like? Ronald. Yes—the fulcrum is in the middle. How does it help you? Well, you can lift something really heavy if you have a long force arm, like a crowbar. When do we use our bodies as third-class levers? (When we throw, kick and strike balls.) I can see you are learning a lot about machines, and as time goes on we'll see more and more examples of how we use our bodies as machines. Bye for now."

ASSESSMENT SUGGESTION

- The work sheets used at each of the stations provide adequate assessment of the children's knowledge of simple machines and the application of that knowledge in movement settings.

LOOK FOR

- Children should be taught to lift heavy objects properly. Rather than bending over and lifting with the arms, children should bend at the knees, keeping the back vertically aligned and the center of mass of the object close to their own center of gravity. They should lift with the strong muscles of the legs.
- Children should stay on task, work together, and all contribute answers on the work sheets. In a cooperative learning experience, no one child should dominate.
- Monitor answers on the work sheets. Make sure children understand the problems being solved and can transfer knowledge to examples of machines in everyday life.

HOW CAN I CHANGE THIS?

- For a simpler lesson, require children to identify only the major category of machine being used at each station. Have them work individually and write their answers on a note card.
- If you don't have all the equipment (scales, dollies, inclined mats, etc.), focus the lesson on levers used in the human body. Emphasize that the body uses mainly a third-class leverage system (figure 5.6) to manipulate objects. Third-class levers offer speed and range of motion (mechanical advantage), but the body has to use a lot of energy to produce force, so it is not a very efficient machine.
- At a higher level, help the children calculate the mechanical advantage gained as a lever arm is extended from one to two to three feet (hand, paddle, racquet, baseball bat).
- Use the formula $R \times RA = F \times FA$ to calculate answers to problems on leverage. Use the known weights of the boxes and the approximate lengths of the resistance or force arms.

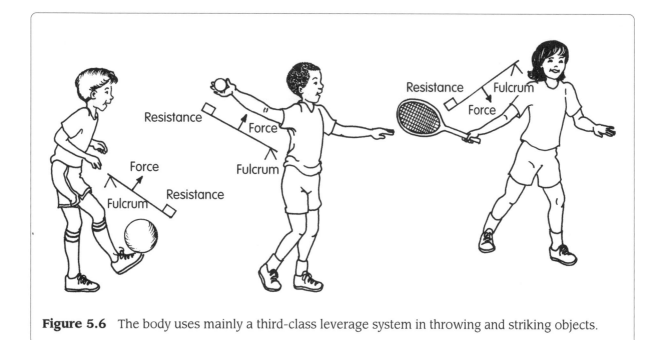

Figure 5.6 The body uses mainly a third-class leverage system in throwing and striking objects.

TEACHABLE MOMENTS

- Bring in pictures from magazines to show different types of machines being used. Have the children bring in their own pictures of different types of machines, and make a collage on the bulletin board.

- Encourage children to find pictures of people doing physical work (chopping wood, using a wheelbarrow, turning a screwdriver, pouring cement, throwing a ball, batting a ball, etc.), and create a small booklet that categorizes work by type of machine: class of lever, pulley, inclined plane, wedge, or screw.

Rainbow Run

SUGGESTED GRADE LEVEL

Intermediate (3-5)

INTERDISCIPLINARY TEACHING MODEL

Shared
Students learning about the body's transport systems in science can use this learning experience to gain practical lessons in how the systems are affected by exercise.

Science
Biological sciences—transport systems

Physical Education
Fitness—cardiovascular running, jumping, skipping

OBJECTIVES

As a result of participating in this learning experience, children will improve their

- physical fitness,
- ability to measure heart rate, and
- understanding of how the body's transport systems are affected by exercise.

EQUIPMENT

Color-coded cones or posters and magic markers, a "rainbow" card for each student (a white index card showing a rainbow found by colors matching cone colors. It is important that cards have different rainbow color sequences, or students will all be going to the same cone at the same time.), rubber bands, and jump ropes

ORGANIZATION

Students work alone and with a partner in a large indoor or outdoor space.

DESCRIPTION

BEFORE students arrive, the teacher has prepared the work area ready for activity. Rainbow cards with rubber bands should be spread out for easy access. Cones or posters for the rainbow run should also be set up at appropriate distances. (The distance of the run is determined by the distance from the starting area to each of the cones.) Jump ropes should be spread so that they do not tangle when students need them.

"Everyone come in and have a seat by a card and rubber band. Hello, everyone! I am very excited because today we are going to explore how the transport systems of the body are affected by exercise. The transport systems are the circulatory system, the respiratory system, and the excretory system. The circulatory system is made up of the heart, blood, and blood vessels. The system that takes air into the body is the respiratory system. It consists of the lungs and the passages through which air travels, such as the nose, throat, larynx, and bronchial tubes. The third transport system is the excretory system. This is the system that takes away waste products from the body and includes the kidneys, the skin, and the lungs.

"We are going to choose only one part of each of the transport systems for our class today. Let's focus on the heart (circulatory), the lungs (respiratory), and the skin (excretory). What happens in one system affects the other. For example, think of a time that something really scared you. Maybe you were lost from an adult in a big store. You were worried, and you were having trouble finding the adult. How did your body react? Your heart, lungs, and skin? Your heart probably began to beat a little faster, you started to breathe deeper and faster, and sweat began to bead up on your face.

"Just for a minute, let's think about how your heart is beating right now. You might know that your pulse is the beating in the arteries with each heartbeat. You can find your pulse by holding your index and middle finger against your wrist at the base of your thumb. This is called your radial artery. Go ahead and try to feel your pulse. Let me know if you can't find yours, and I or some other student will help you. You can also feel your pulse at the carotid artery in your neck or at the temporal artery in front of the ear. Let's take our heart rates for 15 seconds. We will all start together when I say 'go.' Count one for each time you feel your pulse beat. Ready, go.

"Now as you sit relaxed, I want you also to think about your rate of breathing. Are you breathing hard? Are you taking deep or shallow breaths? How about the surface of your skin. Are you sweating? Or is your skin rather dry?

"We are going to exercise now, and after each activity we will examine our selected parts of the transport system: our heart, lungs, and skin.

"Let's look at our activity for the day. We are going to exercise by doing a rainbow run [or walk]. The rainbow run is set up like this (figure 5.7).

"On the field you see a number of different colored cones [or posters] with magic markers beside them. You will go to the different colored cones and use the magic marker beside the cone to make a mark on your card, which you have in front of you. Your card looks like this [hold up]. It has the colors of the cones marked in a certain order. You must move to the cones in the order of the colors of your rainbow. For example, if the first color in my rainbow is red, then I must go to the red cone first, make a mark with the red marker beside the red mark on my rainbow, and continue to my next color until I finish the last color on my rainbow. Who can re-explain this to the class? Good, Joseph, tell the class what we are going to do. . . . Thanks, Joseph. Everyone, remember that you have your own rainbow sequence. Everyone will be traveling a different sequence.

"Okay, go ahead and secure your rainbow card around your wrist with your rubber band. Start off by just walking fast to complete your rainbow. This is not a race to see who finishes first. So as you finish, please walk back over to the starting area and continue to walk fast until everyone is finished. Are we all ready? Go.

"Since everyone is back, let's take our pulse again for 15 seconds. We are taking our pulse for 15 seconds because it is a short time span and easy to count. If we multiply

Figure 5.7 Follow the sequence of your rainbow and mark your card to show you were there.

that number by four we can get our heart rate for one minute. A one-minute heart rate tells us how hard our heart is working (table 5.3). If your heart is beating 75 to 80 beats or fewer in a minute, your body is working easily or is at rest. If it is beating 90 to 120 beats, you are doing moderate exercise like walking. If it is beating 130 to 180, you are exercising vigorously. To get your body fit, you should be able to exercise with your heart beating in the 120 to 160 range for 5 to 20 minutes without stopping. As your body gets in better cardiovascular shape, you can keep exercising for longer periods without stopping. How do your resting heart rate and your walking heart rate differ (figure 5.8)? Can someone tell us what his or her resting and walking heart rates were? Why do think that they are different? What about your lungs? How were your lungs affected by walking? Who would like to share what happened to his or her breathing? Susan. Yes, as you started to exercise, your breathing got deeper. In fact, as you begin to exercise, your heart rate increases and you use more oxygen, which makes you breathe deeper (figure 5.8).

"Let's try the rainbow run again, but this time let's jog or run instead of walking. Turn your rainbow card over, and you will see a new rainbow for you to use. When I say 'go,' we will start. Same as last time, come back over here and continue to jog or run until everyone is finished. Ready, go.

"Let's take the pulse again for 15 seconds. Wow, your pulse was really easy to find that time, wasn't it? Did everyone have a higher rate that time? What has happened to your skin? Have you started to sweat? Does anyone know why most of your skins were dry when we first came into class and now your skin is moist? Jason? Right, as we continue to exercise, our body temperature rises, and we begin to sweat. Sweating provides water to the surface area of the skin, where it evaporates into the air. This causes the skin to cool. So here is another question. Do you think that you should wipe

Table 5.3

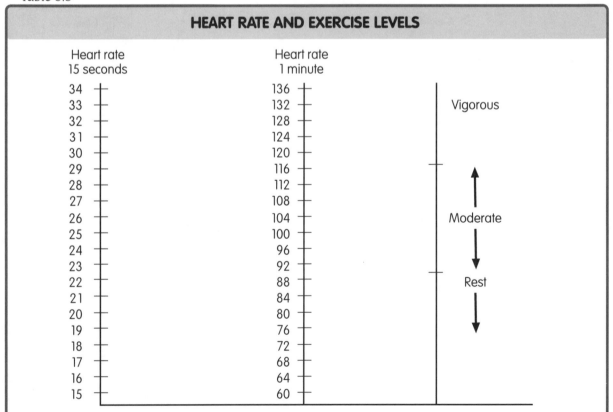

Figure 5.8 Exercise affects the transport system of the body.

sweat off your body while you exercise? In other words, should we all run around with towels in our hands to get rid of our sweat? No. The sweat helps keep us cool.

"Now let's try a new activity. We are going to jump rope. When I say 'go,' I want you to go over and get a rope and then come back and find a personal space. Let's see if we can increase the pace of our jumping. First, we will all jump at an easy pace for a few minutes, then I want you to jump faster for a few minutes. Last, for one minute you will jump as fast as you can—what we call *hot pepper.* Doesn't this sound like fun? Remember, go at your own pace. You know how fast you can go, so pace yourself. Ready, go.

"Let's take your heart rate for 15 seconds. You should be able to find your pulse easily now. Ready, go. . . . Wow, that extra-fast jumping really did something, didn't it? What happened to your transport systems? When I say 'go,' quickly get a partner, and discuss what happened to your heart, lungs, and skin. Go.

"Which partners would like to tell us what happened? Stewart and Jack. Good answer, you could say that as you begin to exercise, your heart rate increases and you also use more oxygen, which makes you breathe deeper. As you continue to exercise, your body temperature rises, and you begin to sweat. Sweating provides water to the surface area of the skin, where it evaporates into the air and causes the skin to cool.

"Now that we have rested for a few minutes, let's take one last look at our transport systems. What happened to your heart, lungs, and skin? This is a good point for us to finish our lesson for the day. Let's review just a little. Can someone tell us what the body's transport systems are? Right, Sharon, the circulatory system, the respiratory system, and the excretory system. What parts of these three systems did we examine? Shane. Okay, the heart, lungs, and skin. You will continue to study the body's transport systems in your science class. I have a list of questions for you to complete in the classroom."

ASSESSMENT SUGGESTIONS

Ask children the following types of questions, verbally or on a work sheet:

- Is your heart rate different when you walk and then run? When is it faster? Why?

- What do you think would happen if you carried two or three books while you exercised?

- What happens to your pulse rate 30 seconds after you stop exercising?

- Why do you think that we took heart rates for only 15 seconds?

- Why do you breathe more deeply when you exercise?

- Why do you breathe faster when you exercise?

- If sweating causes the skin to cool, do you think that you should try to towel off your sweat as much as possible?

LOOK FOR

- Make sure children are taking their pulses correctly at their radial or carotid arteries. Ask children their 15-second counts. If they are in a reasonable range for the type of exercise (resting, moderate, or vigorous using the chart), they are probably counting correctly. A child off the chart probably is making up a number and needs help.

- Make sure children are following the colors on their rainbow and not just following a friend.

- Encourage children to move continuously. This is not a race; it is more about pace. It is not important to be the fastest in class. It is important to maintain exercise over time. Children should learn to monitor their own progress and get in better personal shape over time. They can set their own goals and see improvement over time.

HOW CAN I CHANGE THIS?

- Change the course to a rainbow obstacle course, where the children have to go over, under, around, and through objects.

- Use a similar rainbow run, but children must dribble a ball, jump rope, twirl a hula hoop, and so on at each cone.

- Perform the rainbow run on the playground. Children can go up and down the slide, swing for a certain time, go across the horizontal ladder or monkey bars, and so on.

- Give children a map and compass, and make the rainbow run an orienteering course.

TEACHABLE MOMENTS

- Encourage the children to be active at other times during the day. If there is a fitness course set up at school, talk to the children about walking or running around the course before school, during recess, or at lunch. Make it a social experience. Encourage them to do it with a friend. It should be fun.

- Active lifestyles should be shared with others. Encourage the children to be active with their parents or friends at home. They can share the knowledge they are learning about fitness, body transport systems, and cardiovascular fitness with these people. Prepare handouts for them to take home.

Weather or Not

SUGGESTED GRADE LEVEL

Intermediate (4-5)

INTERDISCIPLINARY TEACHING MODEL

Partnership

Studying about weather patterns, clouds, and storms is common in science at the upper elementary grades. The science teacher and physical education teacher can work together on this theme. Children learn about weather and cloud formations and use that information to develop a movement sequence.

Science

Earth sciences—weather patterns, cloud formations, wind

Physical Education

Body shapes; time, force, and space concepts

OBJECTIVES

As a result of participating in this learning experience, children will improve their abilities to

- create shapes with their bodies inspired by moving clouds (or flowers, trees, or snowflakes);
- demonstrate the contrast of slow, light, indirect movements with fast, strong, direct movements; and
- identify various cloud formations and weather patterns (or discriminate among the sizes, shapes, colors, textures, and patterns of flowering plants and trees in their community).

EQUIPMENT

Pictures of clouds and other weather information provided by the National Weather Service or local TV stations or newspapers (or specimens of various flowers, leaves from trees, and information about the plants and trees); a tape or record player and music for accompaniment

ORGANIZATION

Students begin the lesson dancing individually, then finish the dance in a group shape.

DESCRIPTION

"Good morning. Can you believe this day? What great [lousy] weather we are having! I've been talking to [classroom teacher], and I understand you are studying about weather patterns [plants, trees, flowers] in science. Well, today we are going to create a dance about weather [shapes of plants, flowers, leaves]. Our dance will be about the shapes of clouds, the levels at which they occur, wind and its patterns, and the mood of weather. When the sky is almost completely blue on a calm day, did you ever look up in the sky and see white, wispy clouds just floating about? Those clouds are called cirrus, or sometimes mares' tails or mackerel scales. They are at a high level and are rather friendly clouds. When I say 'go,' I'm going to play some cloud music [e.g., ("Enter Sunlight," Movin, 1973; Palmer, 1973) ("Windsails," Modern Dance

Technique Environments, 1982; Kupka, 1982). What I want you to do is listen to the music and move about the general space within the boundaries of the cones. Make sure your movements correspond to the mood and qualities of the music. Stop occasionally to stretch this way and that, expanding and retracting (getting bigger and smaller), and then move on. Be that cumulus cloud floating across the sky. Go. Yes, Amy, Brett! I see you are really paying attention to the music. Nice slow, calm, indirect, floating movements. Super, Glen. You are showing me soft, gentle movements with moments of swaying and stretching while you are in one spot. Stop. Everyone freeze right where you are. Let's watch Amy, Brett, and Glen as they interpret this cloud music with their movement. Watch their gentle, light, or soft movement. Watch how they move indirectly: stopping, starting, changing directions and pathways, using both floor and air space. Notice how they match the slowness of their movements with the pace of the music. See how they stop to gently stretch up, out, in front, behind, and then move on. Stop. Thanks. As you continue to warm up, pay attention to these details (slow, soft or light, indirect). I shouldn't be seeing any running or any direct, powerful, explosive movements. Start when you hear the music. Much better now. I can just imagine I am floating among those cumulus clouds on a calm day. Stop. Everyone come in and sit down.

"Now that you are warmed up, we are ready to put together our cloud dance sequence (figure 5.9). First, we'll talk about clouds some more. Have you ever noticed that the white clouds are at different levels? They are also all different shapes and sizes. Some are puffy and big, others long and narrow. Do you know what they are called? They are called cumulus clouds. They are rather friendly clouds. For the first part of our dance I want you to choose three cloud shapes. I will play our cloud music again. I want you to float through the sky, using the same type of movements you did during our warm-up. At three different times I want you to stop and hold a cloud shape for five seconds. Make each position different: long or round, wide or narrow, big or small. You may change your levels as well. Then move on. I want you to decide when to float across the sky and when to hold a cloud shape. The critical factors are floating softly and gently and stopping to make how many cloud shapes? Right, three. How long will you hold each shape? Right again. Five seconds. Ready, go. . . . Stop.

"I really like what you are doing, but the music in some ways is hindering what we can do with this dance. So we will continue without music. This time I want us to repeat what we just did, but I want to add the factor of wind. Sometimes the wind is calm and

Figure 5.9　Create a movement sequence based on weather patterns—layered, stratus clouds.

gentle, and other times it is blowing and gusting hard. I still want you to stop and do three cloud shapes, but I want your movements in between to show me calm and gentle versus windy and gusty. You choose the order. Stop and hold your third cloud shape. When everyone is holding their last cloud shape, I'll know you are finished. Start by showing me stillness using your first cloud shape. Go. . . . Stop. I can see you are trying, but you can improve in two ways. First, create more contrast between your calm, gentle wind movements and your windy, gusty movements. Windy movements are more strong, powerful, sudden. Gusty means to blow hard, perhaps swirl, then ease up. Gentle winds are more consistently calm, reserved. Second, really exaggerate your held cloud shapes and make sure you hold them for five full seconds. Let's try again. First shape. Ready, go. . . . Okay, better. One more time. First shape, go. . . . Stop.

"Now we will build the second part of our dance. Did you ever notice the sky when a rainstorm is approaching? What does it look like? Yes, gray, billowing, threatening clouds. These clouds are low, heavy, full of rain. They are often gathered in a definitive line. These clouds are called nimbus or rain clouds or sometimes cumulonimbus or stratonimbus, depending on whether they are puffy, billowing rain clouds or layered, gray clouds. But, the key name is nimbus or rain. This is what we are going to do. After the first part of our dance when we do three cloud shapes and move using two wind conditions, I want you to gather like a rainstorm and create a line here across the floor. The whole class will create a cloud line by individually making the most threatening cloud shape you can think of. If you can, as you come into the cloud line and assume your cloud shape, link your shape to your neighbors. That would be great. Think of a unified cloud line: a nimbus, angry storm line. Hold that shape. Let's try it. Go back to your third cloud shape. Hold it for five seconds. Now we are like the calm before the storm, gathering along this line. Come in slowly, one at a time, gradually gathering mass. Once you come in, link your shape to someone else on either side of you. Touch with different body parts at different levels. Look threatening, menacing. Hold it. Good. Let's try it again. From the beginning this time. Cirrus or cumulus cloud, gentle breeze or gusting wind, another cloud shape, contrasting wind movement, another cloud shape, calm before the storm, nimbus cloud line. Good work. Let's do it again. Start. . . . Stop.

"Now we are ready for the climax. Guess what? Yes, thunder! Powerful, explosive moves. Driving rain. Lots of energy. Sudden movement. The rain and driving wind are moving in one direction across the floor. Show me your energy from the thunder. Explosive runs, jumps, tearing actions. Ready, go. . . . Stop. Let's try that again from the third cloud shape. Ready, cloud shape, gather in a line (calm before the storm), threatening cloud line, hold your shapes (don't worry if you're not always next to the same person). Thunder [drum], explosive movement, driving rain across the floor. Good work. Stop. Come, gather in here for a moment.

"Have you ever seen the destruction after a powerful storm? Do you remember the powerful tornado in Lexington, or hurricane Hugo in Charleston, or the El Niño storms and floods in Malibu? What destruction did you see? (Trees uprooted, houses destroyed, bridges out.) To end our dance, I want you to make small groups of three on this side of the floor and create a group shape that resembles the destructive force of nature. First, find two others with whom you can work responsibly. Let's pretend that the thunder and raging rainstorm turns into a gentle sprinkle. This will allow you to slow your energy and calmly find everyone in your group, then create your final destructive shape. Hold that shape to show me you are finished. Let's try that part several times. Slowly move to find your group of three. Create your shape. Hold it. [Practice this part several times.]

"For our conclusion, we will put our weather dance completely together. It is in three parts. First are the cumulus clouds with varying winds, then the cloud line and thunder with driving rain, and finally a calming of the weather and group destructive shape. What do you think of practicing it twice through and performing it for [next teacher] when he or she comes to pick you up at the end of class? [Practice and performance follow.]

"Before you go. I would like to ask you a few questions about clouds and the weather. What are puffy, white clouds called? (Cumulus.) Gray clouds? (Nimbus.) Layered, gray clouds? (Stratus.) Puffy, threatening, gray clouds? (Cumulonimbus.) I'm impressed. You are really starting to know a lot about the weather. And you have learned to communicate your knowledge and feelings about weather through movement. Before we leave, has anyone ever heard a saying about weather? For example, ,'Pink in the morning, sailor's warning. Pink at night, sailor's delight.' What does that mean? Any others? Yes.'When the wind is from the west, fishing is best.' When you go home tonight, ask your mom and dad if they know any weather sayings or fables. Come back and tell me next class. That's it for now. As you move over to the door to line up, go calmly and gently as a summer breeze."

ASSESSMENT SUGGESTION

- Develop a work sheet with pictures of several different types of clouds. Have the children label each of the different types of clouds.

LOOK FOR

- The focus of this lesson is on body shapes and an awareness of time, force, and space. As children make their cloud shapes, look for variety through changes in level, dimension, symmetry, direction, and base of support. As children add traveling actions to their sequence, look for contrasts between soft, calm, gentle, indirect movements and powerful, sudden, swirling, sometimes direct movements.

- The emphasis on this lesson is on expression using a theme from nature. Look for that expression in the soft shapes, the raging storm, and the destructive shapes at the end.

- Focus on the relationships among science, nature, and body movement terminology. Point out the common ground using shapes, time, force, space, and so on.

HOW CAN I CHANGE THIS?

- This lesson could be adapted to use other themes from nature or the environment. For example, in winter use the shapes of snowflakes as the theme; in spring or fall use the shapes of flowers and tree leaves.

- Use a children's literature book about clouds (e.g., Shaw, 1947; DePaola, 1975) as a stimulus for this lesson, thereby focusing on the integration of language and movement.

- There are many ways to change the content or sequence of this learning experience. For example, children could link cloud shapes together and move across the sky. Children could use traveling actions to represent the change from a soft, gentle, sprinkling shower to a driving rainstorm. They could also create a bouquet of flowers, pile of leaves, and so on as they work on group shapes.

TEACHABLE MOMENTS

- Stress the interrelationships among disciplines. Name the clouds; identify high and low weather fronts and clockwise and counterclockwise flow patterns; describe wind forces (breeze, gust, gale, etc.). How fast are hurricane winds? Why does a hurricane occur? Interpret all these phenomena through a focus on movement factors. Use the interrelationships to enhance and enrich language, science, and dance.

Additional Ideas for Developing Learning Experiences

This section offers additional learning experiences to reinforce the science concepts identified in table 5.1: biological and life sciences, earth and space sciences, and physical sciences. Curricular areas, suggested grade level, and a brief description are provided for each activity. These activities are intended to inspire additional ideas for interdisciplinary work between classroom and physical education teachers. Teachers are encouraged to develop these ideas more completely. Sometimes the connected model will be most appropriate, while other times the shared or partnership model may be used. Your main concern should be to meet the developmental levels and needs of your students; you can adapt activities to accommodate your teaching schedule, equipment, and available space.

Biological and Life Sciences

Body ID

Science
Anatomy—body-part identification

Physical Education
Selected locomotor, manipulative, and nonlocomotor actions

Grade Level
K-2

• Name and touch different body parts. Touch your pointer finger to your nose, fist to elbow, foot to knee, elbow to knee, elbow to tummy, ear to shoulder, chin to knee, and so on. Get a partner and perform the same activities, but touch the called-out body part to your partner's body.

• Tap a balloon into the air with different body parts. Use your pointer finger, ring finger, thumb, fist, elbow, shoulder, head, nose, wrist, knee, and so on. Count how many times you can keep the balloon up with each body part. Change and use a different body part each time. Use a beach ball in place of a balloon.

• With music (with clear, identifiable 4/4 tempo) playing in the background, choose different body parts you can move backward and forward to the rhythm of the music. Start by using the macro beat, the first beat of each measure (front, 2, 3, 4, back, 2, 3, 4). Choose your arm, leg, elbow, hand, foot, head. What body parts can you move side to side? What body parts can you bend, then stretch, move up, then down, twist, swing, and so on? Do each of the preceding activities with a variety of selected body parts using a macro beat, then switch to a micro beat—move to every count of the measure (bend, stretch, bend, stretch).

• Travel across the room on different body parts. When you hear the drumbeat, try a different way: two feet, one foot, hands and knees, two feet and a hand, slide on tummy and pull with hands, slide on back and push with feet. What other ways can you think of?

• Balance on different body parts in a gymnastics lesson. Name the parts. Balance on two knees and an elbow, seat and two hands, forearm and thigh, two shins, shoulders and elbows. What else can you think of (figure 5.10)?

• Balance any way you choose, but make your feet the highest body part. Control the balance for three seconds. Try making your elbow the highest body part. Now try your

Figure 5.10   Balance on different body parts and name them.

tummy, knees, seat. Can you balance with your head, hands, tummy, knees, ankles, shoulders at a medium level? low level?

Oh Deer

Science
What plants and animals need

Physical Education
Locomotor tag game

Grade Level
2-4

The game of Oh Deer! (author unknown) is a game of tag that emphasizes the balance of nature. Students are divided into four equal groups: deer, food, shelter, and water. Deer stand on one side of the gym. The habitat components stand on the other side with their backs turned. Establish three signals used by both deer and habitat components: hands over stomach = food, hands over mouth = water, hands over head = shelter. On the signal to go, the deer choose what habitat component they will search for and put their hands in the appropriate place. They may not change components. In the mean time, the habitat components turn around and show what component they are by placing their hands appropriately. They may not change. Deer run across and join hands with a player representing the habitat component they were in search of. They must match. Together they run, hop, jump, skip, leap, or lope back to the starting line. They then become deer on the next turn. This represents one successful year of reproduction and finding a satisfactory habitat in which to live. However, selected habitat components have been reduced. Play several more cycles. In a year when there are many deer and few habitat selections of a given kind (drought, forest fires, poor growth cycle), some deer will not find what they are searching for. This represents death; deer who have died join the habitat components of the depleted type they were in search of, thus replenishing the source to continue the cycle. Talk about the cycle of life at the end of the game.

Sensitivity Training

Science
The five senses

Physical Education
Selected locomotor, manipulative, and nonlocomotor actions

Grade Level
1-3

- Different sounds are produced by different kinds of vibrations. Objects that are dense and vibrate at a high speed produce a high-pitched sound. Objects that are not dense and vibrate at a slow speed produce a low-pitched sound. Make sounds on several types of homemade and commercial band instruments, such as a glass of water, gourd, steel drum, triangle, maraca, drum, guitar, and tambourine. Experiment with the type of sound each instrument makes. Have the children respond appropriately by moving at high and low levels according to the pitch of the sound. Have them move according to whether the sound is vibratory (shake, quiver), flowing (smooth, curving), percussive (pounding, jerky), and so on. Make a short sequence of sounds, then develop a movement sequence to go with the sounds.

- By listening carefully, a person can tell if a rhythm is even or uneven. An even rhythm or tempo (4/4 time) is one that has the same emphasis on each beat of each measure. For example, one can clap, snap, tap their thighs, step, hop, or jump to each beat of music in 4/4 time that has an even rhythm. An uneven rhythm or tempo (2/4 or 3/4 rhythm) has an unequal emphasis on each beat of music. An uneven rhythm has, for example, a long/short or long/short/short emphasis. A 2/4 rhythm is appropriate for locomotor actions such as skipping, galloping, and sliding. A 3/4 rhythm is more appropriate for a waltz. Play different rhythms on a drum, or use an appropriate record with different types of rhythms. Listen to the beat, clap to the beat, snap your fingers to the beat, move other body parts to the beat, perform locomotor actions to the beat.

- The children listen to a rhythmical sequence you create then make an appropriate movement response. For example, make two loud powerful beats on a drum followed by a long, smooth rubbing on the drum surface. The children should respond by making two quick, powerful body actions followed by one sustained, smooth, flowing action. Make a pattern of long and short squeaking noises out of the mouth of a blown-up but unsealed balloon. The children must listen then respond to the sounds that they hear.

- To help with auditory sequential memory, tell the children to do a sequence of two, three, or four things, for example, do five sit-ups, then get a ball, and bounce it 10 times; or throw the ball up and catch it seven times, dribble it on the floor 15 times, kick it against the wall five times. Observe who listens well and performs the sequence correctly.

- Turn out the lights in the gym, and have the children follow a flashlight beam with their eyes. Then play a game of flashlight tag.

- To develop visual sequential memory, have the children watch you do a movement sequence then copy your sequence. For example, do a forward roll, come out of your roll into a balance on a knee and two hands, go into a sideways egg roll by tucking up into a ball and rolling sideways and finish in a *V* seat resting back on your hands.

- Conduct some taste experiments. Bring in foods to taste that are sweet, sour, bitter, salty, and spicy. After tasting the food have the children show their reactions to it through movement. How do the children's movements change according to the type of food they have tasted?

- Bring in scented items of different types, such as perfume, ammonia, pepper, sassafras, peppermint, rose petals, and charred wood, in unmarked bottles. Have the children open up one of the bottles carefully and smell the substance inside then show their reactions to what they smell with different body movements. Have them put their reactions to several different smells into a short movement sequence.

What Goes Around Comes Around

Science
Cycle of life—growing seeds

Physical Education
Selected locomotor and nonlocomotor actions

Grade Level
2-3

Develop a movement sequence that shows the cycle of life (figure 5.11): "One plants small seeds in the spring. Showers, gentle rains, and proper soil bring growth. Fields of grain sway in the wind. Fruit matures on trees. Harvest comes in the fall. Fruit is picked. Grain is cut, taken to the mill, and ground into flour. Products are eaten to provide energy to continue the cycle of life."

Dem Bones

Science
Anatomy—bones and muscles

Physical Education
Selected locomotor, manipulative, and nonlocomotor actions

Grade Level
3-4

- With a piece of slow, calming music playing in the background (see Brazelton, 1977), have the children place a wadded piece of newspaper in a bent joint for eight counts

Figure 5.11 Create a dance that expresses the cycle of life—a plant sprouting from a seed.

(two measures) then relax and make that muscle loose (shake it out, make it limp) for eight counts. For example, put the wad in the elbow and flex the biceps muscle, in a fist and contract the forearm muscles, behind a knee and flex the hamstring muscle, between two knees and contract the adductors, between two elbows and contract the pectoralis muscles, or under the chin and contract the sternocleidomastoid muscles. Repeat the experience several times on the left and right sides of the body. Talk about what it feels like to have muscles tense and relaxed.

• Develop a lesson that emphasizes the use of major muscle groups of the body. After a good cardiovascular warm-up that elevates the heart rate, perform selected strength exercises and point out the specific muscles used (e.g., triceps in push-ups, abdominals in sit-ups, quadriceps in squats, biceps in chin-ups, gastrocnemius in toe raises). Stretching exercises can identify other muscles (hamstrings in bend at the waist with right leg over left, trapezius when hugging yourself). Then, depending on the lesson (kicking, throwing, striking, etc.), identify the major muscle groups used and what they do. For example, kicking involves mainly hip flexors (quadriceps) and knee extensors (sartorius). Throwing uses mainly the deltoids, biceps, pectoralis, triceps, and forearm muscles.

• Teach children the major bones and joints of the body. As you go over each area, talk about how each part moves. "What can the spine do? (Arch, bend, twist, turn.) The hip and shoulder are ball-and-socket joints. How many ways can you make the arms and legs move? (Bend, swivel, stretch, reach, swing.)" Continue exploring other bones and joints by examining what each can do. Develop a creative movement sequence by combining the elements of shape and time, for example, bend at one joint slowly, then stretch another quickly, and so on.

Flora and Fauna

Science
The ways of plants and animals

Physical Education
Locomotor and nonlocomotor movement sequences

Grade Level
3-4

• Bring several leaves from different trees, different flowers, blades of different grasses. Closely observe the different shapes and arrangements. Some leaves are pointed, others are rounded. Some flowers form in clusters, others are singular. Some flowers are large and colorful, others are smaller and perhaps blander. Some blades of grass are narrow, others are broad. After noticing the similarities and differences among the plants, create a movement sequence about changing shapes. Have the children choose three different shapes. Start in one shape, change rapidly to another shape, then change slowly to the third shape. Shapes should show changes in size, level, formation, and so on.

• Carefully observe one or several different types of animals. For example, horses might be chosen. What kinds of horses are there? How do different horses move? What about a thoroughbred racehorse? (Fast, straight ahead.) A quarter horse? (Meant for cattle ranching, quick starts and stops, zigzag changes of direction.) A draft or plow horse? (Power, pulling heavy loads.) A Tennessee walker? (Elegant, prancing, pulling a fancy cart.) Any other horses you can think of? What other animals can you think of that move in interesting ways? Do not try to be the animal, but try to capture the movement qualities of the animal. What about an ostrich, kangaroo, hippopotamus, elephant? Create a movement sequence that illustrates the type of animal qualities you wish to portray (figure 5.12).

Feel That Rhythm

Science
Transport systems of the body

Physical Education
Rhythmical experiences using the heart and lungs as a movement focus

Grade Level
4-5

• "While resting, feel your heart beat. Silently tap against your chest to the rhythm of your heart. Snap, clap, or tap that steady rhythm. Hop, jump, or step to that steady rhythm." To get every child moving together, play a musical march with a steady, even rhythm. Choose an action with the hands, arms, elbows, knees, hips, or feet to keep the beat. To music in 4/4 time with four beats per measure, slow the children's pace to a movement only to the first beat of the measure (move, rest, rest, rest). Double the time with a movement on beats 1 and 3 of the measure (move, rest, move, rest). Then have them move on every beat of every measure (move, move, move, move). "What else do you know that has a steady beat or rhythm? (Robots, machines, dripping wa-

Figure 5.12 Create a movement sequence showing how animals protect themselves—(a) bull with horns, (b) birds in flight, (c) poisonous snake.

ter, music, sunrise or sunset.) Create a movement sequence using one of these ideas. Make sure to have a definite beginning and ending."

• Think about how you breathe. How does your body move? (Answers will vary from up and down to in and out.) Take that breathing movement into your arms, head, chest, legs. Show how each body part can move up and down or in and out. Bring in the element of time. Take a long breath and several short, panting breaths with a selected body part. Use your whole body to rise with a long, inhaling breath, then collapse quickly using a quick, direct exhale. Create a sequence by combining these ideas.

Earth and Space Sciences

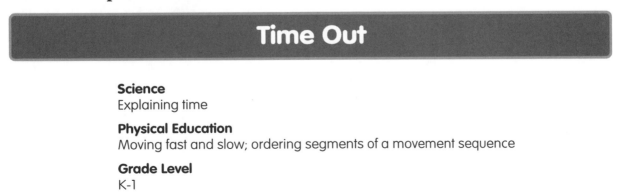

Time Out

Science
Explaining time

Physical Education
Moving fast and slow; ordering segments of a movement sequence

Grade Level
K-1

- Create a time line that represents past, present, and future. Order some significant events (cave dwellers—discovery of fire, wheel; medieval times—Europeans' discovery of America, feudal system; industrial revolution; humanity's first flight; computers; space travel; first space colony; who knows?). Develop a movement sequence that illustrates movement during each of these times.

- How many movements can you make in 10 seconds? Can you make one movement last 10 seconds?

- Create a movement sequence. Which movement in the sequence comes first, second, third? Can you perform the movement sequence in reverse—third, second, first?

Where Are You, Carmen San Diego?

Science
Map and compass skills

Physical Education
Orienteering

Grade Level
4-5

Teach children some orienteering skills. Use a compass to teach north, south, east, and west. Relate these directions to 90, 180, 270, and 360 degrees of a circle. Play a points-of-the-compass drill called the "Silver Dollar Game" (United States Army Infantry School, 1971). Have the children choose the degree bearing of 120 and walk an equal number of steps (or yards) in this bearing three times in a row. Children should return to their point of origin, having walked the path of an equilateral triangle. Use colored cards or poker chips to mark spots. Develop a simple orienteering course with several coded checkpoints around the school. Students should work with partners in a collaborative fashion to correlate their progress.

Weather Channel

Science
Air and water

Physical Education
Locomotor and nonlocomotor movement sequences

Grade Level
1-3

- Describe the types of things you might do when the air is still and calm. What would you do in a soft gentle breeze? What about a gusting, swirling wind? What about a powerful, ripping tornado? Create a movement sequence that shows how you would move differently in each of these air conditions. Show changes of level, energy, speed, pathway, and so on.

- Investigate the types of things you do with or in water: wash dishes, take a bath, swim different strokes, catch the largest fish you have ever seen, raft down a torrent of whitewater, splash in puddles after a rainstorm, and so on. Enhance the experience by using movements that create a mood or feeling about the water: the disgust of having to wash dirty pots and pans, the pleasure of a warm bath, the confidence of learning a new stroke, the excitement of catching record-size fish, the fear of falling out of the raft in the raging rapids, and the glee in getting someone else wet!

Bad Hair Day

Science
Weather

Physical Education
Selected locomotor and nonlocomotor movement sequences

Grade Level
1-4
Weather affects our mood or the way we feel. Show through your movement how you feel on a rainy day; a cold, snowy day; a hot, muggy day; and a damp, foggy day. How and where would you move if a tornado or a hurricane was approaching the area in which you live? Use different directions, pathways, levels, and speeds as you move.

Desert Storm

Science
The environment

Physical Education
Action-word movement sequences

Grade Level
2-3
Create a movement sequence based on action words chosen from an environmental theme. For example, a forest fire, volcano, mountain stream, rain forest, or desert sandstorm could be used as a theme. Themes can be broken down into subthemes according to what happens in each environmental situation. In the case of the forest fire, for example, the concepts of smoke, sparks, flames, destruction, and so on can bring out words such as whirling, swirling, lingering, surrounding, flying, bounding, hurrying, fading, settling, falling, crashing, extinguishing. After exploring each word, the children should develop a movement sequence that depicts the environmental situation. They can also use creative writing to write short paragraphs or poetry about the environment.

In the Zone

Science
Climate

Physical Education
Action-word movement sequences

Grade Level

4-5

• Explore activities you would do in different climates, regions, or areas of the United States or the world. Develop short movement sequences that typify the life of people or animals in a desert climate, frigid zone, tropical rain forest, mountainous region, flatlands area, and so on.

• Create a movement sequence that shows what you do during different seasons of the year. Spring signifies planting, growth, longer days, the return of warmer weather, showers, joy, hope, and so on. Summer means vacations, playing, swimming, fishing, going on a trip, baseball, Fourth of July, thunderstorms, and so on. Fall brings the return of school, harvest, cooler weather, leaves falling, hurricanes, and so on. Winter is typified by cold, snow falling, ice skating, sledding, sliding, and so on.

Spaced Out

Science
Space: the new frontier

Physical Education
Inventing a game, designing a movement experience

Grade Level
3-5

• Create a movement sequence by going on an exploratory space mission. Begin with a rocket takeoff. Include a tethered space walk, landing on the moon, performing a work experiment, a computer glitch and technical engineering resolution, return flight, and landing back on the earth.

• Invent a new game that has never been played before. Play the game as if it were being played in weightless conditions. Write out the rules to the game. Describe how to play the game to some aliens that you meet in outer space. Play the game with the aliens.

Physical Sciences

Did You See That?

Science
Observing things

Physical Education
Fundamental movement patterns, mirroring actions, individual movement sequences in dance or gymnastics

Grade Level
1-4

• Have children observe a partner's performance of a sport or gymnastics skill and check for appropriate cues. For example, the observer can check his or her partner's throwing using a checklist of cues, such as "side to target, opposite foot forward, trunk rotation, long lever arm, and follow-through," provided by the teacher.

• Perform a short movement sequence, for example, clap three times, snap your fingers twice, turn once fully around, and sit down cross-legged on the ground. Challenge the children to observe exactly what you do, then ask them to repeat your sequence.

• While working in pairs, have the children mirror each other's movements. The leader can create different kinds of symmetrical and asymmetrical shapes at selected levels. The follower must be acutely aware of any changes of movement by the leading partner and follow so closely that it is almost impossible to tell who is leading and who is following.

• After developing individual sequences or routines in gymnastics or dance, have the children judge each other's performances. Provide the children with a checklist of items to look for. For example, children can perform a short gymnastics sequence on the floor, consisting of three balances with connecting weight transfers. The checklist can ask, "Was stillness achieved (for at least three seconds) on each of the balances? Were there good lines, extensions, pointed toes and fingers? Was there variety in the choice of balances: upright and inverted, symmetrical and asymmetrical, change of levels, and so on? Were there smooth transitions: no extra or out-of-place movements, no extra steps or adjustments?" Use a rating scale like one used in the Olympics to help the children become critical observers. Have them tell the performer what they liked about the performance. Have them tell the performer how he or she might have improved the performance.

Creating Change

Science
Changing things

Physical Education
Creating designs and shapes then changing them

Grade Level
2-3

• Create a dance showing the molecular movement of water in solid, liquid, and gas forms (figure 5.13). The solid form is ice, where molecules are very close together, moving very slowly in a single direction—back and forth. Little space is used. The liquid form is water, in which molecules are farther apart, moving faster, and slipping and sliding past each other. More space is used. The gas is water vapor, with hydrogen and oxygen atoms in water molecules separating and reforming into new molecules of the compounds hydrogen gas and oxygen gas. Molecules are far apart and moving fast in all directions.

• Have children work in pairs. One partner is a statue or mannequin in a store front, and the other is the designer. The statue assumes one shape, then the designer changes the shape. Work with stretched, curled, and twisted shapes. Have the designer change the statue from one stretched shape to another stretched shape by changing levels. Change the statue from a stretched shape to a twisted shape. Have partners take turns being the statue and the designer.

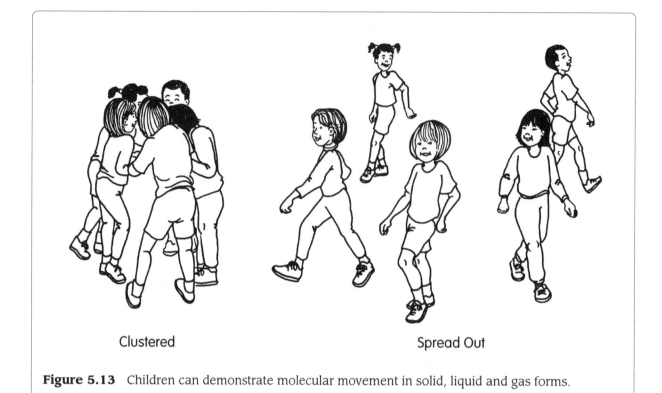

Clustered   Spread Out

Figure 5.13   Children can demonstrate molecular movement in solid, liquid and gas forms.

Balancing Act

Science
Forces in action—principles of stability

Physical Education
Static and dynamic balancing

Grade Level
1-3

• Conduct some simple experiments regarding stability and balance. Static balance is when you are still. Can you balance on one, two, or three body parts and hold each for three seconds? Can you balance at low, medium, and high levels and hold each for three seconds?

• Our body is best balanced when our center of gravity is over our base of support (figure 5.14). Use different body parts as bases: feet, hands and feet, knees, seat, forearms, and hips. Find where your center of gravity is. Use your belly button as a point of reference. When your center of gravity is over your base, you are balanced.

• In general, a wide base is more stable than a narrow base, and a low base is more stable than a high base. Work with a partner. One partner should assume a balance position (e.g., scale, stand on two feet, three-point football stance, kneeling on hands and knees). The second partner should gently push the balanced person from different directions. Working together under control, push until the balanced person is about to topple. Which balances are most stable? Why?

Figure 5.14 Our body is best balanced when the center of gravity is over the base of support.

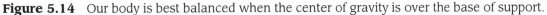

• Sensory organs of the body help a person remain balanced. Stand on one leg. Balance in this position with eyes open, then with eyes closed. Which is easier? Why? (Vision helps orient our body's position in space.) Balance on a knee and hand on the same side of the body, then on opposite sides. Try each with your eyes open, then closed. Try other positions with your eyes open, then closed. Notice that it is much easier to balance with your eyes open. Now try some balances with your arms in close to your side, then spread your arms out. Which position makes it easier to balance? Why?

• To move, people must temporarily, but under control, place their center of gravity outside their base. Stand up straight. Lean in a chosen direction: forward, backward, sideways. Lean until you feel yourself topple. Take a step in that direction to regain your balance. Can you hop forward five times in a row without losing balance? Make one big, long jump and land by bending at the hips, knees, and ankles. Lean forward as you land, and don't let your hands touch the floor. Squat down and place your hands on the floor. Tuck your chin and knees to your chest, bottoms up, and over you go. Return to your feet under control.

• Carry a heavy object, such as a briefcase or a box, as you move across the floor, raised surface, bench, or balance beam. Try holding the object out away from you in front or to the side as you move, then in close. Which way is easier? Why? In general, for best results, lean in the direction opposite the object and hold the object in close to your body.

• Jump in the air and turn a quarter, half, or full rotation. When rotating, pull your arms in for a quick spin. When landing, stretch your arms out to the sides and place your feet wide apart for control. Also bend (give) at the hips, knees, and ankles to absorb your motion. Run, jump, spin and land, or jump from an elevated height to the floor. Each time use good principles of landing to absorb your linear or rotary motion under control—no crashing or falling to the floor.

Do You Measure Up?

Science
Measuring

Physical Education
Selected manipulative and locomotor skills

Grade Level
2-4

• Use a book, string, or newspaper to measure how far you can jump, hop, or step. Put two actions together, such as two jumps or a jump and a hop. Measure the distance of your combined effort.

• Jump as high as you can and place a mark on a wall with a piece of chalk. Measure the height of your vertical jump.

• Throw or kick a ball for distance, and use a tape measure to discover the distance the ball traveled in feet, yards, or meters.

• Use a stopwatch and see how fast the children can run 50 meters, 100 meters, 400 meters.

• Count your resting heart rate using your carotid artery. Then perform a number of different exercises, such as jump rope, step aerobics, and jumping jacks, for 30 seconds or one minute. Count your heart rate again and calculate the difference.

Move Like a Machine

Science
Things on the move

Physical Education
Creative movement sequence

Grade Level
1-3

• The lever, inclined plane, screw, pulley, wedge, and wheel are types of simple machines. Discuss with the children how different types of simple machines are used in everyday life. Examples include hammers, screwdrivers, bicycles, wheelbarrows, axes, wagons, cranes, and cars. As machines help people work, the machines perform tasks such as pulling, pushing, bending, stretching, twisting, and carrying. Create a lesson in which children explore the various movements that machines perform. Use recorded sound effects or electronic music to allow the students to explore the movements of familiar machines and of machines they create in their imagination. For example, the children could move to the percussive sounds of a hammer, the twisting and rotating of a screwdriver, the creaking of an old door slamming shut, and the rolling of a wagon, bicycle, or steamroller.

Understanding Motion

Science
Newton's laws of motion

Physical Education
Selected locomotor and manipulative skills, creative movement sequence

Grade Level
4-5

• Newton's first law of motion is about inertia and momentum. It states that a force is required to start an object in motion, stop it, or change its direction. To help children gain an understanding of this law, conduct a number of experiments in your physical education class (figure 5.15). Some balls, bowling pins, and a box or bench to jump from are needed. (1) An object such as a ball will remain at rest unless acted on by an outside force. When we throw, kick, or strike a ball our body provides the outside force. (2) A push or pull must be exerted for an object to be set in motion. When we roll a ball at a bowling pin, the pin will remain stationary until it is hit by the ball. When the ball hits the pin, it moves in the direction of the applied force. In what direction will the pin move if it is hit straight on, from the right side, or from the left side? (3) Run and then try to come to a sudden stop. From a moving start, jump onto and then off of the box or bench and try to "stick" the landing. Often you have to take extra steps to come to a stop, or you may even lose control and crash to the floor. The reason is that you have acquired momentum that is difficult to control.

• Newton's second law of motion is about acceleration and deceleration. Momentum is directly proportional to the mass of the object and the speed at which the object is moving. Try an experiment with some scooter boards, roller or in-line skates. Push people of different masses or have them build up to different selected speeds on skates

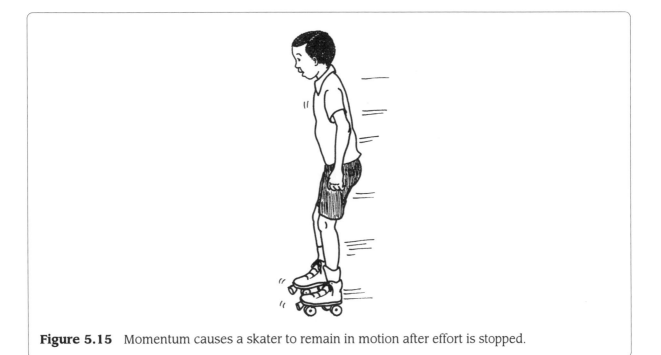

Figure 5.15   Momentum causes a skater to remain in motion after effort is stopped.

when they reach a specific line on the floor of the gym or playground. Then stop and let momentum take over. Help children observe and record the results of the distances rolled before coming to a stop. After analyzing the results, help children discover that if objects have equal mass, a greater speed will yield greater momentum. If bodies are moving at equal speed, a greater mass will yield greater momentum.

• Take several balls of different sizes and masses, such as basketballs, tennis balls, shot puts, medicine balls, and cage balls, out to the playground. First have children toss a ball easily onto the field. Then have them throw the same ball at the same angle but as hard as they can. Observe and record the place where each of the balls lands and the distance each ball rolled. Why did the second throw go farther in the air and on the roll? (More force was applied, it was traveling faster, it had more velocity, it had more momentum.) Next have the children throw balls that differ in weight or mass. They will discover that it takes more force to throw a heavy object a given distance. For example, a child could throw a softball 10 feet with much less force than he or she would need to throw a medicine ball or shot put 10 feet.

• Newton's third law of motion is about action and reaction. For every action, there is an equal and opposite reaction. While sitting or kneeling on a scooter board, if you push backward, which direction will you travel? (Forward.) While swimming, if you push the water backward, which direction will you travel? (Forward.) When jumping, if you push down hard against the floor, which direction will you travel? (Up.) Think of as many other examples of applying Newton's third law of motion as you can.

Push-Pull

Science
Force and motion—work, energy, resistance, friction, linear and rotary motion, centrifugal force

Physical Education
Experiments in human movement

Grade Level
4-5

• A force is a push or a pull exerted against an object to start, stop, accelerate, decelerate, maintain, or change its motion (figure 5.16). To make this point conduct several demonstrations in your class using large pieces of equipment, for example, a piano, balance beam on a transport dolly, horse or parallel bars on a transport dolly, or portable chalkboard. Have the children work in pairs to put the equipment in place before class or put it away after class. Teach them how to lift or push heavy objects safely (straight backs, lift or push with the legs). Try to get them to figure out where force needs to be applied to push the object in a straight line or to make it turn around. In general, to push in a straight line, the force should be applied near the center of gravity. To achieve rotary motion, the push needs to come from the end of the object. After the equipment is put in place, conduct a regular gymnastics class using the equipment.

• Work is a force acting on mass through a distance. In simpler terms, work means the ability to push or pull an object over a distance. Point out to the children that whenever they move their bodies or manipulate an object in physical education or at play, they are performing work. Running, jumping, hopping, skipping, throwing, striking, and so on all are examples of moving mass over a distance.

Figure 5.16 Force should be applied in the direction of the intended movement.

• Energy is required to produce force and move objects from one place to another. The human body applies force in the form of muscular energy, which is derived from burning calories from eating the proper foods. Kinetic energy is the energy of motion. When we lift, push, pull, carry, throw, or strike something we are using kinetic energy. The body applies force to objects indirectly through the use of potential energy. A drawn bow, stretched slingshot, and taut spring are examples of potential energy that becomes kinetic energy on release.

• In order to move a body or an object, the forces acting on it must be unbalanced. Stand in a balanced position. Lean forward, backward, or sideways. Feel the instant that you begin to lose your balance. This is the moment that your center of gravity moves outside your base. Take a step to regain your balance. Squat down and place your hands on the floor. Tuck your head and knees to your chest. Raise your bottom and look under your legs. Once again feel the instant you lose your balance and roll over in a forward roll. This is the moment your center of gravity moves outside your base.

• Resistance is an opposing force that makes it difficult to move a body or an object. Friction is a type of resistance between the surfaces of two objects. Friction is necessary to start and stop motion. To gain efficient movement, it is desirable to create enough friction or resistance for movement to take place but not so much or so little that inefficiency of execution results. Conduct some experiments in the gym by having races under different conditions. Have the children try racing with socks on, bare feet, and gym shoes and consider which ways make it easiest to get a good start and a quick stop. Have the children observe the results of their attempts. Record the results. Point out that athletes use various athletic shoes with special designs, such as football cleats, baseball spikes, and basketball sneakers, to gain traction on the surfaces on which they move. Sometimes it is desirable to reduce the amount of friction between surfaces to enable more efficient movement. Ice skates, in-line skates, and skateboards are examples.

• There are three circumstances in which friction affects motion: starting friction, sliding friction, and rolling friction. Starting friction exists when a person begins to move himself or herself or an object. Starting friction causes the greatest resistance to movement and is the hardest to overcome. Sliding friction exists when an individual attempts to drag or slide one object over another. Rolling friction exists when a person rolls one object over another. Conduct some simple experiments in the gymnasium. Have the children work in pairs. Have one partner try to pull the other a short distance with a jump rope. The resisting partner should be wearing gym shoes and standing with his or her feet wide apart in the direction of movement. The children will find out that starting friction is great under these circumstances. Next, have the resisting child stand, kneel, or sit on a carpet square with the carpet side down. Once again, the pulling partner should try to pull the resisting partner a short distance. Make observations, calculate the force, and record the results. Finally, the resisting partner should sit or kneel on a scooter board. The pulling partner should try to pull the resisting partner a short distance. Make observations, calculate the force, and record the results. The children should discover that it takes much less force to overcome rolling friction than it does to overcome sliding or starting friction.

•   Linear motion is motion in a straight line or a direct pathway. Develop with the children a dance sequence that compares moving in straight lines or direct pathways with moving in curved lines or indirect pathways. Both air and floor pathways should be considered.

•   Rotary motion is movement of a body around an axis. This type of motion may occur in any or all of the three body planes: around the vertical, horizontal, and transverse axes. Conduct a lesson that helps children learn about the principles of rotation around an axis. In general, shortening the radius of rotation causes a faster rate of rotation. Lengthening the radius causes a slower rate of rotation (figure 5.17). Tucking up tight into a ball in a gymnastics roll causes a fast rotation. Opening up at the end of a roll causes a slower rotation. During *V*-seat spins in gymnastics (Werner, 1994a), tucking up tight causes a fast spin, and opening up makes the spin come to a stop. Dancers, roller skaters, and ice skaters all use these same principles to control their spins on a vertical axis. To spin fast, performers tuck their arms in tight. When stopping their spins, performers thrust their arms out to the sides. To help children gain an understanding of these concepts, have them jump into the air from the floor or from an elevated surface such as a box or bench. Have them make quarter, half, or full turns while in the air. To assist in the takeoff and spin, children need to throw their arms in the direction of the spin and then tuck their arms in quickly. To stop the spin and control the landing, the children need to spread their arms and legs out to the sides and flex to absorb the landing. To make this a safe experience, insist that the children always land in control on their feet. Falling and crashing to the floor out of control is not acceptable.

•   Radius of rotation around an axis is also a factor in learning how to pump while swinging. In principle one must lengthen the radius of rotation while working with gravity. When moving against gravity in an upward direction, one must shorten the radius of rotation. One can achieve a long radius by establishing a low center of gravity on the down phase of the swing. One can achieve a short radius by establishing a high center of gravity on the up phase. While this concept may be difficult to explain in detail to children, one can teach them to bend and stretch their legs at the appropriate times to achieve a successful pumping action. For example, when swinging from a sitting position, they should learn to straighten their knees on the down phase and bend their knees on the up phase.

•   Centripetal and centrifugal forces also affect the motion of a person or an object moving in a circular pathway. Centripetal force is the name given to any force directed inward toward the center of a circular path of motion. Centrifugal force is the inertial tendency of a body or object in motion to move out or away from the center of the circular path. Centrifugal force causes a person or an object to travel in a straight line

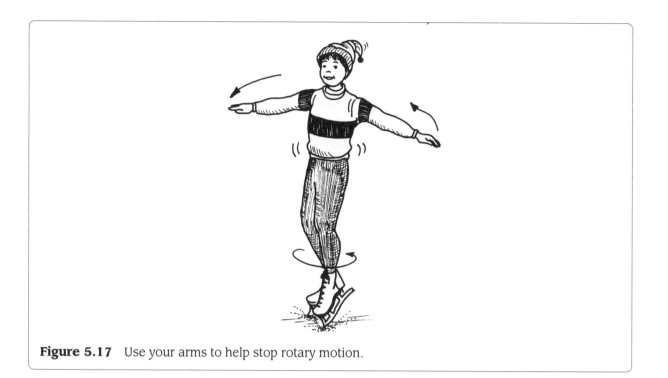

Figure 5.17 Use your arms to help stop rotary motion.

if in some way released from the axis of rotation. Once again several practical examples can be used to help children understand these concepts. When a person throws a ball overhand or pitches it underhand, a windmill-like windup establishes a rotary motion while the ball is held. The muscles of the arm and hand serve as the centripetal force by pulling the ball inward and keeping the ball in contact with the hand as it travels in a circular pathway before release. On release, centrifugal force causes the ball to move away from the body in a straight line tangential to the circle at the point of release. Similar examples may be conducted by having children pivot around a vertical axis using a discuslike hurling action to aim a hula hoop at a traffic cone target or by throwing a Frisbee for distance.

Forces in Action

Science
Force to produce movement, summation of forces, absorbing forces, angle of release, angle of deflection

Physical Education
Using muscles to produce and reduce force (strength), experiments to understand angles of force and deflection

Grade Level
4-5

• The amount of force needed for a particular task depends on the purpose of the movement. Since muscles supply force for each movement a body makes, people should be aware of certain facts about muscles and how they work so that they can use their muscles efficiently. For example, the large, strong muscles of the body are able to exert more force than the smaller, weaker muscles. In general, the muscles of the legs, hips, and thighs are larger and stronger than those in the arms and lower back. Have the children help you when you place large apparatuses (boxes or bags of balls, gymnastics boxes or benches, etc.) as you begin a class. Teach them how to lift heavy objects by keeping a rather straight back and lifting with the larger muscles of the legs (figure 5.18).

• In addition to lifting, teach children how to carry heavy objects. In general, hold the object in close to your center of gravity. Lean away from the resistance (heavy object) in proportion to the weight of the object in an effort to keep your center of mass over your base of support. Have the children experiment by carrying a heavy briefcase, a pail of water, or a heavy box across a balance beam or across the floor.

• Even small-muscle coordination tasks such as cutting, pasting, and writing require each muscle to be as strong as possible to work efficiently. To develop strength, dexterity, and coordination of the smaller muscles of the hands and forearms, provide situations for children to squeeze tennis balls, wad up pieces of paper with their hands, put nuts and bolts together, play with Tinkertoys, and use small muscles in other ways. An excellent recorded resource for these small muscle development activities is "Squeeze and Relax" or "Finger Thumping" (Brazelton, 1977).

• Muscles are able to exert more force when they are placed in a stretched position before they contract. This principle serves as the basis for the windup or ready position of nearly every sports action. Discuss this principle with your students, and then have the children practice their windup before throwing a ball, backswing before stroking a tennis ball, and so on.

• When teaching a lesson to children about throwing, describe to them the principle of summation of forces. The most efficient and effective total force is developed when the force from each contributing part of the body is applied in a single direction in a sequential order over as long a period of time as possible. Try an experiment. Have the children face a target a good distance away. Have them throw toward the target with their arms only—no stepping action, no trunk rotation. Mark and record the distance of the throw. Next, have them throw with a stepping action of the same foot as the throwing arm. Again mark and record the distance of the throw. Finally, with their side to the target have them step with the opposite foot, turn their trunk appropriately, and release the ball with a cracking action of the arm, wrist, and fingers. Mark and

Figure 5.18   Teach children how to lift and carry heavy objects.

record the distance. The children should discover that the last type of throw produces the best results when throwing for distance. The summation of forces from each contributing body part enables a greater number of muscles to apply the force over a longer distance and greater period of time until momentum reaches its maximum at the point of release. The sequential contribution of various body parts to the force of the throw also allows for greater leverage, which will increase the force and efficiency of the throw. The same rules apply when kicking and striking various balls in different sports activities.

• When absorbing the force from a fall or landing from a jump, there should be a gradual reduction of force. Have the children jump from a height such as a box or bench and land on the floor. At first allow them to land rather stiffly on their flat feet. Point out how loud they land as their feet crash to the floor. Next, use the cues "bend" or "give." By creating some tension in their leg and feet muscles (preparation) and coiling like a spring as they bend at the hips, knees, and ankles as they land, they will land softly and make much less noise.

• Teach the children a safety roll to help them learn about how to absorb their body weight over time and surface area. When falling or performing a forward or safety shoulder roll, a person who tries to land and roll by using a large portion of the body and by absorbing the force over as long a distance as possible lands more softly and efficiently.

• Teach the children the principle of absorption of force when teaching a lesson on catching. At first allow them to catch a ball or preferably a beanbag with their hands held rather stiffly out in front or to trap the ball against their chest. Point out that their catches make a lot of noise. Then teach them to reach early to make contact with the ball or beanbag and "give" with the force by bending at the elbows and pulling the object in to their trunks. Have a contest to see who can catch without making any noise.

• The angle at which an object is struck or released will affect the distance it travels (figure 5.19). Have the children conduct a throwing for distance experiment. Each child should throw one or more balls as hard as they can with a rather high trajectory (pop fly). Measure and record their distance. Next, have them throw one or more balls at a rather low trajectory (line drive). Measure and record their distance. Finally, have them throw one or more balls at an approximately 45-degree angle. Measure and record their distance. The children should learn that to project a ball or object into the air over the greatest distance possible, the angle of release should be 45 degrees.

• The angle of deflection equals the angle of approach. This concept is very important in the game of billiards to sink balls after the cue ball rebounds off a side cushion, but the same concept can be used to bounce a ball off the backboard and into the goal in basketball. Stations can be set up to teach about this concept using these or other activities, such as bounce passes in basketball, striking a ball against a wall at an angle and observing the resulting angle of the returning ball, and a chest pass against the wall to a partner five feet away.

Magnetic Field

Science
Electricity and magnetism

Physical Education
Creative movement sequences with a focus on attracting and repelling and appliances that are run by electricity

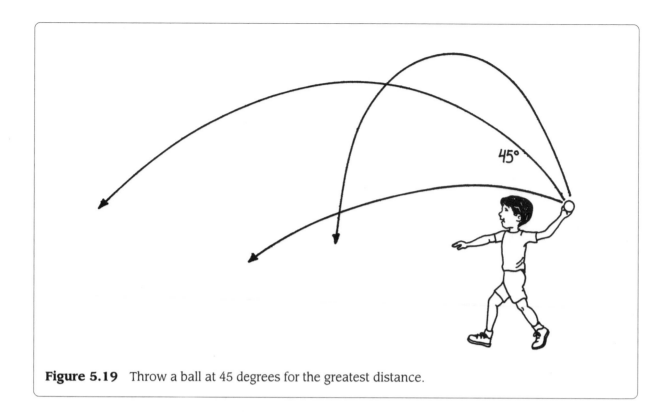

Figure 5.19 Throw a ball at 45 degrees for the greatest distance.

Grade Level
3-4

• Create a short dance sequence by having the children move about the room as if they were all magnets with only a north pole. What would happen? They would repel each other, and as a result, the magnetic force would become so great as children approach one another that they could get only so close before they would move off in different directions. The children's movement selections should show choices in moving on different levels, in different directions, and at different speeds. They can also experiment with bringing specific body parts close together, showing greater tension as parts come closer together, and moving quickly away in different directions.

• Pretend that the whole class is working in a magnetic field (figure 5.20). Have each child choose whether they want to be a north or south pole. Use a signal or code for identifying poles, for example, red band or pinny or thumbs up for north, green band or pinny or thumbs down for south. Children should move around the room in different ways such as hopping, skipping, sliding, crawling, and so on. As they approach another person, they will come closer and attach to each other by holding hands if they are opposite poles. They will repel and move away from each other if they are like poles. Once two poles attach they must move around together while linked. Eventually the whole class will end up attached to each other.

• "What appliances in your home are run by electricity?" While the children work in small groups, have them choose a specific appliance and develop a short movement sequence that shows how the appliance works. As groups take turns, have the observing groups guess what appliance is being demonstrated.

Figure 5.20 Opposite magnetic poles attract.

Summary

The scope and sequence chart in table 5.1 shows that there are many science concepts taught to children in elementary school. Concepts taught in science include those within the biological and life sciences, the earth and space sciences, and physical sciences. We have experimented in our classes with different ways to integrate these concepts in movement settings using different models of interdisciplinary programming. We have always tried to stay true to the principles of maintaining the integrity of each discipline and teaching active lessons. We have shared with you both complete learning experiences and short vignettes of additional learning experiences for you to try with your students.

Try our ideas. Some will work for you. Some will not. Some you may have to modify. Share your ideas with other teachers both in the classroom and in physical education and dance. Try your own new ideas of ways to integrate science with movement concepts. Make science come alive through practical applications in movement.

© Jack Vartoogian

Active Learning Involving Social Studies

In this chapter we examine the integration of movement with social studies. We describe what elementary social studies entails and provide a scope and sequence for each grade level. Several full learning experiences are presented. They are structured to be used as guides for a class period. "Moving Through the Years" focuses on various locomotor patterns to express the movement in types of transportation; "Have a Good Day" uses locomotor patterns to express greetings of different cultures; "Games From Other Countries" presents games from around the world; and "Heave, Hurl, Fling" deals with throwing events from the Olympics of the past. The additional ideas for developing learning experiences are divided into curricular focus areas: family, school, and community; citizenship; transportation; jobs; history; mapping and globe skills; national identity and cultures; and geography.

It is clear that integrating movement and social studies provides a fertile environment for achieving many of the goals of the contemporary education, such as fostering critical thinking and collaborative learning. Students can have learning experiences in social studies that influence the way that they live their lives at school and at home.

Even very young children are involved in social relationships. As they grow, these social relationships expand. When young learners enter school, they are involved mostly in relationships within the family and neighborhood. As they mature, students come to know more about the community, region, state, nation, and world. The social studies curriculum helps students focus on people and their interactions with one another in the past, present, and future. As a result of learning social studies, students should be able to participate more effectively in their world.

Unlike other curricular areas presented in this book, the social studies comprise a number of different disciplines. According to Banks (1985), social studies in the elementary curriculum has the primary responsibility to "prepare citizens who can make reflective decisions and participate successfully in civic life of their communities, nation and the world". At least eight disciplines make up the content foundation of elementary social study's programs: history, geography, civics, economics, sociology, anthropology, political science, and philosophy. Recently, history, geography, and civics have been emphasized most.

Evans and Brueckner (1990) explain that students can experience social studies by reading about social studies, internalizing data, formulating attitudes, practicing human relation skills, and participating and sharing in group activities. The scope and sequence of elementary social studies topics can be divided into three categories: product skills, process skills, and human relation skills (table 6.1). Product skills are the topics that are actually studied, while process skills are gained as a result of learning about the topics of social studies. The human relations skills are skills that help students live effectively in their society.

Scope and Sequence for Social Studies

The scope of elementary social studies usually includes specific topics by grade levels. Because social studies is made up of so many disciplines, the scope and sequence are quite elaborate. It might be helpful to examine the content of elementary social studies by grade level (table 6.2).

Primary-Grade Social Studies Skills and Concepts

The focus in kindergarten is on awareness of self in a social setting. Kindergartners begin to connect their home life with group life at school. They also study neighborhoods, communities, ways to travel, and the need for rules in social settings. First graders learn about themselves in primary social groups, including family (past and present), school, neighborhood, and community. Within communities, first graders study citizenship and the differences between urban, suburban, and rural life. Second graders study about neighborhoods, communities, famous people, citizenship, and how people live and work. Third-grade social studies focuses on communities and emphasizes sharing earth and space with others who are working and changing. Third graders are introduced to their own country and continue to study citizenship.

Table 6.1

SOCIAL STUDIES TOPICS

Product skills

Geography	Cities
History	Labor
Famous Americans	The world
Government	States and regions
Economics	Maps and globes

Process skills

Read graphs, diagrams, time lines, charts	Make decisions
Recognize and use specific social studies terms	Read social studies textbooks to determine important information and supporting details
Interpret graphics	Use the inquiry process when appropriate
Plan and participate in research projects	Use the library and media centers appropriately
Write and present reports	Transfer social studies knowledge to other subject areas
Participate actively in a group or committee	Recognize points of view, bias, generalizations
Think, plan, and do	Compare and contrast
Recognize main ideas, sequencing of events	Estimate
Outline	

Human relations skills

Accepting	Feeling
Becoming	

Intermediate-Grade Social Studies Skills and Concepts

The major emphasis in fourth grade is on the United States, including citizenship, the first Americans, and settling the land, and on their own state. The fifth-grade program highlights the United States and focuses on geography, history, economics, and the political system. The subject of study in sixth grade is usually the people, cultures, and geography in the western hemisphere and the world.

Students can profit greatly from the integration of social studies experiences with physical education experiences. This integration causes the learning experiences to be more meaningful in both disciplines. Relationships within families, school and community, citizenship, history, mapping and globe skills, national identity and culture, and geography can be studied and enriched through participation in physical education activities.

Both contemporary elementary social studies and physical education curricula emphasize critical thinking and collaborative learning. The Houghton Mifflin social studies curriculum (*Social studies,* 1991) stresses critical thinking as a goal in teaching social studies so that students become citizens who make informed and reasonable decisions. The text notes that teachers can help students become better critical thinkers when they help students in

- seeking a clear statement of the question,
- using and mentioning credible sources,
- seeking reasons,
- looking for alternatives and alternative viewpoints,

Table 6.2

SCOPE AND SEQUENCE OF SOCIAL STUDIES CONCEPTS TAUGHT IN ELEMENTARY SCHOOLS								
Concept	**Grade**							
	K	1	2	3	4	5	6	
Family	X	X						
Home		X						
Neighborhoods	X	X	X					
Communities	X	X	X	X				
School	X	X						
Travel	X							
Necessity of rules	X							
Urban, suburban, and rural life		X						
Family life, past and present		X						
Citizenship		X	X	X	X		X	
United States				X	X	X		
Famous people			X					
How people live and work				X	X			
First Americans					X			
Settling the land					X			
Own state					X			
How people change				X				
Geography of the United States						X		
History of the United States						X		
Economics of the United States						X		
Political system of the United States						X		
History of western hemisphere						X		
Geography of western hemisphere							X	
The world, past and present							X	
The world, regions							X	

- being open-minded, and
- changing their position when the evidence merits.

No doubt integrating movement and social studies contributes to the actualization of these characteristics of critical thinking. Consider the ways in which students could be encouraged to think critically in the following movement activity.

Learning About the Statue of Liberty

The Statue of Liberty has welcomed immigrants to the United States for more than 100 years. The Statue of Liberty was the first sight of America for many immigrants as they made their way to Ellis Island. On the base of the statue are the words, "I lift my lamp beside the golden door." After studying about the Statue of Liberty and looking at pictures of the statue, pretend that you are a statue designer. You are going to design other Statues of Liberty and create new messages to be written on the base of the statue. Explore making your body into different statues. Model for a partner your two best statue designs. Explain exactly what your statue represents, and tell your message for the base. Have your partner critique your statue. Make changes and show your best design to a group or to the class.

To perform this movement challenge well, students need to

- work collaboratively,
- seek reasons,
- look for alternative viewpoints,
- be open-minded, and
- be persistent until the statues and messages are refined.

The teacher needs to

- provide a good model to give the students a concrete idea of the task,
- ask thought-provoking questions about the students' work, and
- hold students accountable for credible solutions.

Learning Experiences

Each of the four learning experiences (see table 6.3) demonstrates one of the interdisciplinary teaching models presented in chapter 1. The learning experiences have been designed to include skills and concepts from physical education and social studies. Each learning experience includes a name, suggested grade level, interdisciplinary teaching model, objectives, equipment, organization, complete description of the lesson, and assessment suggestions. In addition, tips on what to look for in student responses, how teachers can change or modify the lesson, and ideas for teachable moments are offered to provide further insights into each learning experience.

Table 6.3

SOCIAL STUDIES LEARNING EXPERIENCE INDEX			
Skills and concepts	Name	Suggested grade level	Interdisciplinary teaching model
Social Studies: Modes of transportation, with a focus on the development of the bicycle Physical Education: Locomotor patterns	Moving Through the Years	K-3	Shared
Social Studies: Customs and cultures: greetings from around the world Physical Education: Locomotor patterns and axial, gesturelike patterns	Have a Good Day	1-2	Partnership
Social Studies: Customs and cultures: games children from various countries play Physical Education: Locomotion, balance, and coordination	Games From Other Countries	4-5	Shared
Social Studies: Olympic history Physical Education: Throwing using force	Heave, Hurl, Fling	4-5	Partnership

Moving Through the Years

SUGGESTED GRADE LEVEL

Primary (K-3)

INTERDISCIPLINARY TEACHING MODEL

Shared
Studying transportation is common in elementary social studies. Students can use what they learn in this lesson to better understand the historical development of transportation, and improve expressive movement skills.

Social Studies
Modes of transportation, with a focus on the development of the bicycle

Physical Education
Various locomotor patterns to express the movement in types of transportation

OBJECTIVES

As a result of participating in this learning experience, children will improve their ability to

- move like different types of transportation,
- develop and perform a movement routine that focuses on the evolution of the bicycle,
- move in ways that reflect an understanding of the concepts of fast and slow movement,
- move in ways that reflect an understanding of the concepts of bound and free-flow movement, and
- identify the different types of bicycles in the evolution of the bicycle.

EQUIPMENT

A picture file of the evolution of bicycles will be needed for this lesson. Some social studies textbooks include such pictures.

ORGANIZATION

The students will work individually in mass or scattered formation. They will also work with partners in scattered formation.

DESCRIPTION

"Hello! Today we are going to take a look at transportation, which is how we travel. Every day our lives are affected by different types of transportation. Can you think of ways the transportation has affected your life since you woke up this morning? Some of you were transported to school in cars, buses, trucks, trains, subways, or on bicycles or skates. Maybe you even transported yourself here by using your own two feet. Another way that transportation has affected you is by the food you eat in the cafeteria. The food was transported here in some way. The bananas that are served might have come by boat, freight train, or truck. We can think of many ways that transportation has touched our lives in the hours that we have been awake this morning.

"Let's get moving. I want you to pick some type of transportation. You might choose a car, boat, helicopter, skateboard, or something else. When I say 'go,' move like your method of travel. For now you are not, for example, riding in the car or the boat, but you are moving like the car or boat. You don't need to sound like your type of transportation. Let's move quietly. Who would like to show us what we are looking for? Erin. Everyone, let's see if we can figure out Erin's transportation. Thanks Erin. What were you moving like? Okay. You were a jet. You had a takeoff that started off slowly but very quickly increased speed until you were moving very fast. Once you reached your traveling speed you stayed at that speed for a while. Now everyone, go. . . . Freeze.

"Think about the speed of your movement. Were you going fast or slowly? Did your speed truly represent the speed of your mode of transportation? This time I want you to think about the way your mode of transportation changes speeds. Think of your type of transportation, for example, a huge flatbed truck, moving from still (or parked) up to full speed and gradually back to parked. Really think about your mode of transportation. Usually the larger modes of transportation take longer to arrive at top speed and also take longer to slow back down. Ready, go. . . . Freeze.

"When I say 'go,' make a bridge with a partner by the time I count to five. Ready, go. Show your partner your change of speed sequence. See whether your partner can tell what you are moving like. Then switch and have your partner take a turn. When you have finished, stand beside your partner so that I'll know that you have completed the task. Now ask you partner what you can do to make your sequence look more like your type of transportation, from parked, to full speed, to parked. When I say 'go,' each of you work to improve your routine. Ready, go. . . . Freeze.

"We had so many ways to travel. Let's get to know a little more about transportation. There are three areas in which we can travel: on land, over water, and in the air.

"Let's focus on land travel. This is very interesting! The invention of the wheel started real land transportation. Guess how long humans have had the wheel? About five thousand years. Once people understood the wheel, they could transport themselves and their belongings more easily. What would be some of the first kinds of transportation that used wheels? Oxcarts, chariots, covered wagons, buggies. Later came the bicycle and horseless carriage, or automobile. *Automobile* means 'moving by itself.'

"The bicycle was popular well before the car was invented. Bicycles were the most popular way to travel in cities. The first bicycles had no pedals, the riders sat on a seat and moved by walking [show picture]. These cycles were called *hobbyhorses* (figure 6.1). The next cycles, which were invented in the 1860s, were *velocipedes*, and they looked like this [show a picture of a velocipede]. As you can see, the velocipedes had a big front wheel and two very small rear wheels. The larger the front wheel, the faster the cycle could go. Gradually the front wheel became smaller, and the bicycle came to look more like the bicycles that we ride today. The bicycles of today are really awesome. With the technology that we have, some bicycles are designed to go very fast. Have any of you seen bicycle racing? Those athletes are really moving, aren't they?

"Let's move like different types of cycles. First, take a look at the velocipedes again [shows picture]. How do you think that those velocipedes moved? I'll tell you that riders had to be careful not to run over rocks or holes because they could crash very easily. Now when I say 'go,' I want you to begin to move like a velocipede over a city street. Ready, go. . . . Freeze. I notice that many of you are going slowly and are moving in what we call a bound flow. You want to stay in control, avoiding other cycles, bumps, and rocks. Let's move again like those early cycles. Ready, go. . . . Freeze. Molly, please show us the way that you were moving. She is doing a nice job of moving like a velocipede in a slow, bound flow. Thank you, Molly. Everyone, let's give that movement another try. Ready, go. . . . Freeze.

"Different cycles emerged over the years. The *ordinary* could go much faster than the velocipedes [show picture]. Next came the *safety* [show picture], which looks much like the bicycles that we ride today.

Figure 6.1   A picture of a "hobbyhorse."

"Let's move like the ordinary and the safety. The ordinary we can see still had a large front tire and smaller back tires (figure 6.2). Riders sat over the front wheel about five feet off the ground. When a rider fell off, it was difficult to get back on. Sometimes a rider would have to push the ordinary a good distance before he or she found something to stand on to mount the bike. The wheels were rubber and had wire spokes with steel rims. How do you think that the movement on the ordinary was? Probably more like the velocipedes than the bicycles that we ride today. More bound than free flow. Bound flow is really controllable, like the jump you would make from one slippery rock to another in a creek. Free flow is almost unstoppable, like a child running down a hill.

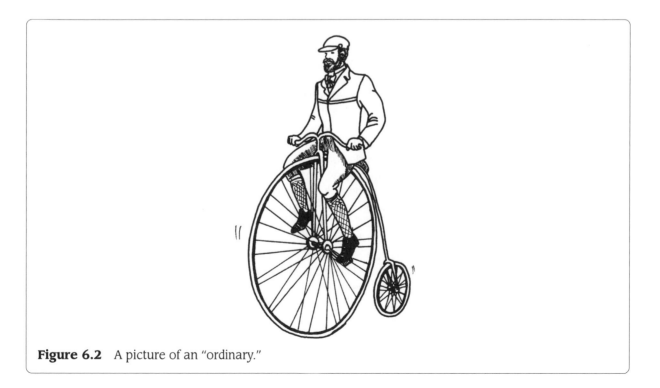

Figure 6.2   A picture of an "ordinary."

"The safety (figure 6.3) looks similar to the bicycles that you might have at home. Of course, they did not have all the modern features that we have today. What do you think that the movement of the safety over a city street was like? More bound or free? Yes, more free flow.

"When I say 'go,' I want you to move like an ordinary until you hear the drumbeat. Then begin to move as a safety would move. Who can tell us what we are going to do? Jeff? Right, move like an ordinary until the drumbeat, then like a safety. Ready, go.

"Freeze. I want you to keep the same idea, but now begin with an interesting starting position, move like an ordinary bicycle, then on your own change into a safety bicycle. Gradually increase speed, then slow down and stop in a finish position. Who can quickly tell us what we are going to do? Phillip? Okay, good answer. Everybody ready. Go.

"Freeze. You all are moving very well. Let's add another part to your sequence. Again you will begin with an interesting starting position, but then move like a velocipede (with caution, you need to avoid those potholes, rocks, and debris), gradually transition into an ordinary cycle (you are still somewhat cautious), then into a safety, increasing speed and then gradually slowing to an interesting finish. So the sequence is like this: starting position, a velocipede, ordinary, safety, ending position. Ready, go.

"Freeze. Adam and Lauren have agreed to show us the sequence that they have come up with. . . . Thanks, you two. Now I want you to continue to work on this sequence. Focus on making the first part of your sequence slow with bound flow, which is cautious and restrained, just as Adam and Lauren did. This is sort of like learning to ride a unicycle, a cycle that has only one wheel. Have you ever seen someone ride a unicycle? Have you ever tried to ride a unicycle yourself? Think about the way you would ride if you were trying to balance on a unicycle, which would be much like trying to ride a velocipede. Ready, go.

"Freeze. You are working hard. Let's add a final part to your sequence. Remember that at the start of the lesson we talked about modern bicycle racing. Racers go very fast. Most of you have probably ridden your bicycle very fast down a hill. Well, that is what I want you to add to the last part of your sequence. So let's say that your safety

Figure 6.3 A picture of a "safety."

bicycle turns into a current-day racing bicycle [show picture]. You are going to be moving very fast, as if you are traveling down a big hill. This is called free flow. For the ending, you must slow down and finish in an interesting way. So, Sarah, tell us what we are going to do for our whole routine? Good. Ready, go.

"Freeze. Students, you are going to continue to work on your routines. I want to emphasize starting your routine with a slow, bound movement and gradually changing into a free-flow, fast movement. Ready, go.

"Freeze. Let's show our routines. We will have six or seven of you go at a time. The others of you can just have a seat on the floor until you are asked to show you sequence. . . . I enjoyed seeing your sequences, but I would like you to refine your routines a little more. When I say 'go,' I want you to get with a partner to work on your routines. Ready, go. Now I want you to show your routine to your partner and ask for help in making it look better. Then switch and have your partner show his or her routine. Remember, we are telling a story here. What is our story? It is the development of the bicycle, which is a form of land travel. . . . Freeze. Let's show our routines again.

"You are going to find this next task very interesting. How many of you have heard of a bicycle built for two? They are also called tandem bicycles. They have two seats, two sets of handlebars, two wheels, and two sets of pedals. The tandem bicycle was popular during the late 1800s and early 1900s. Many couples dated, or courted, on tandem bicycles. With the same partner you are going to come up with a "tandem routine." Choose one of your routines and perform it as if you are on a tandem bicycle. Remember, this is leading and following. The person on the front of the bicycle is the leader. Ready, go.

"Freeze. Students, let's show what we have so far. We will have four sets of partners go at one time.

"You did very well at working with your partner on your tandem routines. That is about all the time we have today. Let's review. What were the first bicycles called? The next one? And the next? On what type of movement did our routines focus?

"Let's end on a funny story. At first, automobiles were unpopular with farmers. Drivers who were not careful ran over dogs, cats, and chickens. Cars also scared horses that were pulling wagons or buggies. I think that this next part is funny. When farmers saw a car that was broken down, they would often yell, 'Get a horse!'

"Okay, thanks for the hard work on your routines. See you tomorrow."

ASSESSMENT SUGGESTION

- After the sequence is completed, ask students to write their sequences. Have an observer check that his or her partner followed the written sequence and that all parts are included. Encourage the observer to provide feedback about the inclusion of all parts and about the expressiveness of the sequence.

LOOK FOR

- Emphasize that all routines (or movements that are connected) should be repeatable, have a starting and ending position, and use smooth transitions from one movement to the next.
- A focus of this lesson is on moving fast and slowly. As children move like their chosen modes of transportation, look for gradual changes in speed. Also look for speeds that are really representative of the type of transportation. For example, a huge ocean liner never would move as fast as a small speedboat.
- A focus of this lesson in on bound and free-flow movement. Look for students to make their bound flow really bound. A good example of bound flow is jumping on slippery, wet rocks in a creek. Also look for free movement to be almost unstoppable, like a child running down a hill. Point out the contrast in bound and free movements as the children move.

- When students work on leading and following, look for accurate matching of movements.

HOW CAN I CHANGE THIS?

- The lesson could focus on the evolution of other types of transportation, for example, the evolution of the automobile.
- Students could be asked to mirror, instead of match, movements in the partner sequence.
- Students could develop a sequence that focuses on different types of transportation during a certain time period, for example, the early 1900s. The sequence could include moving like trains, airplanes, bicycles, and automobiles of that era.

TEACHABLE MOMENTS

- Stress the relationship between the disciplines of physical education and social studies. Emphasize how types of transportation move and how our bodies move through space.
- Be sure that students can identify the specific types of bicycles. Ask which bicycles would emphasize different types of movements: slow, fast, bound, free.

Have a Good Day

SUGGESTED GRADE LEVEL

Primary (K-2)

INTERDISCIPLINARY TEACHING MODEL

Partnership
It is strongly urged that this lesson be a part of a collaborative effort by several teachers in a school. Themes of study including important life milestones (births, religious rites of passage such as baptisms or bar mitzvahs, weddings, funerals), seasons of the year (new year, planting, harvest), holidays, and so on clearly are interdisciplinary in nature. As children explore customs and cultures of different people around the world through a theme approach, they can celebrate similarities and differences among groups of people.

Social Studies
Customs and cultures: greetings from around the world

Physical Education
Locomotor patterns of walking and skipping and axial, gesturelike patterns involved in greetings

OBJECTIVES

As a result of participating in this learning experience, children will improve their ability to

- perform simple locomotor and gesture patterns to the rhythm of music,
- move using the specific rhythms designated in each part of the dance,

- perform selected folk dances that reflect greeting customs from other cultures, and
- recognize a variety of ways that people from different cultures and vocations greet each other.

EQUIPMENT

A record, CD, or cassette player and music for the French folk dance "Bridge of Avignon" (Michael Herman's Orchestra, 195) or the Danish folk dance "Dance of Greeting" (Michael Herman's Orchestra, 1958) or the African folk dance "Jambo" (Weikart, 1989, record 7).

ORGANIZATION

To learn the specific steps of the dance and the greeting customs, the children will work individually in mass or scattered formation. Then the children will form a single, large circle with an assigned partner and corner to perform the selected folk dance.

DESCRIPTION

"Buenos dias. Bon jour. Jambo. Guten tag [guten morgen]. Do you know what any of those phrases mean? Ashley? (Good day or hello.) Right. Buenos dias is a greeting in Spanish. Good day. The other three are the same greetings in French (bon jour), Swahili (jambo), and German (guten tag). What do we say to each other in the United States when we greet each other? (Hi, hello, how ya' doin, what's up, what do you say, man.) You're right. Those are all verbal ways of greeting each other.

"In our school we are studying the theme of customs and cultures of different people around the world. This will help us come to understand that while we all may do things differently, we are alike or similar in many ways. For example, as you have learned in your class with Ms. Crosse, most cultures celebrate or honor specific important life milestones, such as births, namings, graduations, weddings, and funerals. Most cultures also celebrate the beginning of new seasons of the year, such as New Year's Day, planting, blessing of the fleet, and harvest. Most countries also celebrate special holidays. Can you name any we celebrate here in the United States? (Martin Luther King Day, Valentine's Day, St. Patrick's Day, Memorial Day, Mother's Day, Father's Day, Fourth of July, Columbus Day, Washington's and Lincoln's Birthdays, All Saints Day or Halloween, Hanukkah, Kwanza, and Christmas.) Why do we celebrate them? Yes, some are religious holidays, others celebrate our war dead, our independence, national heroes, and so on.

"The reason I greeted you in different ways today is because we are going to learn to physically greet each other in different ways and put those greetings into a dance. What is one way we often greet someone we know using our bodies? Kelly. (Wave hello.) A wave is one way, any others? (Hug, high five, give skin.) We'll use those ways of greeting each other, plus some other ways of greeting people from different historical time periods, different vocations, and different cultures as we develop our dance.

"Let's begin by spreading out into general space. The music I have selected ["Bridge of Avignon"] has two parts, A and B. In part A, or the chorus, there are eight measures or 32 counts. During that time we will skip 16 times. To make it easier to remember we will count eight skips two times. Let's put the music on, and do just part A. Then we'll stop and listen to part B. Ready [music on], skip, 2, 3, 4, 5, 6, 7, 8, skip, 2, 3, 4, 5, 6, 7, 8. Listen (da, da, da, da, da-da), Skip. . . . Stop. Remember, this is not a race. Try this again, and skip to the music. . . . Stop.

"Now we are ready to do part B. You have already heard the special music signals (da, da, da, da, da-da) for part B. That is the time we will greet each other. Because this is a French dance, we'll start with some French greetings. This dance originated in Avignon during the 14th to 16th centuries. The royalty used to dress very formally in fancy costumes [bring in pictures of Louis XIV or other pictures showing period dress].

They would greet each other by bowing or curtsying (figure 6.4). [Demonstrate.] As the music indicates, we will offer a greeting to someone nearby two times: boys bow, girls curtsy. Let's practice this much: part A and B one time. Ready, [music on], skip, 2, 3, 4, 5, 6, 7, 8, skip, 2, 3, 4, 5, 6, 7, 8, greet, greet, stop.

"Very good. You're getting it, but as you can tell, there is more music and more ways to greet each other. This time try a different way of skipping—forward, backward, while turning, and so on—each time the chorus plays. And each time part B comes on, we'll do a new greeting. The first time we'll be French mademoiselles and messieurs and curtsy or bow. The second time we hear part B, we'll salute like the gendarmes (French military soldiers or police). The third time we'll do a prayerful, holy greeting (hands folded) like the Catholic priests, monsignors, or nuns. The fourth time we'll pretend we are greeting our good friend with a big wave. Remember to skip about in general space during the chorus each time and to greet (look someone near you in the eye) two different people near you on part B. I'll help you with my cues. Ready, [music on], skip, skip, bow/curtsy, bow/curtsy, skip, skip, salute, salute, skip, skip, prayerful, prayerful, skip, skip, wave, wave, stop. Very good so far.

"Now I want you to get a partner and stand next to your partner as we form a single, large circle. Stand, face your partner, and shake his or her hand. Say hello. Stand with your back to your partner. The person you are now looking at is your corner. Take a step toward your corner, shake hands, and say hello. I want us to do the greeting dance as we now know it from this formation. For the first eight skips in part A, we'll join hands and skip clockwise in a large circle. Then we'll do eight skips counterclockwise. On part B we'll greet our partner, then turn and greet our corner. Who can tell us the order or sequence of the greetings? Jennifer. Bow or curtsy, salute, prayerful, wave. Can everyone remember that? I'll give you word cues to help you remember. Ready. . . . Stop.

"There are still three more times for part A and two more times for part B before we get to the end of the record. We'll keep part A always the same, but I'm going to give you and your partner one minute to agree on two new ways to greet each other. Think about how people from other time periods, cultures, and so on might greet each other, for example, American Indian, high five, give me some skin, hug, and cool wave. Go. . . . Stop. Now turn and talk to your corner for one minute and agree on two more ways you'll greet each other.

"Okay. Let's try the whole dance. Remember, skip clockwise, skip counterclockwise, greet, greet. I'll cue the type of greeting each time. There will be one extra part A or set

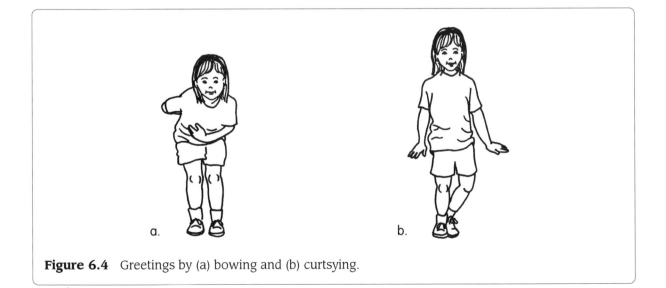

Figure 6.4 Greetings by (a) bowing and (b) curtsying.

of skipping steps after our last greeting sequence. Ready, [music on], skip, skip, bow/curtsy, bow/curtsy, . . . stop. Good hard work, children. You performed the sequence quite well. I saw only a few mistakes that we can polish up, but for now we'll stop. Bring your partner over here and gather around me in front of the board.

"You now know how to say hello or greet each other at least six different ways. Who can tell me one way and who might greet that way? Heather? (A soldier salutes.) Mike? (A religious person bows in a prayerful way.) John? (A French person might say *bon jour*.) Ira? (A person from the Middle East might hug and bring cheeks close together on both sides.) Simon? (An American Indian might raise his arm in a peaceful way.) Maria? (A Spanish person might say *buenos dias*.) Judi? (An American youth might give a high five or some skin [pound fists together].) Very good, everyone. What I'm hoping that you are learning from your study about cultures and customs is that while people have some differences in the way they do things, we all have a lot in common that makes us alike. We all celebrate similar occasions and have the same needs and interests as humans. Good-bye for now. *Au revoir. Abientot. Adios, hasta la vista. Syonara.*"

ASSESSMENT SUGGESTION

- Videotape small groups of learners and ask students to complete a self-evaluation of the dance.
- The teacher can also complete an analysis of the video.

LOOK FOR

- Watch to see if children have beat awareness and skip to the music. If some students are having trouble, reduce the skill to walking to the music or take some time to clap to the music.
- Make sure children understand that their greetings are to occur for the whole duration of part B. Racing through just to get done then waiting for part A to start again is not proper.
- After having done the dance sequence individually, the children might show some confusion in getting a partner, forming a circle, and learning about a corner. Be an especially good manager during this transition.

HOW CAN I CHANGE THIS?

- Teach a different international dance of greeting, such as the Danish "Dance of Greeting" (Michael Herman's Orchestra, 1958) or the African "Jambo" (Weikart, 1989, record 7).
- Develop a creative dance about a birthday party (Purcell, 1994), planting or harvest season, a celebration of victory or independence, or other special event.
- While teaching about the culture or customs of another country, teach a game or sport from that country (Kirchner, 1991.)

TEACHABLE MOMENTS

- Invite others from the community with different cultural heritages to share their language, costumes, food, life in their culture, cities, special festivals, and national heroes and heroines.
- Use a globe or map to point out where the countries are located. What other countries are near? What are the major bodies of water and other major geographical features of a country? What are each country's main industries?

Games From Other Countries

SUGGESTED GRADE LEVEL

Intermediate (4-5)

INTERDISCIPLINARY TEACHING MODEL

Shared

Studying characteristics of different countries is common in upper elementary social studies. Students can learn children's games from various countries to enhance their understanding of the cultures of the countries.

Social Studies

Customs and cultures: games children from various countries play

Physical Education

Locomotion, balance, and coordination

OBJECTIVES

As a result of participating in this learning experience, children will improve their ability to

- teach and learn new moving games,
- move to meet the objective of a game, and
- appreciate and understand the origin of a variety of moving games.

EQUIPMENT

Individual games have different equipment requirements. The following equipment is needed for the games suggested in this lesson: handkerchiefs, beanbags, long ropes, small objects to represent bones.

ORGANIZATION

Throughout this lesson children will work in groups of four or five.

DESCRIPTION

This interdisciplinary lesson requires cooperation with the students' other teachers. The class is divided into groups of four or five students. Each group chooses a different geographic area from a list of areas, which could include Egypt, China, Scandinavia, Arctic, Nigeria, and Brazil. Students are given time to research their geographic areas. This lesson would ideally be a culminating experience after the different geographic areas have been studied.

Each group is given the description of several games that are commonly played in their chosen country or region. The group selects one game, then reads the directions, and begins to play the game. When the groups are ready, one group teaches their game to the others. In teaching the game, the group in charge should identify the national or regional origin of the game, describe characteristics of the country or region, and explain why they believe the game is so popular in its native country or region. Next, the group will demonstrate the game and explain all rules and procedures. (It is important for the teacher to closely monitor as the group teaches; students might need help focusing on the most important aspects of the game. Time efficiency in giving directions is essential.) All the students then play the game within their group.

Many games are played in their native countries in large groups. In an educational setting, however, it is more appropriate for students to play in small groups to increase individual participation and activity time.

Following are examples of games from different nationalities (Hunt, 1964).

Egypt

The horse-and-rider theme is popular in Egypt. Games with universal appeal such as leapfrog and blind man's bluff are common among Egyptian children.

FOX

Players: Any number   Equipment: Handkerchief

Activity: Hunting, chasing, dodging   Appeal: Dramatization, problem solving

One player, the fox, walks around the circle formed by the other players carrying the handkerchief. The fox walks around the circle and tries to distract the other players. At some point the fox drops the handkerchief behind a circle member and quickly tries to stand beside that player before being tagged. If the fox is tagged, he or she must be "it" again. If the fox is not tagged, the circle player must become the fox.

HORSE

Players: Any number in groups of three   Equipment: None

Activity: Stunt-balance, coordination   Appeal: Dramatization, strength

Two players form the horse by having one player stand behind another. The player in back puts his or her hands on the shoulders of the front player. The third and lightest player is the rider. The rider mounts the horse and rides astride the arms of the player in back. This is frequently used in a relay.

China

Games of China with origins in the pre-Communist era show the amicable attitude of the Chinese people before their domination and indoctrination by the Communists. It is interesting to note that the games show an attitude of readiness to follow a knowledgeable leader. Games played by Chinese children seldom include relays.

FISHING BY HAND

Players: Any number   Equipment: Handkerchief

Activity: Clapping, grasping, running   Appeal: Dramatization, problem solving

One player, the fisherman, is blindfolded and extends the right arm out with the palm facing up. The other players and the fish verbally make noises to tease the fisherman and try to tag his or her palm with their index finger. If the fisherman closes his right hand on a finger of the fish, the fish is caught. If the fisherman can guess the name of the caught fish, they change places.

During the game, the fisherman may say, "The tide is high." At this time the fish must move as if they are playing in deep water. When the "tide is low," fish move as if playing in shallow water.

Scandinavia

The games of Scandinavia usually focus on friendly play and competition. Most of the games are representative of a history of a physically strenuous past.

STEALING THE BONE

Players: Any number

Equipment: A small object for a bone

Activity: Hunting, chasing, dodging, running

Appeal: Competition, skill

"Doggie Doan," who is "it," sits with his or her eyes closed in the center of the circle of players. The bone is placed behind Doggie Doan. The circle players skip as they say,

You'd better watch the bone,

Doggie Doan, Doggie Doan,

I'll take it away for my own, for my own

When I've snatched it and away I've gone.

The player nearest the bone the second time the word *own* is sung snatches it and runs. Doggie Doan chases this player. If the player with the bone returns to his or her place without being tagged, the same player is Doggie Doan for the next game. If the runner is tagged, he or she is Doggie Doan for the next game.

Nigeria

A common characteristic of games from Nigeria is that the player caught in chasing games is expected to accept a playful beating from the one who catches him or her.

JUMPING THE BEANBAG

Players: Any number

Equipment: Beanbag, long rope

Activity: Jumping

One player is "it." He or she stands in the center of a circle formed by the other players. "It" holds a beanbag that is tied to the end of a rope that he or she swings and gradually lets out until the players have to jump to avoid being hit by the bag. When a player fails to jump and is hit by the bag, he or she is out of the game. As the players decrease in number, the speed of the bag increases. The last player in the circle is the winner.

Brazil

Some of the popular games of Brazil are singing games played in a circle.

***COELHO NA TOCA* (CO-EL-YO NA TO-CA)**

Players: Any number in groups of three

Equipment: None

Activity: Hunting, running

One player is chosen to be "it," or the rabbit without a house. The other players are in groups of three. Two form a house by holding hands. The third player is inside the house and is also called a rabbit.

At a signal all rabbits run to another house. The rabbit without a house tries to find a home. The rabbit left outside then waits for or gives the signal and tries to become a *coelho na toca*, or rabbit in the burrow.

ASSESSMENT SUGGESTION

• Have group members explain the rules of the game. After all games have been taught, have students name the game, the geographic origin, and rules.

LOOK FOR

- Encourage students to work well together to learn, play, and teach their game.
- Make sure that students make good connections between the characteristics of the people of their geographic area and the games.

HOW CAN I CHANGE THIS?

- Focus on only one country or geographic area. Each group of students could find a different game for the specific country or area. Students spend an entire lesson learning and playing games from, for example, Nigeria.
- Instead of providing a list of games from which the students can select, have students do the research to find the games themselves. It would be helpful to work with the media arts teacher to ensure that adequate resources are available.
- This same lesson could be done using dance or popular leisure activities.

TEACHABLE MOMENT

- At the end of the lesson, review and have students match the game with the geographic area.

Heave, Hurl, Fling

SUGGESTED GRADE LEVEL

Intermediate (4-5)

INTERDISCIPLINARY TEACHING MODEL

Partnership

Few themes offer the richness of the Olympic experience to pull the efforts of teachers of the whole school together. It is suggested that, if not the whole school, at least the teachers at a particular grade level unite around an Olympic theme in teaching all subjects to their children. Teachers are encouraged to get a copy of the suggested reference as a springboard for generating ideas on integrating language arts, mathematics, science, social studies, art, music and physical education.

Social Studies, Mathematics, Language, Science, Art, and Music

Themes of the Olympics with a partnership of all of the disciplines. Suggested references: United States Olympic Committee (1984), Atlanta Committee for the Olympic Games (1994-95).

Physical Education

Throwing events from track and field in this example (but any Olympic sport can be used)

OBJECTIVES

As a result of participating in this learning experience, children will improve their ability to

- use the muscles of the arms, shoulder girdle, back, and abdomen to develop muscle strength;
- throw a variety of objects using different styles of producing force;
- know about the history and the spirit of the Olympics; and
- comprehend relationships among disciplines when studying information related to a theme.

EQUIPMENT

One each: playground ball, basketball, Frisbee, hula hoop, and javelin (six- to eight-feet-long, one-inch-wide PVC tubing with taped handles in the middle for balance and grip); two traffic cones or markers for every pair of students

ORGANIZATION

The children work in pairs, lined up along the sideline of a basketball court or football field with plenty of space between pairs. The active partner stands at the line. The marking or retrieving partner stands behind the performer. For safety purposes, a signal is used for simultaneous retrieval of objects.

DESCRIPTION

THE FOLLOWING introduction to the history of the Olympic Games could take place at a convocation of all teachers and children in the gymnasium or cafeteria.

"Good morning, girls and boys. We are about to begin a new unit of work in which all teachers in our school/grade level will combine their efforts to help you learn about the Olympic experience. Did you know that for the second time in the last 12 years the Olympics have been held here in the United States—in 1984 at Los Angeles and in 1996 at Atlanta? The Atlanta Olympics were special because they celebrated the 100th anniversary of the modern Olympic Games. In 1896 Baron Pierre de Coubertin initiated the modern Olympic Games in France. He was inspired by the concept that 'the important thing in the Olympic Games is not to win but to take part; the important thing in life is not the triumph but the struggle. The essential thing is not to have conquered but to have fought well. To spread these precepts (beliefs) is to build up a stronger and more valiant and, above all, more scrupulous and more generous humanity.' Since that time the Olympics have been held every four years.

"The Greeks began the Olympics in 776 B.C. with a single foot race of 200 meters. The winner of the race got to carry a torch to the altar in Olympia to initiate a celebration of sacrifice by neighboring communities. The distance of 200 meters, then called a stadion, is still significant today as track races are held in multiples of the stadion measure. In fact, football or soccer fields with oval tracks built around the outside with seating for spectators are called stadiums after the Greek word. For the first 13 Olympiads the stadion (200-meter) run was the only contest.

"Gradually, the Olympics became more popular and events were added. Chariot races around a hippodrome (800-meter track), horse races, pentathlon (discus, standing long jump, javelin, 200-meter sprint, and wrestling), boxing, and *pankration* (judo) are examples. The Olympic Games gained strength because of the ideals or beliefs they embodied, and they remained popular for over a thousand years, unchanged by fashion or political and cultural forces.

"The word *athlete* comes from the Greek word *athlon*, which means competitor. To the ancient Greeks an athlete was someone who entered a contest for any sort of prize. Competing was what counted. In fact, interest in measuring and recording individual feats does not appear to have been important. Eventually there were many classes in which to compete. If you were not going to measure yourself against the sprinters or boxers, you could try poetry, dance, speech making, or music. The ancient Greeks did not separate physical competitions from competitions in other forms of skill. In fact, they believed in the concept of a sound mind in a sound body. Olympia was not merely a mecca for athletics, but also a human proving ground for the Greek ideal of strong, able, beauty-loving, and wise citizens (Umminger, 1963).

"It is because of these high ideals that the Greek civilization was a dominant force in history for hundreds of years. As you will learn in the next several weeks, the contributions made by the ancient Greeks continue to influence what we learn today, for example, modern medicine is influenced by the work of Hippocrates; philosophy, by that of Plato, Socrates, and Aristotle; math, by Euclid and Pythagoras; literature, by Homer.

"We can learn some important lessons in history through our study of the Olympic Games and the ancient Greek culture. It was only when the influence of politicians and the wealthy was permitted to make itself felt that corruption crept in and athletes began to think of themselves as professionals. (Do you see any parallels occurring in politics or sport today that illustrate corrupting forces?) Athletes began to think not of olive-branch but of cash prizes to be earned for victory.

"The decline of the Olympic Games was slow. The official end of the unbroken series of games was in A.D. 393 under the Christian ruler Theodosius I, who banned the Games. They occasionally recurred until A.D. 529, when Justinian I reissued and enforced the ban. It was at this time that the Greek civilization in its classical form officially came to an end.

"As we work together in the next few weeks, we are going to hold our own Olympics of sorts. Not only will you learn about the contributions of the Greek civilization in literature, philosophy, math, science, history, art, and music, but also each class will choose a modern country to study and adopt. Then, as a fitting end to our studies, we will conduct our own version of the Olympic Games. We will have events of all sorts, and everyone will compete in the ideal of the Olympic spirit."

CLASSROOM teachers are encouraged to discuss with their students at this time any visions they may have for assignments or projects in language, mathematics, science, social studies, art, and music to make this a true partnership project of the whole school or grade level.

"*Citius, altius, fortius*—does anyone know what that means? [Show a picture or statue of the discus thrower or winged victory.] It is the Olympic motto and means 'swifter, higher, stronger.' Over the next few weeks we are going to learn about competing in the Greek tradition to enter a contest and to do our best. There will be many events, and everyone will be able to select a contest in which they can excel.

"We know from studying the history of the Olympics that the pentathlon was one of the early events. It consisted of five contests, two of which were throwing, one jumping, one running, and one wrestling. Eventually we will get to running and jumping contests, and we may even get to bicycle races around the track to symbolize chariot races, but first we are going to focus on throwing events.

"The ancient Greeks did not have metal balls called shot puts or metal and wooden discs to throw. In all probability they used stones of different weights and shapes. And they probably used different styles of throwing in different events. Today we are going to use basketballs, soccer balls, playground balls, hula hoops, and javelins (PVC tubing) to heave, hurl, and fling objects for distance from a line. As we do that we will simultaneously be working on the fitness concept of arm and shoulder strength because it takes a lot of strength to throw well.

"When I say 'go,' I want everyone to get a partner with whom you feel you can cooperate and line up on the sideline of the football field [basketball court], one in front of the other. The first partner will be the performer and should be at the line. The other partner is the retriever and should be three to five meters behind the performer for safety. Also for safety, each set of partners should be about three to five meters apart. Go. . . . Good. You did that quickly. Now when I say 'go,' I want the retrieving partner to get one basketball [soccer ball, playground ball] and two markers and bring them back to your partner at the line. Both partners stand side by side so you can see when you get back. What are we going to do when you hear the word 'go'? Right, Susan. Retrieving partner gets one ball and two markers and returns to the line beside his or her partner. Go. Quickly now. Good work. I like it when everyone pays attention to directions.

"Our first throwing event will be a form of throwing called heaving. We define heaving actions with our arms in several ways. First, we will sit with our backs to the line. Our legs will be bent and spread apart. We will hold the ball in our hands at or near the floor. Then, with a powerful heaving action, we will lift the ball up and over our heads, releasing it at about 45 degrees to project the ball as far as possible. [Demonstrate.] The observing partners will stand safely in front of the throwers. They will observe where the ball lands, and on my signal they will mark the spot with a marker and retrieve the ball. Does everyone understand? How do you get a good heaving action? (Lift with power quickly, then release at 45-degree angle.) Observers, go to your places, get a marker ready. Heavers, ready. Go. . . . Retrieve. Change. Observers, in your place with a marker. Heavers, ready. Go. . . . Retrieve. I am noticing that several of you are having trouble with the release. You are either letting go of the ball too early so that it goes up toward the ceiling [demonstrate incorrect form], or you are holding onto the ball too long so that it lands on the floor too soon [demonstrate incorrect form]. Remember to release the ball at 45 degrees [demonstrate correct form]. First heavers and observers in your places. Observers, watch where the ball lands. If it is farther this time, move the marker to the new position. Otherwise, leave the marker alone. Then, on my signal, everyone retrieve your balls. . . . Second heavers and observers ready. Go. . . . Retrievers, remember to mark only throws that are farther and get your ball. [Repeat once more for a total of three throws.] Measure and record the distance of the farthest throw on a provided recording sheet.

"Next we will stand up with our backs to the line. We will heave using the same motion as we did while sitting. [Demonstrate.] Lift and release at 45 degrees. Each thrower gets three heaves using the same procedure. Observers, mark and record the farthest effort. Ready, go. . . . Stop. Everyone close ranks by staying on the line, but gather toward the middle of the line. Quickly! One, two, three. Good. I like it when you respond fast so we don't waste time.

"Our next heaving effort will involve facing the line. Watch me. You will straddle your legs some. You will hold the ball with both hands and swing it down and back between your knees. Then, you will lift forward and up forcefully and release the ball (figure 6.5). [Demonstrate.] What do you think will be the best angle of release to get the farthest distance? (45 degrees.) You're learning application of a concept from math and science. Everyone spread back out. First heavers and observers ready. Go. [Repeat until everyone has three turns. Mark, measure, and record everyone's best effort.] Stop. Come in again.

"This last heaving action was very similar to one used in the Scottish Highland Games where strong individuals balanced a long pole or tree trunk in their arms and heaved it, sending it toppling end over end as far as they could. It is called 'tossing the caber.'

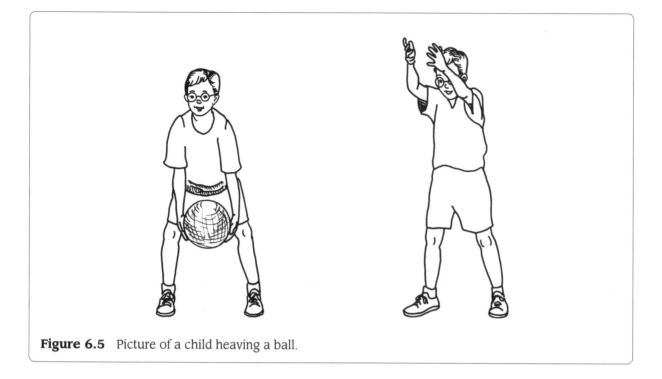

Figure 6.5   Picture of a child heaving a ball.

"Our next heaving action will be very similar to the shot-put action. Watch again. You will stand with your side to the line. You will place the ball under the side of your chin against your neck. The ball will be supported by your throwing or heaving hand. The elbow will be out away from the body. Next, you crouch down. [Demonstrate.] Without a ball, everyone do that much. Cradle, elbow out, crouch. [Check students' form.] Okay, stop and watch again. After the crouch, the body will begin its heaving action. Led by the elbow of the nonthrowing arm, the body will turn, lift, and heave as forcefully as it can. The action of the arm is a push or lift, not a throw. Make sure you lift the ball up and away from your chin at a 45-degree angle as you push the ball as far as possible. When you finish the turning action, you should be standing on the leg of your heaving arm with that side of your body closest to the line. You have rotated 180 degrees. [Demonstrate.] Remember, ready position, turn, lift, heave. Everyone go back to your positions. First heavers and observers ready. Go. [Repeat until everyone has had five turns. Watch carefully for heaving actions. Do not allow children to throw the ball. Mark, measure, and record everyone's best effort.] Stop. Come in again.

"Next, we are going to think about the concept of a hurling action. Like heaving, hurling is a forceful throwing action. But for our purposes we will define a hurl as a forward, overhand action. We can do this with one or two hands on the ball. Thus, we sometimes call a baseball pitcher a hurler. We can also think of a soccer throw-in as a style of hurling. First, we'll try a two-handed hurl. Watch. Place the ball in both of your hands and bring it back over your head. You face the line and step forward. As you step, you forcefully hurl the ball forward. Back, step, hurl. [Demonstrate.] Everyone, go with your partner back to your space. First hurler ready. Observers stand back. Go. Retrieve. Second hurler, go. Retrieve. I see some people standing still when they are hurling. For this action it doesn't make a difference which foot you use, but you must remember to step. It helps establish momentum. Also, remember to hurl up at a 45-degree angle. Three more times each. Retrievers, adjust markers to mark the best effort. Then measure the best score. Go. . . . Stop. Come in.

"The second hurling action will be an overhand throwing pattern that you already know. However, we are going to throw javelins [PVC tubing]. [Softball throw for distance could be substituted.] First, a point about safety. When retrieving a javelin, lift it at the end and walk it up to vertical. Grab the handle and always carry it in a vertical position. [Demonstrate.] We don't want anyone getting poked or stabbed. Stand at least 10 feet behind your throwing partner to give them plenty of room. Rember, safety is important. If I see anyone being unsafe, you'll be asked to sit out.

"For the javelin hurling action, face the line. Hold the javelin back over your head, arm straight. Hold the javelin between your thumb and base of your fingers or between your pointer and middle fingers supported with your thumb. Do not cup your fingers or hold it like a baseball. [Demonstrate.] Next, step forward with the opposite foot. Then bring the arm through, leading overhead with the elbow. Arm back, step, hurl. [Demonstrate.] Everyone, go back to your space with your partner. As before, take turns, five tries each. Measure and record the best score. Retrieve only on my signal. Ready, go. . . . Stop. Come in.

"Last, we're going to try a flinging action. Like heaving and hurling, flinging is a forceful throwing action. For our purposes we will define a fling as a sidearm motion. Thus, throwing a discus is a fling. As a substitute, we are going to use hula hoops. Watch. You will place the hoop in your dominant hand between your thumb and the base of your fingers. Again, be careful not to cup your fingers tightly around the hoop. [Demonstrate.] Stand with the nonthrowing arm close to the line. Place your feet shoulder-width apart. Twist or coil your body back, and get lower into a crouch. Begin to forcefully uncoil (fling) by leading with the free elbow. Your flinging arm should be relatively straight and trail the leading action of the arm and chest. Play crack the whip with the hoop arm as you release the hoop in an upward, sideways arc. Follow through as your body spins around at the line by landing on the same foot as the flinging arm. Coil, elbow lead, spin, fling, recover. [Demonstrate.] Go back to your space at the line with your partner. As before, five flings each. Take turns. Retrieve only on signal. Mark and record your best effort. First person ready. Go. . . . Stop. I'm noticing several errors. If you are flinging your hoop out to one side or the other, you are letting go too early or too late. If your hoop wobbles through the air, try to make your sideways arc smoother and release the hoop smoothly from between your thumb and palm. Also, make your flinging action at a rising 45-degree arc to get the most distance. Ready again, go. . . . Stop. Come in.

"We have tried several styles of heaving, hurling, and flinging today. Now as we end the class, we are going to set up two stations for each action along the line. I want you to look at your score sheets and choose one of the actions you liked best or in which you had your best score. Go to that station and practice that event several more times, and see if you can get an even better score. Mark and record your performances. Ready, go. . . . Stop. Let's collect all the balls, hoops, javelins, and markers and put them in their proper box. Then sit down in front of me. Go.

"Today we began work on an Olympics unit. We started with throwing actions called heaving, hurling, and flinging. What Olympic events do we know that use these actions? Catherine? Yes, javelin. Steve? (Shot put.) Lauren? (Hammer throw.) Benjamin? (Caber.) Well, that is an interesting point. I mentioned that the Scottish toss the caber, but that is a sport unique to their country. In order to be an Olympic event, a sport must be sanctioned by the Olympic governing body and practiced in many countries. Each time the Olympics are held, the host country gets to choose three activities or sports as exhibition events. Then all the countries get to vote on whether to include these events in competition. That is how events are added to the Olympic Games. As we continue our Olympic unit, we will continue to practice the throwing events. We will also add running and jumping events and several sports. At the same time you will be learning about the Olympics, the Greek culture, the contributions of the Greeks throughout the ages, and other countries in all of your classes. We will finish our unit with our very own Olympics at our school. Remember, you are all *athlons*, or contestants. Do your best. Be true to the Olympic motto: *Citius, altius, fortius* (swifter, higher, stronger).

ASSESSMENT SUGGESTIONS

- Develop a mechanics checklist for each type of throw. Have students evaluate each other.
- Have students measure their throws and work toward improving throwing distance.

LOOK FOR

- Place an emphasis on the use of good technique by having the children model your demonstrations and use the learning cues that stress process characteristics. Some children (particularly the stronger ones) will be able to use their strength to achieve the best product results (distance) while using poor form. This will only hurt them over time. For example, when heaving using the shot-put style, some children will take the ball away from their chin and just throw it overhand. While they may get a good distance score, they are not developing good technique. Over time they will hurt their arms, and when they heave real weights, distance scores will also suffer.
- Encourage all children to challenge themselves. Each child should try to improve his or her own score. That is what it means to be a competitor, an *athlon*.

HOW CAN I CHANGE THIS?

- Include the use of a real (eight-pound) shot put, discus, javelin, hammer, or even a heavy medicine ball.
- Focus other classes in this Olympic unit on jumping events, for example, the high jump, standing long jump, running long jump, triple jump.
- Focus other classes in this Olympic unit on running events, for example, the 50-meter sprint, 100-meter sprint, 200-meter sprint, 4 × 100-meter sprint, 800-meter run.
- Develop some novelty events, such as a gladiator run in armor (cardboard), chariot race around the track on bicycles, and three-legged run with a partner.
- Investigate games from other countries. Learn them, and include them as contests in your Olympics.

TEACHABLE MOMENTS

- Emphasize interdisciplinary work throughout this unit. The initial focus may be on the richness of the early Greek culture and its many contributions to art and architecture, government, philosophy, literature, science, and math.
- As classes adopt a country, attention may focus more on modern society. Children can research facts about a given country's flag, anthem, population, economy, government, sports, and so on.
- Develop specific interdisciplinary projects with classroom teachers. For example, record metric scores for throws, jumps, or runs in physical education. Calculate average scores and plot or graph increases in performance over trials or days. In language arts children can select and research a favorite Olympic sport individually or in groups. They should find out the equipment used, training needed, clothing worn, countries that compete in this sport, the current Olympic champion. They could write a report about their findings or develop a cartoon strip to depict their results. Finally, they should do some training in the sport to improve their performance. Suggestions for hundreds of interdisciplinary projects can be found in the references listed (USOC, 1984 and Atlanta Committee, 1994).

Additional Ideas for Developing Learning Experiences

This section offers additional learning experiences to reinforce the social studies concepts identified in table 6.2. Curricular areas, suggested grade level, and a brief description are provided for each activity. These activities are intended to inspire additional ideas for interdisciplinary work between classroom and physical education teachers. Teachers are encouraged to develop these ideas more completely. Sometimes the connected model will be most appropriate, while other times the shared or partnership model may be used. Your main concern should be to meet the developmental levels and needs of your students; you can adapt activities to accommodate your teaching schedule, equipment, and available space.

Family, School, and Community

If You're Happy and You Know It

Social Studies
Showing emotions about being part of a group

Physical Education
Expressive movement with music

Grade Level
K-2
Teach the class the song "If You're Happy and You Know It." Have students focus on really showing emotions as they perform the physical actions called for in the song. Add verses that require large body movements, such as "jump up and down" or "run in place." Help students understand that they should feel happy about coming to school and being part of a family and community.

Wake Up, Let's Get Ready for School

Social Studies
Getting ready for school

Physical Education
Creating and performing movement sequences

Grade Level
K-3
Make a movement sequence that reflects the steps involved in getting ready for school, such as waking up, getting out of bed, brushing teeth, eating breakfast, riding the school bus, greeting friends.

Let's Be Happy at School

Social Studies
Showing emotions about school

Physical Education
Creating and performing movement sequences

Grade Level
K-6

Physically act out the happy and sad emotions related to school. Prompt students for situations that make them happy (when you do well on a paper, when you kick a ball high on the playground, when your teacher tells you that you are special, when your friend asks you to sit with her at lunch) and sad (when you miss the bus, when you don't do as well as you had hoped on a test, when your best friend eats lunch with someone else, when you get in trouble for something that you did not do).

Moving Through the School Day—Now and Then

Social Studies
Parts of the school day

Physical Education
Creating and performing movement sequences

Grade Level
K-3

Make a movement sequence representing the parts of the school day, such as arriving at school, going to class, doing class work, going to a particular class, having lunch in the cafeteria, going out for recess, checking books out of the media center, and getting ready to leave school.

   Now, make a movement sequence of the parts of the school day that your great grandparents might have experienced (if possible ask grandparents or great grandparents for information), such as arriving at school after a long walk or a horse-and-buggy ride, going to class with students of all ages, eating a lunch brought from home, getting firewood or coal to help keep the schoolroom warm, going out for recess, getting ready to leave school, and walking home.

Meet My Family

Social Studies
Family

Physical Education
Creating and performing movement sequences

Grade Level
K-3

Make a movement sequence that portrays the members of your (nuclear) family. Start with the youngest members and move through the oldest. Can a partner tell how many people are in your family? Now make a movement sequence that shows favorite activities of each of your family members, for example, your mother might like to jog, your father might enjoy working in the yard, your sister might spend lots of time reading. In a group of three people, try to figure the family member and activity for each movement sequence.

Watch Me Change

Social Studies
People grow and change

Physical Education
Creating and performing movement sequences

Grade Level
K-6
All the people that we know are growing and changing. Make a movement sequence that represents the changes that you have made since you were born until today. You can think about drinking from a bottle, learning to sit up, learning to roll over, learning to stand, learning to walk, learning to drink from a cup, learning to throw and kick a ball, learning to ride a tricycle or bicycle.

Citizenship

Working With My Friends

Social Studies
Working with friends

Physical Education
Creating and performing movement sequences

Grade Level
K-3
Physically show ways that you can work well and poorly with friends, such as sharing or not sharing equipment, helping or not helping when your friend has many things to carry, taking or not taking turns.

Let's Play by the Rules

Social Studies
Importance of rules

Physical Education
Game play

Grade Level

K-3

Participate in a game. Talk about the rules in the game and how we have rules at school, at home, and in our communities. Discuss the need for rules in these settings.

I Am Important in My Community

Social Studies

Caring for your community

Physical Education

Creating and performing movement sequences

Grade Level

K-3

You want to help take care of your community. Show through movement things that you can do to help take care of your community, such as throwing paper in the garbage can, turning the lights out when you leave the room, planting flowers at the city park. Show your partner five different actions, and have your partner show his or her five actions. Select the five best of your and your partner's actions. Make a movement sequence to show the five actions. Now use the same procedure to show ways that you can be unhelpful in taking care of your community.

I Get by With a Little Help From My Friends

Social Studies

Helping others

Physical Education

Creating and performing movement sequences

Grade Level

K-3

In families, schools, and communities we need to help others. With a partner, make a movement sequence that represents ways that you can help each other. Next, make a sequence where you are not being helpful to each other. Talk about which way of being makes you feel better.

It All Depends on You and Me

Social Studies

Depending on others

Physical Education

Creating and performing movement sequences

Grade Level
K-6
We depend on others and they depend on us. We especially depend on others for the food that we eat. Make a movement sequence that represents the people on whom we depend for the orange juice that we may have had for breakfast. The sequence could include someone planting the orange tree, watering and pruning the tree, picking the oranges, driving the truck full of oranges to the packing plant, cleaning the fruit, operating the machine that squeezes the oranges for juice, bottling the juice, driving the juice to the store, and unpacking the juice and placing it on shelves.

You Can Depend on Me

Social Studies
Depending on others

Physical Education
Creating and performing movement sequences

Grade Level
K-4
We depend on others for all types of services in our community. Think about a job in your community on which you depend. Physically show what a person in that job does, and ask a partner to guess the work that you are doing. Explain to your partner how you depend on the job that you demonstrated. You and your partner find another pair of partners and show your jobs to each other.

I Like to Obey Rules

Social Studies
Obeying laws

Physical Education
Creating and performing movement sequences

Grade Level
K-2
"We must obey traffic laws because there are certain laws for driving or walking on public roads. I have set up a traffic area, and you must follow the signs." Set up different pathways and traffic signs. Have students move through the course under control.

I'm a Safe Driver

Social Studies
Obeying laws

Physical Education
Creating and performing movement sequences

Grade Level

K-2

We must obey traffic lights to travel safely. Line up across the starting line. You will move or stop movement according to the color that I hold up. When you see green, you may move fast, but under control. When you see yellow, you should move slowly and cautiously. When I hold up red, you must stop. Always move safely. No one wants to get a ticket or be in a wreck.

Transportation

The Wheels on the Bus Go Round and Round

Social Studies

Transportation to school

Physical Education

Expressive movement to music

Grade Level

K-2

We will learn the song "The Wheels on the Bus Go Round and Round" and use whole-body movements to act out the song. For example, when you sing, "The wheels on the bus go round and round," make big circles with your arms or feet or do rolls. Now we'll talk about riding a bus and other forms of transportation to and from school. [The teacher can also emphasize the need for safety in transportation.]

Let's Travel to School

Social Studies

Transportation to school

Physical Education

Creating and performing movement sequences

Grade Level

K-3

Show through movement ways that you are transported to school. Think about the type of transportation that you chose. What is the speed of your type of transportation? What is the size of your mode of transportation? Does size effect speed? Could you transport yourself to school? Show a partner three ways that you might transport your-self to school. (Students might show skateboarding; walking; riding a bicycle, unicycle, or tricycle; roller skates or in-line skates; hopping on a pogo stick.)

Transportation in My Community

Social Studies

Transportation in the community

Physical Education
Expressive movement

Grade Level
K-2
Show through movement four different types of trucks in your community. You might show a garbage truck, a moving van, an ice cream truck, a cement mixer, or a mail truck. Be sure that your movement actually matches the movement of the truck. Does the truck move fast or slow? Does it start and stop frequently? Is the truck large or small? Now show through movement four different types of movement of trucks from outside your community (urban, rural, suburban). Do the trucks primarily seen outside your community move differently from the ones in your community?

Jobs

So Many Jobs at School

Social Studies
Jobs at school

Physical Education
Creating and performing movement sequences

Grade Level
K-3
Make a movement sequence that represents the different jobs at school, such as the cooks in the cafeteria, the janitor, the bus driver, the nurse, the teacher, the principal. Link at least three different job actions that the person you have chosen might do. See whether a partner can guess your job.

So Many Jobs at Home

Social Studies
Jobs at home

Physical Education
Creating and performing movement sequences

Grade Level
K-3
Show through movement some of the jobs that are done at home, such as washing dishes, mowing the lawn, cleaning windows, cooking, writing checks to pay bills. Show a partner your job and see whether he or she can guess the job. Now link two movements that represent different jobs at home. Now link three movements. Can your partner guess all three of your jobs? Did you and your partner show any of the same jobs?

So Many Jobs in Our Community

Social Studies
Jobs in the community

Physical Education
Creating and performing movement sequences

Grade Level
K-4
There are many different jobs in our communities. Pick the job you like best, and make a movement sequence of tasks that you might perform at your job. Include three different actions that would be performed in your job. Can members of your class guess your job?

Working on the Night Shift

Social Studies
Jobs in the community

Physical Education
Expressive movement

Grade Level
K-3
Some jobs in our communities are performed at night. Physically show three examples of jobs that might be performed at night, for example, printing a newspaper, being a nurse in a hospital, or driving a mail truck. In a group of three, show your jobs and have the others in your group guess what the jobs are. Have your group choose the three most interesting jobs and show them to the class.

Working From Country to City

Social Studies
Jobs in city and country

Physical Education
Creating and performing movement sequences

Grade Level
K-4
People in the city can have different jobs than people who live in the country. Work with a partner. One of you show through movement three different city jobs and the other show three country jobs. Now switch roles, and come up with three different jobs.

History

Hello, I Am From Ireland

Social Studies
The immigrant experience

Physical Education
Creating and performing movement sequences

Grade Level
K-4
An immigrant is a person who moves permanently from one country to another. With a partner, make a movement sequence that represents the experience of an immigrant coming to the United States. The immigrant is your age and is coming from Ireland in the year 1900. Be sure to research the immigrant experience from leaving their homeland to settling in the United States.

Please Meet Harriet Tubman

Social Studies
The immigrant experience, Harriet Tubman

Physical Education
Creating and performing movement sequences

Grade Level
K-6
Harriet Tubman in the late 1800s was a conductor on the Underground Railroad. She helped more than 300 slaves to freedom from slavery in the South. In groups of three, make a movement sequence that represents Harriet Tubman helping two slaves to make their escape. Remember that most of their travel was done at night.

Take a Walk on the Moon

Social Studies
Looking to the future

Physical Education
Creating and performing movement sequences

Grade Level
K- 6
On July 20, 1969, Neil Armstrong became the first person to take a step on the moon. He said of his step, "That's one small step for man, one giant leap for mankind." Develop a movement sequence showing what you think that it would have been like to take that first step off the spacecraft and onto the moon's surface. Follow that by taking more steps on the moon. Next, pretend that you are exploring a new planet for the first

time. Develop a movement sequence for a new planet that has a very soft, spongy surface.

The New Deal

Social Studies
U.S. history

Physical Education
Creating and performing movement sequences

Grade Level
4-6
In 1932 Franklin D. Roosevelt was elected president of the United States. This was during the time of the Great Depression, when many people were out of work. He established the New Deal, through which millions of jobs were created for unemployed workers. Many of these workers planted trees and built dams and roads. Develop a movement sequence that shows how an unemployed worker might feel about being offered a good job. Begin your sequence with being poor and out of work; show the worker hearing about the potential job, being offered the job, and then beginning his or her new job.

Carrying the Olympic Flames

Social Studies
History of the Olympics

Physical Education
Creating and performing movement sequences

Grade Level
2-4
Many of you have seen the Olympic flames at the Olympic Games. Some of you might have seen the torch bearer running up to light the Olympic flames. Usually many people are involved in transporting the flame across the country to the Olympic site. In groups of three, design a movement sequence that represents running with the torch, arriving at the Olympic site, and lighting the Olympic flames.

I Move Like an Olympian

Social Studies
History of the Olympics

Physical Education
Creating and performing a movement sequence

Grade Level
3-6
Athletes can participate in many different activities at the Olympic Games. Choose your favorite activity and develop a movement sequence that represents this activity. Your sequence should have an interesting beginning, a middle part that includes several actions, and an interesting ending. Show your sequence to a partner and see if he or she can determine your activity. Next, teach your sequence to your partner and also learn your partner's routine.

Mapping and Globe Skills

Maps of Pathways

Social Studies
Mapping skills

Physical Education
Traveling over pathways

Grade Level
3-6
You are going to draw a map. I will give you and a friend three traffic cones and two short ropes. You can make a pathway with your equipment. Now walk beside your pathway, and then draw your pathway on the paper that I will give you. Be sure to include all three cones and the two short ropes in your map.

Moving in Different Directions

Social Studies
Mapping skills

Physical Education
Traveling in different directions

Grade Level
1-6
Students should learn movement concepts such as right, left, far, near, up, and down. The teacher can design movement activities to help teach and reinforce these concepts, for example, "slide to the left, now to the right, and back to the left" or "stand near a partner, now use a locomotor movement to move far from your partner."

Butterfly Time Line

Social Studies
Using a time line

Physical Education
Creating and performing a movement sequence

Grade Level

3-6

Time lines show the order that things happened. Draw a time line of a butterfly's life from egg, larva, chrysalis (cocoon), through the butterfly stage. Now design a movement sequence that reflects your butterfly time line.

Kicking Line Graph

Social Studies

Constructing a line graph

Physical Education

Creating and performing a movement sequence

Grade Level

3-6

Working in groups of four, record the number of times out of 10 tries that each person in your group is able to kick a ball to a large target on the wall. Everyone can kick at the same time and record his or her own scores. Construct a line graph that represents your scores. You can place students' names at the bottom of the graph and the numbers ranging from 0 to 10 on the left side of the graph.

Exercise Time Line

Social Studies

Using a time line

Physical Education

Cognitive focus

Grade Level

3-6

Make a time line of the months of the year. Mark the months when you are able to exercise comfortably outside in shorts. Mark the months when you exercise inside. Mark the months when you have physical education at school. Mark the months when you participate in some kind of sporting activity, dance lessons, or gymnastics lessons.

Moving in Cardinal and Intermediate Directions

Social Studies

Moving in cardinal and intermediate directions

Physical Education

Performing motor skills

Grade Level

4-6

"In order to use maps effectively, you must be able to determine direction. The cardinal directions are north, south, east, and west. The intermediate directions lie halfway between the cardinal directions. They are northeast, southeast, southwest, and northwest. Follow my directions as I have you move in certain ways in different directions." It is important to use good start and stop signals here. The teacher should begin with the cardinal directions. Once students are all oriented in the same direction, they can, for example, skip south; run north; leap east; bear-walk west. The intermediate directions can be added when students are ready.

Scaling the USA

Social Studies
Using a map scale

Physical Education
Performing motor skills

Grade Level
3-6
This activity requires that a large map of the United States be painted, drawn, or project by an overhead projector on a floor surface. Perhaps your class could volunteer to paint the map on the blacktop surface at your school. The students, with the help of the teacher, should determine an approximate scale for the map. The scale can then be gauged to individual students' feet (or hands). If working in inches, a child can measure his or her foot, or use his or her shoe size as an approximate number of inches. Have students walk to and from certain destinations with a heel-to-toe gait, count the number of steps, and multiply by the length of their foot. For example, if a child's foot is five inches and each inch equals 100 miles, then in one step the child travels five hundred scale miles.

National Identity and Culture

Ethnic Games

Social Studies
Ethnic groups and games

Physical Education
Participating in games

Grade Level
2-6
Different ethnic groups have special games that they play. Ask your relatives for games that might represent your ethnic group. Show this game to your class and have everyone play.

Play in Different Cultures

Social Studies
Play in different cultures

Physical Education
Play

Grade Level
2-6

Ask your grandparents, older aunts and uncles, or older people in your neighborhood what they did for play when they were your age. Describe and then show these activities to your classmates. Have them participate in the activity.

Do You Get My Message?

Social Studies
Communicating with those from a different culture

Physical Education
Expressive movement

Grade Level
2-6

We sometimes need to communicate with those who speak a different language. Pretend that your partner does not speak your language. Try to communicate a message without using words. You may use only body language to send your message. After your turn, give your partner a chance. (Possible messages: "I want you to play a game with me"; "I am lost from my family"; "I have a dog and a cat at home.")

Activities From Across the World

Social Studies
Activities from other cultures

Physical Education
Performing motor skills

Grade Level
K-6

It is fun to learn about activities from other countries. Arrange for an immigrant or person who is very knowledgeable about a country that you are studying to come to class. Ask the person to demonstrate games, dances, or leisure-time activities to the class. Have students participate in these activities.

I Love the USA

Social Studies
Celebrating living in the United States

Physical Education
Creative dance with music

Grade Level
3-6
Select a patriotic song, such as "My Country 'Tis of Thee," "This Land Is Your Land, This Land Is My Land," or "The Star-Spangled Banner." With a partner, create a dance that represents the song. Present your dance with the music for a small group or to the class.

Sing a New Song, Dance a New Dance

Social Studies
Celebrate other nationalities

Physical Education
Creative dance with music

Grade Level
3-6
Select a patriotic song from a country that you are studying in social studies. Find out the English interpretation, if necessary, and create a dance that represents the song. You and a partner can present your dance with the music for a small group or to the class.

Jumping Rope With Chants

Social Studies
Ethnic groups and exercise

Physical Education
Jumping rope with chants

Grade Level
K-6
People in many cultures jump rope. Double Dutch was first played in the Netherlands. In China, children jump a rubber rope, which you might call a Chinese jump rope. In the United States we often jump a turned rope to jump rope chants. Lets form three different stations: one Double Dutch, one Chinese jump rope and one for self turned jump ropes to chants. Practice at each station. Which station did you like best?

Ethnic Groups and Exercise

Social Studies
Ethnic groups and exercise

Physical Education
Physical fitness

Grade Level
2-6
It is interesting to examine exercise around the world. Choose a culture and discover the types of exercise that are popular there. For example, the Chinese participate in an activity called Tai Chi. Be prepared to demonstrate and have the class participate in your activity.

The Best Birthday Party Ever

Social Studies
Celebrating holidays

Physical Education
Create and perform a movement sequence

Grade Level
K-6
Write a story about the birthday party of your dreams. Now make a movement sequence that goes along with your story.

The Johnny Appleseed Apple Dance

Social Studies
Celebrating holidays

Physical Education
Create and perform a movement sequence

Grade Level
K-6
Johnny Appleseed is often associated with Arbor Day, a day that celebrates planting trees. Johnny Appleseed lived in the late 1700s and early 1800s and traveled around planting apple trees and giving seeds to others for planting. Create an "Apple Dance" that reflects the actions of Johnny Appleseed.

Dances From Around the World

Social Studies
Dances from around the world

Physical Education
Creative dance

Grade Level
K-6
Learn dances from cultures that you are studying. Analyze the dances to determine characteristics of the culture that are represented in the dance.

Geography

Moving Through the Seasons

Social Studies
Activities during different seasons

Physical Education
Creating and performing a movement sequence

Grade Level
K-6
You participate in different activities during each of the four seasons. Show us some of the activities that you do in the spring, summer, fall, and winter. Discuss how the seasons affect what we do.

Let's Travel in February

Social Studies
Climates in the United States

Physical Education
Create and perform a movement sequence

Grade Level
3-6
The temperature of a region or state plays an important role in the climate. You are going to go through an imaginary trip through the United States during February. Take a good look at the big map of the United States. You will travel in a straight line from Florida to Washington State. With a partner, make a movement sequence that represents how the temperature change affects your journey.

Jump for the Temperature

Social Studies
Climate in the United States

Physical Education
Physical fitness

Grade Level
K-6

This task is divided into two sections. First, make a bar graph of the average monthly temperature in your county during last year. Include all 12 months. Second, for each degree Fahrenheit of temperature, you will jump a self-turned rope one time. Begin with January: If the average temperature is 32, then take 32 jumps. Progress through each month. Discuss when you jumped the most and why there was a gradual increase and decrease in temperature through the year. Next, come up with your own physical activity for each month.

Traveling Through Your State

Social Studies
Traveling to different parts of the state

Physical Education
Physical fitness

Grade Level
K-6

You are going to pretend to travel to different cities in your state. Each 10-minute time period that a member of your class exercises represents a mile in your travel across the state. For example, if all 25 members of your class run or walk the fitness trail at your school for 10 minutes, then you have traveled 250 miles toward your destination. Once you arrive at your designated city, study the area and discover more about your own state. [This can be a year-long project.]

Move Around the World

Social Studies
Moving around the United States (or state or world)

Physical Education
Physical fitness

Grade Level
K-6

This activity requires that a large map of the United States be painted, drawn, or project by an overhead projector on a floor surface. Perhaps your class could volunteer to paint the map on the blacktop surface at your school. With the map you can do all sorts of fun activities. You could do an exercise routine that includes activities such as running and standing on states that begin with an *M* and doing 20 curl-ups there, bear-walking to a state that borders on the Atlantic Ocean, skipping to the last five states to join the Union, crab-walking to states that produce wheat, or sliding to states that border on another country.

There are many potential movement activities for using these large maps. The teacher can select the activities or students can help. Students could each write an activity and place them in a box, and then the activities can be drawn at random.

Shape the States

Social Studies
Making the shapes of the states

Physical Education
Expressive movement

Grade Level
3-6
Work with a partner or partners to form the shape of designated states with your bodies. See how closely your bodies can match the shape of the state. Now make your shape on a different level.

Summary

Many ideas for integrating movement and social studies are presented in this chapter. You can use these ideas in integrated lessons, and you may want to expand on the ideas according to your own goals for the lesson. You should be especially conscious of requiring quality movement from students. Students need to understand that the purpose of their movement generally is to communicate a concept. A challenge in each lesson should be to perfect movement as much as possible.

Active Learning Involving Music, Theater Arts, and Visual Arts

The arts—music, theater arts, and visual arts—are embedded in our daily life (figure 7.1). They provide means of expression that go beyond ordinary speaking and writing. They can express intimate thoughts and feelings. They are a unique record of diverse cultures and how these cultures have developed over time. The arts provide distinctive ways of understanding human beings and nature. The arts are creative modes by which all people can enrich their lives by both self-expression and response to the expressions of others (College Board, 1983). Dance is also considered one of the arts and is a content area within physical education. It is included as an essential part of the physical education discipline in this book.

Most students have some exposure to the arts during their formal education. These experiences are as varied as the content presented. Some may simply observe art as an illustration in a picture book, others may participate in a sequential music program, and still others are involved on a daily basis through arts magnet schools. Learning through and in the arts engages the imagination, fosters flexible ways of thinking, develops disciplined effort, and builds self-confidence. Art experiences will permanently enhance the quality of a student's life, whether he or she continues artistic activity as an avocation or a career or maintains an appreciation of the arts as an observer or audience member.

The arts are characterized by three artistic processes: creating, performing or interpreting, and responding to one's own art or the art of others. The arts provide important lessons in communication and offer a means for students to record and express their feelings, ideas, and observations about life. Through the arts, students gain a greater self-awareness and a deeper understanding of the world in which they live.

This chapter addresses the integration of music, theater arts, and visual arts with physical education. The content for the music, theater arts, and visual arts disciplines, included in the scope and sequence section of this chapter, is defined by the *National Standards for Arts Education* (Consortium of National Arts Education Associations, 1994). Additional information gathered from various state standards documents, curriculum guides, and program activities is included in this chapter. You may find a slightly different approach or version in your state or school district, one that has undoubtedly been designed to address your local perspectives and needs.

According to Elliot Eisner (1980), the development of literacy and the use of one symbol system bears on the development and use of literacy in other symbol systems. Eisner's words are particularly applicable to the integration of the arts and physical education. Children discover new ways to learn, communicate, interact, create, understand, and perform when they experience the concepts and skills learned in music, theater arts, and visual arts programs through movement.

Music is a basic expression of human culture and is perhaps the discipline most integrated with physical education. It comprises singing, performing on instruments, composing and arranging music, reading and notation, and listening and evaluating. Music naturally accompanies dancing and is frequently used to provide a rhythm for jump-rope routines, warm-up exercises, or simply bouncing a ball.

The theater arts enable students to learn about themselves and others, about actions and consequences, and about customs and beliefs. It is a complex discipline that encompasses many different areas, including acting, directing, playwriting, and set designing. Some of these areas, such as acting and directing, can be easily integrated with physical education, while playwriting and set designing can be re-

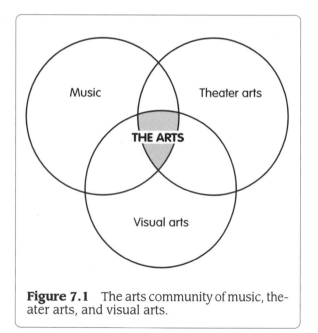

Figure 7.1   The arts community of music, theater arts, and visual arts.

lated indirectly. Sport themes can be used as the inspiration for an improvised or scripted scene, or movement can be used to convey a message, as actors do with their bodies.

Education in the visual arts includes a wide range of media, techniques, and processes. Personal experiences are translated into visual form, from which the child can discover clues about himself or herself. The child can be actively involved in drawing, painting, sculpture, design, architecture, film, video, and folk arts. When developing learning experiences that integrate the visual arts and physical education, you can focus on the elements of art and principles of design, the different types of media, and the historical and cultural context. You can discuss how changes in design elements have affected the development of sports equipment (e.g., color of balls, shapes of sticks, clothing fashion), a fitness bulletin board can be filled with students' drawings and paintings, or you can create a dance about how a sculpture might move in space.

Scope and Sequence for Music

"Music is one of the great pleasures of life. It has the power to command our attention and inspire us. It speaks to our spirit and to our inner feelings. It provokes thoughts about the mysteries of life, such as why we exist, the vastness of the universe, and our purpose on earth. Music reaches deep into our nature to console us, to reassure us, and to help us express who and what we are as human beings" (Fowler, 1994, p. 5).

The matrix in table 7.1 indicates the grades in which specific music skills and concepts are presented. Skills and concepts introduced during the primary grades are continued during the intermediate grades at higher levels and with more complexity.

Primary-Grade Music Skills and Concepts

Students in the primary grades are learning to enjoy and explore a variety of music. Their early hands-on experiences allow them to gain musical skills and knowledge while singing, playing instruments, creating music, and moving to music. Learning to read and notate music are introduced, along with opportunities to explore music independently and with others. As students listen to a variety of music from various cultures and different time periods, they begin to identify common musical elements and characteristics and the role that music plays in their lives. They understand how to use music as a means of individual expression and are developing the ability to listen to

Table 7.1

SCOPE AND SEQUENCE OF MUSIC CONCEPTS TAUGHT IN ELEMENTARY SCHOOLS							
Concept	**Grade**						
Music	K	1	2	3	4	5	6
Singing independently and with others	x	x	x	x	x	x	x
Performing on instruments	x	x	x	x	x	x	x
Improvising melodies, variations, and accompaniment	x	x	x	x	x	x	x
Composing and arranging music	x	x	x	x	x	x	x
Reading and notating music	x	x	x	x	x	x	x
Listening to, analyzing, and describing music	x	x	x	x	x	x	x
Evaluating music and musical performances	x	x	x	x	x	x	x
Making connections between music, the other arts, and other curricular areas	x	x	x	x	x	x	x
Understanding music in relation to history and culture	x	x	x	x	x	x	x

the creations of other people with respect, curiosity, and pleasure.

Intermediate-Grade Music Skills and Concepts

Students at the intermediate level build on the skills they developed in the primary grades. They can generally sing a melodic line with accurate use of pitch and rhythm using some expressive quality. Instruction in playing instruments becomes more complex with the study of keyboard, band, and orchestral instruments. The students can compose and improvise simple melodies and rhythms that demonstrate their understanding of the structure of music. Through their own performances, they attempt to communicate ideas and feelings and to recognize ideas and feelings in the performances of others. They enjoy listening to a wider variety of music and can discuss their personal response to it.

Scope and Sequence for Theater Arts

"Theatre is . . . a study of life. It is the study of things that motivate people to do the things they do and live as they do" (Baker and Wagner, 1977, p. 24).

The matrix in table 7.2 indicates the grades in which specific theater arts skills and concepts are presented. Skills and concepts introduced during the primary grades are continued during the intermediate grades at higher levels and with more complexity.

Primary-Grade Theater Arts Skills and Concepts

Young children eagerly engage in theater arts activities through acting out favorite stories, creating original situations from life experiences, and imagining themselves in fantasy worlds. Frequently, they create events and costumes, assign roles, and develop dialogue individually or with one or two other children. As a socializing activity and a means of learning, the children explore the skills and knowledge related to acting, writing, designing, and researching and begin to develop an aesthetic awareness necessary for analyzing and critiquing.

Intermediate-Grade Theater Arts Skills and Concepts

At the intermediate level, students begin to develop scripts and scenarios that describe characters and environments and improvise dialogue to tell a story. They use movement and

Table 7.2

SCOPE AND SEQUENCE OF THEATER ARTS CONCEPTS TAUGHT IN ELEMENTARY SCHOOLS							
Concept	Grade						
	K	1	2	3	4	5	6
Theater arts							
Making and writing plays	x	x	x	x	x	x	x
Acting in formal or informal presentations	x	x	x	x	x	x	x
Designing and arranging environments for informal and formal presentations	x	x	x	x	x	x	x
Directing by planning improvised and scripted scenes	x	x	x	x	x	x	x
Researching information to support improvised and scripted scenes	x	x	x	x	x	x	x
Comparing and integrating art forms	x	x	x	x	x	x	x
Analyzing and explaining personal preferences and constructing meanings from dramatizations and theater, film, television, and electronic media productions	x	x	x	x	x	x	x
Relating theater arts to cultures, times, and places	x	x	x	x	x	x	x

vocal expression to define characters and design scenery, props, costumes, lighting, and sound to communicate the locale and mood. The intermediate-grade student is able to identify and use the elements that make a dramatic work successful and to provide rationale for their personal choices in their creative and performing work. Collaborative initiatives develop during this period. These efforts bring all the elements of theater together to produce an improvised or scripted presentation on a stage or for a film, television, or other electronic media. When students create a dramatic work, they are able to use perspectives from various cultures, time periods, and places to project their own understanding of life.

Scope and Sequence for Visual Arts

"The visual arts interpret and reflect life. Through studying art, children gain valuable insights about the world along with knowledge and skills they can use throughout their lives" (National Art Education Association, 1991, p. 1).

The matrix in table 7.3 indicates the grades in which specific visual arts skills and concepts are presented. Skills and concepts introduced during the primary grades are continued during the intermediate grades at higher levels and with more complexity.

Primary-Grade Visual Arts Skills and Concepts

In the primary grades, children enjoy experimenting with many different art materials. The school environment may be the first place where children receive visual arts instruction and learn to make choices that enhance communication of their ideas. Creating is the key to this instruction. Skills of observation, eye-hand coordination, and manipulation of various tools are developing. Children begin to understand the purpose of visual arts in their lives and the role the visual arts play in different cultures.

Intermediate-Grade Visual Arts Skills and Concepts

Students in the intermediate grades continue to explore various art media, techniques, and processes. Visual expressions become more individualistic and imaginative. The students continue to formulate their own understandings and criteria for making critical judgments related to structure and function, content, techniques, and purpose. Through increased exposure to art works from a variety of historical periods and cultures, students gain a deeper awareness of their own values and the values of other people. They begin to understand that art is influenced not only by aesthetic ideas but also by many societal customs and beliefs.

Table 7.3

SCOPE AND SEQUENCE OF VISUAL ARTS CONCEPTS TAUGHT IN ELEMENTARY SCHOOLS							
Concept	**Grade**						
Visual arts	K	1	2	3	4	5	6
Understanding and applying media techniques and processes	x	x	x	x	x	x	x
Using knowledge of structures and functions	x	x	x	x	x	x	x
Choosing and evaluating a range of subject matter, symbols, and ideas	x	x	x	x	x	x	x
Understanding the visual arts in relation to history and cultures	x	x	x	x	x	x	x
Reflecting on and analyzing the characteristics and merits of their work and the work of others	x	x	x	x	x	x	x
Making connections between visual arts and other disciplines	x	x	x	x	x	x	x

Learning Experiences

Each of the four learning experiences (see table 7.4) demonstrates one of the interdisciplinary teaching models presented in chapter 1. The learning experiences have been designed to include skills and concepts from physical education and music, theater arts, and visual arts.

Each learning experience includes a name, suggested grade level, interdisciplinary teaching model, objectives, equipment, organization, complete description of the lesson, and assessment suggestions. In addition, tips on what to look for in student responses, how teachers can change or modify the lesson, and ideas for teachable moments are offered to provide further insights into each learning experience.

Table 7.4

MUSIC, THEATER ARTS, AND VISUAL ARTS LEARNING EXPERIENCE INDEX			
Name	**Skills and concepts**	**Suggested grade level**	**Interdisciplinary teaching model**
The Circus Performers	Theater arts: Acting as circus animals and performers	K-1	Partnership
	Physical education: Traveling movements and balances		
Patterns in Action	Visual arts: Repetition in patterns	3-6	Shared
	Physical education: Tossing, catching, and bouncing to self		
Tempo Dance	Music: Tempo and rhythm	2-4	Connected
	Physical education: Shapes—straight, twisted, and round		
Lines of Expression	Music: Choosing or creating music to express a mood or feeling	4-6	Shared
	Theater arts: Creating a character that will travel on a pathway		
	Visual arts: Drawing different types of lines to express an idea		
	Physical education: Creating a dance emphasizing pathways		

The Circus Performers

SUGGESTED GRADE LEVEL

Primary (K-1)

INTERDISCIPLINARY TEACHING MODEL

Partnership

The students, while studying the circus, create their own circus as part of the unit of study. The theater arts and physical education teachers research and collect information on the circus and plan a series of learning experiences. They will both teach in the classroom and the gymnasium.

Theater Arts
Acting as circus animals and performers

Physical Education
Traveling movements and balances

OBJECTIVES

As a result of participating in this lesson, the students will

- travel using different directions (forward, backward, sideways);
- practice using forward, backward, and sideways rolls;
- practice balances using different body parts;
- be exposed to basic acting skills; and
- present an improvisational scene based on the actions and characteristics of a circus animal or performer.

EQUIPMENT

Mats, hoops, tape lines, individual jump ropes, and circus music

ORGANIZATION

Small groups of three, four, or five students

DESCRIPTION

THIS learning experience represents one class in a series of sessions in which the physical education and classroom teachers have integrated their curricula around the theme of the circus. In preparation for this class, previous classroom activities have focused on the characters, history, events, and activities that constitute a circus. The physical education gymnastics curriculum has prepared the students for this event, and the gymnastic skills will be used to facilitate the movements of the circus performers and animals. The teachers will use creative dramatics as a means for the children to express their knowledge and understanding of a circus and its components.

"During the next few classes, we will create our own circus. Some of you will be the circus performers, some will be the tightrope walkers, others the trapeze artists, and still other the juggling clowns. You will also have the chance to perform as a lion or a horse doing tricks in the circus. Let's begin to warm up our bodies so that we can move in many different ways."

THE PHYSICAL education teacher leads the children in a warm-up that prepares the children for balancing, rolling, and traveling movements.

"Now that we are warmed up, let's start creating movements for the lions and horses."

ONE of the teachers leads the children in a discussion about the characteristics of the lions and horses and records the responses on the chalkboard (figure 7.2).

"Your ideas about lions and horses were great. Let's practice some of the movements you described. First, let's show how the lions travel on their hands and feet. Can someone show us how a lion would walk? How will the lion hold its head? Show me how you take big, strong steps. How can you change your hands into the shape of a lion's paws? How will your arms and legs move when you roar like a lion? When I raise my hand, everyone practice your loud roar and lion movements, and when I lower my hand, you should stop."

THE TEACHER asks several children to demonstrate their roar and movements using their voice and body. The class observes and discusses how the students use their voice and body to make the roar and movements of a lion.

"This time when you perform your lion roar and movements, decide what kind of lion you will be. Are you a small, shy lion? a big, ferocious lion? a scared lion? or maybe you are a silly lion? Show me how your lion will move."

Figure 7.2 Brainstorming about lions and horses.

THE CHILDREN practice their lion roar and movements, and the teacher asks each one to demonstrate.

"Now it's time to practice jumping through the hoop and rolling on the mat. I will hold the hoop as you jump through using your hands and feet. Then you may choose to roll forward, backward, or sideways on the mat. Now let's put all our lion actions together into a short scene. First, all the different kinds of lions walk out of their cages and sit in a big circle. I will play the lion tamer, and when I raise my hand, you will stretch up and use your hands as paws when you roar. Then when I point to you, you will jump through the hoop, roll over, and return to your cage."

 **SEVERAL** children can play the part of the lion tamer—each assuming this role with their own small group of lions.

"Now let's create the movements for the horses using the words on the board. We are going to gallop to demonstrate the prancing rhythm of the horses. You will hold your hands up to act as the front legs of the horse. How can you position your hands to show the shape of the hooves? Amy, would you please show us your creation. Wonderful, now let's practice galloping in a big circle, thinking about how the horses love to perform and show off for an audience."

 **CHILDREN** practice galloping in a big circle.

"The horses stop and slowly turn in place to show their favorite trick of balancing on their rear hooves and turning around. They end the trick by pawing the ground with their rear hooves and bowing to the audience. They are very proud of this trick. Now try standing on your toes and the balls of your feet with your front arms and hands reaching to the ceiling, and slowly turn in place. How can you move your feet to show the horses pawing the ground? Juan, can we see your idea. Excellent, now let me hear from all of you. What type of sound you will make as you do a bow? You are doing a good job of balancing as you make a small turn. Now continue to gallop around in the circle."

THE TEACHER describes the sequence of movements for the horses: galloping out into the circle, stopping to turn and balance, pawing the ground, taking a bow, and galloping off to the stables. Children practice the traveling and balancing movements as the teacher relates the sequence.

"Next, we are going to create movements for the juggling clowns, the trapeze artists, and the tightrope walkers. First, let's create the clowns."

 **THE CHILDREN** have previously written descriptions and drawn pictures of the type of clown they would like to be. They take a moment to read their description and view their drawing. Now they will use this information to bring their clown to life. The teacher leads the students through an imaginary scene in which the children put on their clown costume and makeup. The children practice smiling and laughing in different ways that represent the type of clown they have become.

"Wow! The clowns look great, very funny. I am sure the audience will have a wonderful time watching these clowns juggle. Now let's invent many different ways to pretend we are juggling. First think about what you will be juggling—balls, scarves, rings. What else can you juggle? How many objects will you have? What size and color are they? Do you juggle high, low, in front of your body, in back of your body, standing on one foot, using one hand? Do you drop any of the objects? When I turn on the circus music, you can create your own way to juggle. Ready, go."

STUDENTS practice different juggling movements; some pretend to drop an object, some juggle with other clowns, others fall down while juggling, and others create different ways to juggle.

"For this part of the circus performance, the clowns will skip out into the circus ring and begin their juggling acts, then they will take a bow together, fall down, and roll over sideways. Then they get up, brush themselves off, take a second bow, and fall and roll over again. Finally, they stand up, bow together, and do not fall down. They skip out of the space waving to the audience. Let's practice this scene."

 **THE CHILDREN** practice the scene together and then participate in a discussion about the different ways they juggled.

"The next two circus acts will take us high above the circus ring. First, we will move as a tightrope walker, and then we'll pretend to be the high-flying trapeze artist swinging across the space. Let's look at these pictures of people walking on the tightrope."

 **THE TEACHER** presents three pictures: one from a picture book about a circus, a second from a printed program distributed at a circus, and a painting of a tightrope walker that one of the students brought to school. The children discuss what the performers are wearing, what type of people they might be, where they live, how they became interested in tightrope walking, and what happened to them if they have ever fallen. They create a background for the character.

"You are going to become tightrope walkers and pretend you are many, many feet up in the air walking on a rope. Now, each person should find a tape line to stand on, with space in front of you to walk forward. Slowly begin to walk forward, stepping only on your line. Try walking backward, sideways, turning, balancing on one foot, or in a squat or a straddle position. Now create a tightrope routine that uses walking, turning, and two balances. Practice your routine, staying on the line the entire time."

 **BOTH** teachers visit each of the children, observe their practice, and make suggestions to help the students improve their performance.

"The last performer is the amazing, high-flying trapeze artist. We can't really fly across the space; however, we can create the feeling of flying across the space using rocking, running, and leaping. Now, let's look at a video of a trapeze circus act."

THE TEACHER shows a video of a trapeze act and leads a discussion with the children about the cooperation and trust needed between the performers to ensure their success. The discussion continues about how cooperation and trust help people attain success in everyday life.

"Now you will practice rocking, running, and leaping, first by yourselves and then with a partner. Find a space so you have some room in front of you to complete a short run and a leap. To begin rocking, place one foot in front of the other and shift your weight forward and backward. Reach up with your hands as if you are holding on to the trapeze bar. Let's practice rocking forward and backward for eight counts. Ready, one, two, three, four, five, six, seven, eight. At the end of the eighth count, you will take six running steps and leap up into the air. Then take a couple of steps to recover from the leap, stop, turn around, and repeat the rock, run, and leap going back across the space. Let's try it together. Ready, rock, two, three, four, five, six, seven, eight; run, run, run, run, run, run, and leap; recover; and stop. Turn around, and let's try it again. Now I will give each of you a jump rope. Fold the rope in half and hold each end like a trapeze bar. Now try the trapeze movement again holding the rope."

STUDENTS practice the trapeze movement sequence individually, moving smoothly from one movement to another.

"The next part of the trapeze movement will be done with a partner. After I give you a partner, stand side by side with him or her. Practice performing the trapeze movements so that you both are moving at exactly the same time. You and your partner should rock forward and backward at the same time, run at the same time, leap into the air at the same time, and recover and stop together (figure 7.3)."

STUDENTS practice together to match their movements as closely as possible. The teachers visit each pair and comment on the positive cooperation exhibited by the two students that has enabled them to successfully move together.

"Now that you have tried each of the different circus acts, we are going to put together the entire circus. You will be asked to select a role as either a lion or a horse, and then you will choose to perform as either one of the clowns, one of the tightrope walkers, or one of the trapeze artists."

Figure 7.3 Partners performing trapeze movements simultaneously.

THE TEACHERS organize the students into small groups that represent the selected circus performers. Several students are selected to be the lion tamers, horse trainers, and ringmasters. Over the next several days, in their classroom space, the students finalize the development of the sequence of circus scenes, create a script for the ringmasters, add simple costumes, and create scenery. On returning to the gymnasium, the students are ready to bring their circus to life.

"Today we will practice each part of the circus so that the movements are performed well and everyone is clear about the order of the performance. First, the ringmasters will make their announcements, then each circus act will be performed."

THE STUDENTS acting the part of the ringmasters read their scripted introduction. They welcome everyone to the circus and introduce the first act, the tightrope walkers. Students who have selected to perform in this act do their walk, turn, and balance sequences and take a bow. The ringmasters continue to introduce each of the acts: the lions, the clowns, the horses, and finally the trapeze artists. Each student makes the necessary costume and scenery adjustments for each act. The audience is composed of the classmates in the other acts.

ASSESSMENT SUGGESTION

- The teachers have a checklist of the movement sequences for each act. A record is kept indicating whether the students can perform the complete sequence or only parts of the sequence. In addition, the students can represent through some form of visual arts one of the acts they selected to perform, or they can write about their experience and choices in an entry in a journal.

LOOK FOR

- Whether students are able to perform combinations of movements smoothly.
- Correct use of the body in rolling and traveling movements.
- Students using control moving in and out of balances. Students should not fall out of a balance.
- The different ways students use their body and its parts to express the animals and human performers in the circus.
- The ability to cooperate and move with other children in pairs and small groups.

HOW CAN I CHANGE THIS?

- Use other circus performers, such as elephants, tumblers, bears, or equestrians.
- The teacher acts as the ringmaster, and all the students perform in all the acts.
- Each group of students creates a mini-circus.
- Involve the visual arts teacher to help with scenery, costumes, drawings, paintings, or three-dimensional representations of the circus.
- Ask the music teacher to recommend different types of music or percussion instruments that can accompany each circus act.

TEACHABLE MOMENT

- Students can create their own gymnastic sequence that represents the movements in each of the circus acts. This is a good learning experience to teach making smooth transitions between movements and creating a sequence of movements.

Patterns in Action

SUGGESTED GRADE LEVEL

Intermediate (3-6)

INTERDISCIPLINARY TEACHING MODEL

Shared
The visual arts teacher and the physical education teacher teach about patterns in their own programs at more or less the same time. They meet to discuss how they will teach patterns in their respective disciplines. When teaching, they will be able to refer to the other discipline to help students make the connection.

Visual Arts
Repetition in patterns

Physical Education
Tossing, catching and bouncing to self

OBJECTIVES

As a result of participating in this lesson, the students will

- practice tossing a ball to different heights;
- practice catching a ball from different heights;
- practice bouncing a ball while stationary and while traveling;
- practice coordinating the transition from bouncing to tossing a ball and from catching to bouncing;
- create patterns that can be accurately repeated using tossing, catching, and bouncing to self; and
- understand how the concept of patterns are used in physical education and the visual arts.

EQUIPMENT

One 8 1/2-inch playground ball for each student

ORGANIZATION

Students work individually.

DESCRIPTION

"Good morning! Today we are going to create a pattern as you toss, catch, and bounce a ball to yourself. The art teacher and I have agreed to teach patterns over the next several weeks. This will give you the chance to experience the different ways patterns exist in the world, and it will also give you the opportunity to create your own patterns in art and in physical education. First, let's look around the room and at our clothing for patterns. Tell me about one of the patterns you see."

SEVERAL students describe patterns in their clothing, the patterns of the cement blocks forming the walls, and the patterns of the lights in the ceiling.

"You are going to warm up by repeating the pattern of running for 30 seconds and walking for 15 seconds. I will give you a signal when it's time to change the pattern. Begin with the run. Ready, go."

STUDENTS repeat the run and walk pattern for several minutes.

"Now I would like you to warm up your arms by creating a pattern composed of three different arm movements. Each arm movement is performed three times. Keep repeating your pattern until I signal you to stop."

STUDENTS create an arm pattern and practice the sequence.

"Now I would like for each of you to get a ball and practice tossing and catching the ball to yourself without dropping it. Change the height of the toss each time, sometimes only a foot above your head and sometime as high as you can toss the ball without hitting the ceiling. Practice catching the ball falling from the different heights. What are some of the different ways to toss the ball into the air? How are your hands placed on the ball, and where is the ball when you begin the toss?"

SEVERAL students demonstrate tossing the ball in different ways and describe how they change the force to attain different heights. The other students observe and try the different strategies suggested by the demonstrators.

"You are now going to practice bouncing a ball while stationary and then while traveling. I will call out a series of bouncing tasks for you to practice. Ready, find a space. Begin bouncing with your dominant hand with the ball at waist level. Try the same with your other hand, now alternating hands. How fast can you bounce the ball while alternating hands? Bounce the ball around your body, keeping your feet still. Now lift your right leg and bounce the ball under it, now under the left leg. Can you alternate bouncing under your right leg and then under your left? Can you bounce the ball while changing the height of the ball, sometimes very low to the floor and sometimes at waist height? Travel forward and then backward while bouncing the ball. Now try sliding to the right and then to the left while bouncing. Can you move forward, backward, right, and then left while doing five bounces in each direction? Create your own bouncing idea that alternates using bouncing in a stationary space with bouncing while traveling."

 STUDENTS practice their bouncing idea, and the teacher circulates among the students to observe their progress and offer feedback.

"The next task is to create a pattern that uses tossing, catching, and bouncing to yourself. You can choose your own arrangement; however, you must have control of the ball at all times. Having control means that you do not drop the ball when tossing and catching. You are using control when you are bouncing if the ball does not roll away from you as you bounce it."

 **TEACHER** demonstrates what losing control looks like.

"Combine ways to toss, catch, and bounce the ball that you can do well, and practice a smooth transition between the toss, the catch, and the bounce."

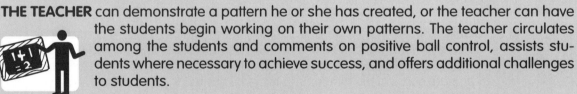 **THE TEACHER** can demonstrate a pattern he or she has created, or the teacher can have the students begin working on their own patterns. The teacher circulates among the students and comments on positive ball control, assists students where necessary to achieve success, and offers additional challenges to students.

"Now I will assign you to a group of three or four, and each person will take a turn to demonstrate his or her pattern to the group. After you perform your pattern, you complete the self-assessment form."

ASSESSMENT SUGGESTION

- The physical education teacher has a checklist to assess the students' ability to accurately perform the pattern without losing control of the ball. For example, a plus sign indicates students who can accurately repeat their pattern twice without losing control of the ball. A check indicates a student who loses control of the ball once in two repetitions of the pattern, and a minus sign marks a student who repeats the pattern twice but loses control of the ball two or more times. Students can practice their pattern and repeat the assessment to demonstrate improvement.

LOOK FOR

- Control when tossing, catching, and bouncing to self.
- A controlled transition between the toss, catch, and bounce.
- Students who need help to organize their ideas into a repeatable pattern. Some children may have many wonderful ideas but need help to select only two or three for the pattern.

HOW CAN I CHANGE THIS?

- Students teach each other their patterns.
- Use a different type of ball.
- Add traveling movements to the pattern, such as walking, skipping, galloping, hopping, or jumping.
- Students work with a partner to create a pattern and perform the same pattern in unison.
- Add music to the performances.

TEACHABLE MOMENT

- Students can draw symbols that represent the different parts of their pattern, such as a star to represent the toss and catch and a circle to represent the bounce. They create a visual pattern on paper that represents the sequence of their pattern (figure 7.4).

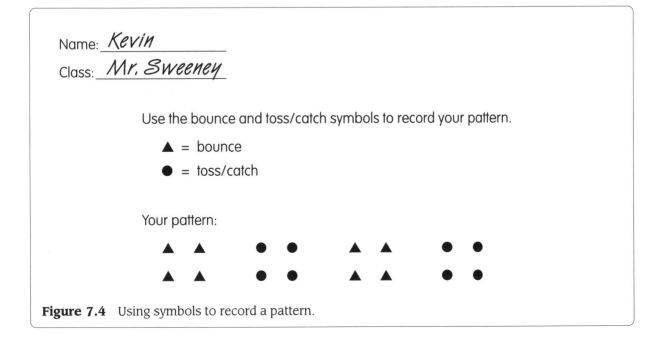

Figure 7.4 Using symbols to record a pattern.

Tempo Dance

SUGGESTED GRADE LEVEL

Primary/Intermediate (2-4)

INTERDISCIPLINARY TEACHING MODEL

Connected
Music is used to accompany dance movements.

Music
Tempo and rhythm

Physical Education
Creating shapes—straight, twisted, and round

OBJECTIVES

As a result of participating in this lesson, the students will

- create straight, twisted, and round shapes with their bodies;
- practice traveling movements in a forward, backward, or sideways direction;
- design a short dance that has a beginning, a middle, and an end;
- coordinate the tempo and rhythm of the dance movements with the tempo and rhythm of the music; and
- change dance movements to reflect different types of music.

EQUIPMENT

Tape or CD player; two pieces of music: one with a fast tempo and a strong rhythm and the second with a slow tempo and a light quality; a handheld drum and mallet

ORGANIZATION

Students work individually.

DESCRIPTION

"In this lesson you will compose a short dance that uses straight, twisted, and round shapes with traveling movements, and then you will perform the dance using two very different pieces of music. You will explore how the same movements can be performed to fast music and then to slow music. Let's begin with a warm-up using slow and fast music."

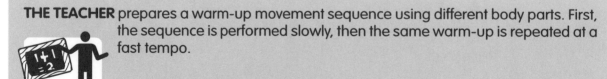

THE TEACHER prepares a warm-up movement sequence using different body parts. First, the sequence is performed slowly, then the same warm-up is repeated at a fast tempo.

"Now that you are ready to move, I want you to create a straight shape with your whole body. Practice making different straight shapes. Find a way to move very slowly from one straight shape to the next. I am going to play a slow, steady beat on the drum as you move from one straight shape to the next. Let's try it. . . . Great job! Now, you'll try making a different straight shape as quickly as you can. I will beat the drum once and you will quickly make a straight shape. Ready, go. Now make another straight shape and another different straight shape each time I beat the drum. . . . Fantastic! Now we'll alternate slowly making a straight shape and quickly making a different straight shape. I will play four slow, soft beats on the drum for the slow shape and one strong, loud beat for the quick, straight shape. . . . Nice straight shapes!"

THE TEACHER plays the alternating sequence several times.

"Now let's try the same idea of making shapes quickly and slowly using round shapes, and then we'll make twisted shapes."

THE TEACHER repeats the same sequence of tasks used for the straight shapes for making the round and then the twisted shapes.

"Next let's explore different ways to travel in the space using a fast and slow tempo. First, the fast tempo. I will play a tape of fast music. I want you to listen to the music and think about three ways you can travel to the music."

THE TEACHER plays the music for 30 seconds and then asks the students to share their suggestions for traveling fast with the class. Students can demonstrate and verbally explain their answer.

"Now each of you will try your first answer. When I play the music, you travel, and when the music stops, I want you to stop and slowly make a straight shape. Ready, travel."

THE TEACHER plays the music, and the students travel quickly around the space and slowly make a straight shape when the music stops. The teacher can ask several students to demonstrate how they changed from the fast traveling movement to making a straight shape slowly. Then the students repeat the sequence twice, using their second and third ideas for traveling fast. The teacher instructs the students to add a round shape after the second way to travel and a twisted shape after the third way to travel.

"The next way to travel in the space is using the slow music. First, listen to the slow music I have selected, and picture in your mind how you can travel slowly."

TEACHER plays the slow music and leaves it on as the next task is presented.

"Now as the music continues, I want you to slowly begin to move your arms and then your whole body. Use one of your traveling ideas to move slowly in the space. Think about what steps you will use. Add a slow turn as you travel. Now change direction, moving forward sometimes, then backward, and maybe sideways."

STUDENTS explore different ways to travel slowly forward, backward, and sideways. The teacher circulates among the students and comments on the different types of steps students are using.

"In the next part of this lesson, you will create a dance using the sequence I have written on the chalkboard." (See figure 7.5.)

"Begin your dance in a straight shape, slowly move out of the shape, and then travel to another place in the space. Stop and quickly make a twisted shape, holding the shape as you count to four, then travel to another place in the space, and end your dance by slowly making a round shape. Now you have five minutes to create the

Figure 7.5 Using straight, twisted, and round shapes in a sequence as you travel.

shapes and the traveling movements and to choose where you will move and make the shapes in the space."

THE STUDENTS begin to create their dances using the sequence outlined by the teacher. No music is played while they are working on the dance.

"Now that you have completed your dance, I will play two different types of music, and I want you to make changes in your movements to coordinate with the tempo and rhythm of the music. Listen to the first piece of music, and picture in your mind how you will perform your dance to the music. The first selection is a slow piece of music."

THE STUDENTS listen to the music.

"I will play the music again, and this time try your dance to the music. Everyone take your places and begin in your straight shape. Ready, begin."

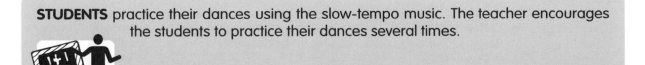

STUDENTS practice their dances using the slow-tempo music. The teacher encourages the students to practice their dances several times.

"The next music selection is fast music with a strong rhythm. Listen and think about how your dance movements will be performed to this type of music."

THE STUDENTS listen to the music and then try their dances several times to the music.

"Would anyone like to share how you changed your dance movements to fit the different tempo and rhythm of the music? Tonya, what a wonderful change, great job! Is there anyone else who would like to share their changes?"

SEVERAL students verbally share their perceptions, and several volunteer to demonstrate their dance using the two types of music. The class comments on the similarities and differences they have observed in the dances.

"The last part of the lesson requires each of you to make a personal choice about which type of music you would prefer to use for your dance. Think about your choice as I play each piece of music once more."

THE TEACHER plays each selection once more. Then students are asked to perform their dance to the music they have selected. The slow music is played first, and the students who selected this music perform their dance. Then the second group performs to the fast music.

ASSESSMENT SUGGESTIONS

- Students can describe in writing the type of music they selected for their final dance and include a statement on why they chose the slow or fast music.
- The students can accompany the writing with a drawing of their body in a straight, twisted, or round shape.

LOOK FOR

- Clarity in making the straight, round, and twisted shapes. Is the whole body involved? How is the student using his or her torso, arms, legs, and head to express the shape?
- A variety of traveling movements, more than walking to the slow music and running to the fast music.
- The ability of the student to accurately repeat the dance using the shapes and traveling movements he or she has selected.
- Active participation in the discussions by many different students.

HOW CAN I CHANGE THIS?

- Use levels to define the shapes, such as a high-level, straight shape; a medium-level, twisted shape; or a low-level, round shape.
- Use music from different cultures that emphasizes changes in tempo and rhythm.
- Have students create their own dance sequence. First they can write the sequence and then practice the dance.
- Students can collaborate in pairs or small groups to create the dance.
- Students can select their own music that reflects two different types of tempo and rhythm.

TEACHABLE MOMENT

- The teacher can show videotapes of professional dancers performing to different types of music. A discussion can follow describing how the movements of the dancers coordinate with the music's tempo and rhythm. Dances from different cultures or different forms of dance can be used, such as tap dance, ballet, hip hop, or dancing while ice skating.

Lines of Expression

SUGGESTED GRADE LEVEL

Intermediate (4-6)

INTERDISCIPLINARY TEACHING MODEL

Shared
The visual arts, music, theater arts, and physical education teachers have agreed to focus on the concept of how lines represent a feeling or a mood. The students complete their study of lines in the visual arts class, compose music in the music class, and write descriptions of characters and scenes during a lesson in the theater arts. These lessons precede the dance lesson on lines taught in the physical education class.

Music
Choosing or creating music to express a mood or feeling

Theater Arts
Creating a character that will travel on a pathway

Visual Arts
Drawing different types of lines to express an idea

Physical Education
Creating a dance emphasizing pathways

OBJECTIVES

As a result of participating in this lesson, the students will

- learn to draw different types of lines using pencil, chalk, and pastels;
- interpret a feeling or a mood based on a line drawing;
- create a character and scene based on a line drawing;
- choose or create music that represents a feeling or a mood;
- use the line drawing to create a floor and an air pathway; and
- create a sequence of movements that is performed using a floor or an air pathway.

EQUIPMENT

Line drawing from the visual arts class, music selected or created in the music class, character and scene descriptions developed during a theater arts lesson, chalkboard or chart paper, chalk or markers, 8 1/2 × 11 paper and crayons, four or five tape recorders

ORGANIZATION

Individuals, partners, or small groups

DESCRIPTION

"Over the next few lessons you will create a dance using the line drawing from your visual arts class, the music you selected or created in your music class, and the descriptions of characters and scenes you wrote during your theater arts session. Before you get started on creating your dances, you will need to warm up your body. You are going to organize into small groups of five or six and stand in a circle. Then each person will perform a warm-up exercise, and the rest of the group will follow. After each person has had a turn as the leader, you may add any other exercises you feel will help your own body warm up."

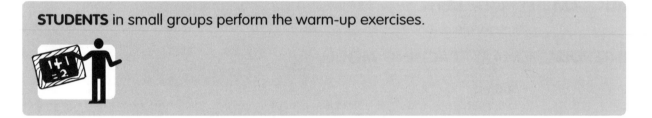

STUDENTS in small groups perform the warm-up exercises.

"Now I will explain how you will create your dance, and then you can choose to work by yourself, with a partner, or in a small group of three or four. The line drawing you worked on in the visual arts class will become a floor and air pathway for your movement. Let's try an example together. Look at this line drawing (figure 7.6)."

"What types of lines do you see?" Carmen responds, "Lots of curvy lines all over the page. "Can someone show the class how you can move your arm in a pathway in the air that would look like one of the curvy lines in the drawing?"

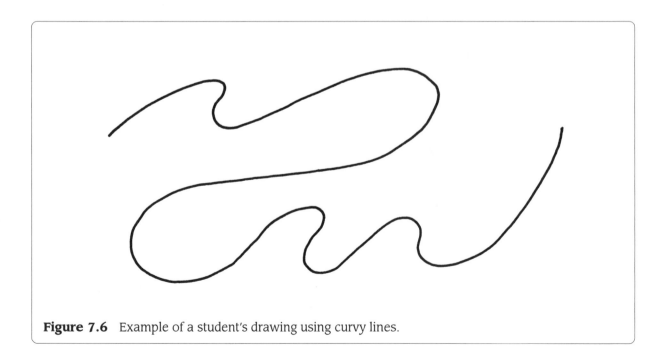

Figure 7.6   Example of a student's drawing using curvy lines.

CARMEN volunteers to demonstrate, then the teacher has all the students move their arms in a curving pathway. The class and teacher discuss possible musical selections.

"Has anyone brought music with them today that could accompany moving on a curvy pathway?" Ryan responds, "We could use slow, smooth, violin music." "Great! Let's use your tape. Now try moving your whole body on a curvy floor pathway and at the same time use your arms to draw the air pathway. Move all around the room, just as the drawing filled the whole page. Describe the small and big curves in the drawing with your feet. Move your feet in different ways: Run, skip, or walk and use different directions—forward, backward, or sideways—as you move on the curvy pathway."

STUDENTS practice and make changes as the teacher suggests.

"Now let's add a character and a scene that would be represented by the movement on a curvy pathway. Did anyone write a character description or can you suggest one now?" Rashad suggests, "Someone is digging in a field, and a strong wind blows by, and the person is blown all over the field." "Thank you, Rashad. Now try your curvy line movements again, and this time begin moving as if you were digging in a field. As the music comes on, begin to move as if you are being blown around by the wind. Travel on a curvy floor pathway changing directions. Your arms are moving in a curvy pathway and have the feeling of being blown around by a strong wind."

THE STUDENTS begin the dance with a digging movement and travel on the curved pathway when the music begins. They return to the digging movements when the music stops. Next, the students can try a second example using a similar series of directions and a drawing of zigzag lines.

"Now I will help you organize to create a dance. You can choose to work as an individual dancer, in partners, or as a small group of three or four."

SOME students are in pairs, several students want to work individually, and the rest of the class is organized into small groups.

"Now that you are organized, let's create your dance. First, select a drawing from your collection that you did in the visual arts class. Then think about the different characters and scenes you wrote in the theater arts session. Remember, they reflected the different types of drawings. You can use the writing ideas or think about a feeling or a mood that the drawing represents. Then create movements that follow the lines in the drawing. Some of the lines can be a floor pathway and others can be an air pathway. Use different traveling movements and directions. Consider the tempo of your movements."

STUDENTS spend a few minutes looking at the drawing, talking with each other about what character or feeling they will use, and begin to try out different movements. The teacher visits each student, pair, or group to offer suggestions or ask questions about how they are using different lines in the drawing.

"Now I want you to add a still beginning and ending shape to your dance. Use a line or part of a line from the drawing in your shape. Perhaps you can use your arms or back to demonstrate the shape of the line. Think about using a different level for the beginning shape and the ending shape. Maybe the beginning shape is standing, and the ending shape is low or on the floor. Your character or feeling may help you determine a good shape for the beginning and ending of your dance."

STUDENTS continue to work on their dances, and the teacher asks to see what movements the students have completed.

"The final addition to your dance is the music. Choose one of the selections from your music class and try performing the dance to the music. You may want to make some changes to fit the dance to the music."

STUDENTS share tape recorders, taking turns using the music as they practice their dance.

"After each person, pair, or group has finished creating their dance and has practiced the movements so that they can remember the dance, we will perform for each other. I will group the class so some people are the audience and others are performing. You will share your dance with a couple of people, not the whole class. Before you perform, show the audience the drawing you have selected, and talk about the characters, scene, or feeling represented in the dance."

THE CLASS is divided into four groups. Each group includes individuals, pairs, and one or more small groups. The students take turns performing for each other.

ASSESSMENT SUGGESTIONS

- Students as audience members or as performers can answer the following questions in writing: What part of the dance was the most interesting? Why? What changes would you make in the dance?
- The teacher can also assess the dance to see whether all the components of the dance were present (figure 7.7).

LOOK FOR

- Students who need help with suggestions to vary their movements.
- Controlled movement in and out of the beginning and ending shapes.
- The different ways students use their body and its parts to draw the lines in the drawing. Do they need help engaging more of the body parts in the dance?
- Accuracy with which students represent the line with their bodies.

HOW CAN I CHANGE THIS?

- Use the same drawing for all students as you did in the examples.
- Students can use percussion instruments instead of recorded music.

Date:_____   Class:_____

Student:_____

	Yes	No
Dance component?	❏	❏
Still beginning shape?	❏	❏
Still ending shape at a different level?	❏	❏
Floor pathway follows some of the lines?	❏	❏
Air pathway follows some of the lines?	❏	❏
Uses change of direction?	❏	❏
Uses two or more different traveling movements?	❏	❏
Can remember the sequence of the dance?	❏	❏

Figure 7.7   Teacher checklist for assessing dances using line drawings.

- Students can use the drawing of another student instead of their own.
- The students can add props or costumes.

TEACHABLE MOMENTS

- Students working individually can perform their separate dances at the same time in the same space and find commonalities where their individual dances match or coordinate.
- Students in pairs can start the same dance at different times, as if one person is the echo of the other.
- Students in groups can work on unison movement and practice moving together at the same time.

Additional Ideas for Developing Learning Experiences

This section offers additional learning experiences to reinforce the skills and concepts identified in tables 7.1, 7.2, and 7.3 for music, theater arts, and visual arts, respectively. Curricular areas, suggested grade level, and a brief description are provided for each activity. These activities are intended to inspire additional ideas for interdisciplinary work between classroom and physical education teachers. Teachers are encouraged to develop these ideas more completely. Sometimes the connected model will be most appropriate, while other times the shared or partnership model may be used. Your main concern should be to meet the developmental levels and needs of your students; you can adapt activities to accommodate your teaching schedule, equipment, and available space.

Music

Music and Movement Rounds

Music
The round form

Physical Education
Repetition of movement sequences

Grade Level
4-6

Students create a sequence of movements in 12 counts. Then, they practice the sequence to memorize the movements. The students organize into groups of three and designate themselves as first, second, or third. Then, using the music form called a round, they perform the movement sequence to demonstrate a round. The first person begins the 12-count sequence and continues to repeat the sequence three times. On the fifth count of the first person's sequence, the second person begins his or her movement sequence and repeats the sequence three times. The third person begins his or her sequence on the fifth count of the second person's sequence and continues to perform the sequence three times.

Jump Rope and Singing

Music
Learning to sing songs as part of a group

Physical Education
Practicing jump-rope skills and moving in unison

Grade Level
2-6
During the physical education class the students sing songs learned in the music class while individually jumping rope or jumping as other students turn the rope.

Movements and a Song

Music
Learning to sing songs as part of a group

Physical Education
Creating movements and moving in unison

Grade Level
2-6
During the physical education class the students create movements to illustrate a song. The students perform the movements in unison as they sing.

Changing Pace

Music
Tempo changes using classical music terms

Physical Education
Jump-rope skills or bouncing a ball

Grade Level
4-6
In the music class the students are learning the Italian terms for tempos used in classical music: *largo, adagio, andante, allegretto, allegro, presto, accelerando, ritardando,* and a *tempo*. During the physical education class students practice the different tempos as they jump rope or bounce a ball. They can also practice jump-rope skills or bounce a ball by beginning very slowly and accelerating to a very fast tempo (*accelerando*), or from a fast to a slow tempo (*ritardando*).

Music for Ballet

Music
Music that conveys a story using music written for a classical ballet

Physical Education
Study of how dance can tell a story through the dance form of ballet

Grade Level
3-6

In the music class students are listening to ballet music and learning about how the composer conveys the story through music. Students then view different classical ballet performances, such as *The Nutcracker, The Firebird, The Sleeping Beauty, Peter and the Wolf,* or *Rodeo,* to study how ballet movements express the characters and events in a story. Students can write their own stories and create movements and music that express the characters and events of the story.

Musical Composers

Music
The study of different composers, their background, and their process for composing

Physical Education
The study of different choreographers, their background, and their process for composing

Grade Level
4-6

The music teacher has selected to focus on American composer John Cage (1912-1992). During the music class students learn about his life and his innovative process of music composition, view musical scores, and listen to music he composed at different times of his life. Students create dances using the change process used by Cage to create some of his compositions and by American choreographer Merce Cunningham in his choreography. In the physical education class students are also introduced to the dances of Cunningham, who worked closely with John Cage for many years.

Guitar Dances

Music
Study of timbre in different instruments

Physical Education
Creating and performing dance movement

Grade Level
K-6

Students explore skipping or galloping in different directions; pausing in different straight, curved, and rounded shapes; and turning at different levels. Next, students create a short dance using the following movement sequence: Skip or gallop, pause in a shape, and turn around. Once students have created the dance, they listen to three types of music played on three types of guitars: classical, played on a 6-string Spanish guitar; folk, played on a 12-string acoustic guitar; and heavy-metal rock, played on a 6-string electric guitar. Then they perform their dance to the three different types of guitar music. Discuss with students how their movements changed to fit the three different types of guitar music.

Music in the Movies

Music
Study of how music sets a mood, establishes a character, and enhances the drama of a film

Physical Education
Manipulative skills: bouncing a ball

Grade Level
4-6
The students use different movie themes to create ball-bouncing routines that use stationary and traveling movements. The routine can reflect the tempo, rhythm, mood, or changes in the music. Students can imagine they are a character from the movie and use the bouncing skills to express the character's actions. Music from silent movies can also inspire students to create their own characters and actions.

Theme and Variation

Music
Theme and variation

Physical Education
Locomotor and nonlocomotor movements

Grade Level
4-6
This activity works best after the concept of theme and variation has been introduced in the music program. The students select three locomotor and two nonlocomotor movements and organize the movements into a repeatable sequence. This sequence becomes their theme. They create variations by changing the order of the movements, changing the tempo, making the movements bigger or smaller, or altering the amount of force.

Warm-Up Music

Music
Listening to music from various cultures, different time periods, and disparate styles

Physical Education
Rhythm and tempo for warm-up exercises

Grade Level
K-6
Select music for warm-up or cool-down exercises. Choices such as African drumming music provide a strong rhythm to initiate movement; popular music that students enjoy is great for motivation; a jazz piece, a classical selection, a movie theme, or a children's song can also be used. Listen to the music before using it in class so that you are familiar with the rhythm, tempo, melody, and lyrics.

Music Interpretation Through Dance

Music
Interpretation of music through narration

Physical Education
Creating a dance based on images evoked from listening to a musical selection

Grade Level
3-6
The students are focusing on listening to different styles of music in their music program. The music teacher asks students to interpret the music through creation of a poem, painting, or dance. During the physical education class the students experience how to create short dances based on their interpretation of the music. The students complete a list of words that describe images or feelings interpreted from the music and then illustrate them through movements using space, time, and force. For example, using the words *scared* and *afraid*, the teacher guides the students by asking what shape the body would have if someone were afraid. The teacher can follow up with questions about how fast or slow they would move, what type of steps they would take, in which direction they would go, or where they would be looking.

Echo Rhythms

Music
Reproduction of different rhythms

Physical Education
Reproduction of different rhythms using body movements

Grade Level
K-3
The teacher plays a tape of different rhythms or plays the rhythms on a percussion instrument. Students respond to the rhythms using different body movements such as clapping, jumping, twisting, making shapes, running, or shaking. Students can also create their own movements and rhythms.

Percussion Instruments

Music
Learning to play a percussion instrument

Physical Education
Dancing to percussion instruments

Grade Level
K-6
The students create dances and use various percussion instruments for accompaniment, or they can create dances reflecting the sound of various percussion instruments.

Theater Arts

What Is It?

Theater Arts
Acting skills with a prop

Physical Education
Creating movements to communicate an idea

Grade Level
4-6
Students are arranged in circle formations in small or large groups. One student holds an object, such as a hockey stick, tennis racquet, baseball glove, or Frisbee. The student demonstrates with actions only, no words, a way to use the object that is different from its intended use in a game or sport. The hockey stick can become a broom, giant spoon, or helicopter blade. The other students in the circle guess what the new action with the prop might be. Then another student in the circle takes the same object and tries another idea.

Create a Character Using a Prop

Theater Arts
Creating different characters

Physical Education
Creating movements using shapes and gestures

Grade Level
K-6
The teachers collaborate to present a lesson that focuses on movements used by different types of characters. The students and teachers bring in many different props (e.g., hats, broom, lab coat, newspaper, football helmet, long piece of material, frying pan). Each student selects a prop and creates a character who uses the prop in some way. The student considers how the character walks, stands, performs various

actions, and shapes his or her body. After students practice, their characters are shared with the class. The teachers lead a discussion about how the movement communicates information about the character. Students can also write scripts and scenes for their character. Different characters can be grouped together to create a scene.

Gymnastic Dramatics

Theater Arts
Creating a scene using an environment and characters

Physical Education
Gymnastic skills

Grade Level
K-3
The students and the teacher create an environment, such as a jungle, a food store, a vegetable garden, a candy factory, or an undersea environment, using gymnastic mats and large and small apparatuses. The students create characters who move through the environment by rolling, walking on a balance beam, swinging on a rope, climbing over the vaulting horse, performing cartwheels, jumping, or using other traveling and turning movements. For example, characters could be bugs traveling through a vegetable garden or ingredients for a piece of candy that are mixed, rolled, made into different shapes, and wrapped up.

The Moving Machine

Theater Arts
Acting the characteristics of inanimate objects

Physical Education
Creating a dance to reflect repetition of movement

Grade Level
2-4
Students select a machine, list the parts, and create repetitive movements that represent how the machine moves. Each student can be a different part of the machine, or students can collaborate to move together as a machine part. The machine can be imaginary, such as a machine that would make your bed, or one that is familiar, such as a car wash or washing machine.

Creating With Pantomime

Theater Arts
Creating movements to communicate a scene and characters

Physical Education
Creating movements for communication

Grade Level

2-6

Students work in small groups using pantomime to create a scene. The scene depicts a problem to be solved by a small group working together. The scene should stimulate the imagination and suggest action. Students discuss how the scene will occur then perform the scene using only movement. The scenes can be developed by the teacher, by the students, or both. Here are three example scenes: Several children are skating on a pond when one of the skaters falls through the ice; the others must decide what to do. People are taking the elevator to the top floor of a department store when suddenly the elevator stops between floors; they must decide what to do. You are a lion tamer at the circus, but one of the lions is not cooperative and runs off into the audience. What do you do?

The Seasons

Theater Arts

Pantomime movements

Physical Education

Creating movements for communication

Grade Level

K-3

Students individually create movements to express actions that are related to seasonal activities, for example, spring: planting bulbs, watering and caring for the growing plants, becoming a growing plant, birds building a nest, birds sitting on the eggs, a young bird learning to fly; summer: having fun at the beach, running in the waves, building things with sand, going on a picnic, swimming in the pool, riding a bike, playing baseball, mowing the lawn; fall: raking leaves, jumping in a pile of leaves, playing football or soccer, carrying pumpkins, picking apples; winter: building a snowman or snow fort, making angels in the snow, ice skating, sledding, wrapping gifts, or walking on ice.

Caught in Action

Theater Arts

Acting characters in a scene

Physical Education

Creating action positions from sport scenes

Grade Level

4-6

Students identify several sport scenes or action shots in magazine or newspaper photographs. The photos can contain one or more figures. In pairs or small groups, the students discuss how they will create the scene or photo using their bodies in the different positions. After they have assigned positions, they collaborate to present a tableau using still shapes. The other students in the class observe and make comments about what they see happening in the tableau.

Dance a Scene

Theater Arts
Telling a story and directing actions in a scene

Physical Education
Listening and moving to a set of directions

Grade Level
4-6
The students have written several scenes using sports as the theme and have practiced telling a story during their theater arts sessions. Now, the students will act out the scenes as a storyteller verbally describes the scene like the announcer at the sport event. You could use scenes such as the final minute in a close basketball game, a gymnastics routine in which the gymnast loses and regains his or her balance, or a challenging relay race in track.

The Emotional Voice

Theater Arts
Using the voice as an instrument for the expression of meaning and feeling

Physical Education
Creating movements that express a vocal sound

Grade Level
2-6
The students develop a list of objects, animals, and emotions and create a vocal sound to accompany each word. Then they create movements that express the sound. Students can make the sounds as they perform the movements, or some students can be the voices while others are the movers. Consider creating a fire engine sound accompanied by running and leaping; a jackhammer accompanied by jumping and shaking; a purring cat accompanied by slow, stretching movement; or an angry yell expressed through a sequence of jumps.

Imaginary Ball Pass

Theater Arts
Developing acting skills using an imaginary prop

Physical Education
Performing manipulative skills with an imaginary ball

Grade Level
2-6
The students stand in a circle with one student holding an imaginary ball. This student shows the size and weight of the ball through the movement of his or her hands and body. He or she throws, rolls, kicks, volleys, or bounces the ball to another person, who

pretends to catch the ball. That person then changes the size and weight of the ball. Each time the ball is passed, it changes size and weight, and the person doing the passing changes his or her body to reflect the new size and weight of the ball. The ball can be very big and light, like a giant balloon, and held by two hands, or it can be very tiny and pushed across the floor with one finger.

Visual Arts

Pathway in the Air and on the Floor

Visual Arts
Line drawings

Physical Education
Pathways

Grade Level
K-3
Students draw horizontal, vertical, diagonal, zigzag, or curved lines with colored pencils on a piece of paper to form a design using only one type of line or a combination of types. The drawings can be used as floor or air pathways for movements. Students can also pretend to draw designs in the air. Students can perform different movements such as walking, skipping, running, galloping, bouncing a ball, or foot-dribbling a ball along the pathway.

Partner Balances

Visual Arts
Symmetrical and asymmetrical balance

Physical Education
Balance

Grade Level
4-6
In this activity students create several symmetrical and asymmetrical partner balances. Then they develop a gymnastic sequence emphasizing a smooth transition between the partner balances.

The Sculpture Garden

Visual Arts
Free-standing sculpture and modeling for a sculpture

Physical Education
Balance and shape

Grade Level
4-6
Students working in pairs designate one partner to be the clay and one partner to be the artist. The clay person can begin lying on the ground, sitting, or standing. The artist creates a sculpture by moving the clay person's head, arms, legs, fingers, back, and feet into different positions. Students can switch roles several times to form different types of sculptures. Themes for the sculptures can be sport actions, emotions, monsters, or dancers.

The Playground

Visual Arts
Design in nature

Physical Education
Creating shapes

Grade Level
K-2
The students observe clouds and paint pictures of the different cloud shapes. The paintings are used to inspire the creation of a dance about clouds. Individual students move slowly, changing from one cloud shape to another, and join with other students to form larger clouds.

Circles

Visual Arts
Principles and elements of shape and form

Physical Education
Shapes and targets

Grade Level
K-2
In art class the students have been exploring different-size circles, practicing different ways to arrange circles to create a design, and observing the different ways circles appear in the environment. In physical education class the students explore how different circular objects can move. Students explore hoops, Frisbees, balls of various sizes, deck-tennis rings, Styrofoam cylinders, ropes, and tires. Students can create games that use circular objects and circular targets.

Native Americans of the Southwest

Visual Arts
Art history of the Native Americans of the Southwest

Physical Education
Native American games and dances

Grade Level
4-6
The students study the architecture, sculpture, painting, and crafts of the Native Americans of the Southwest United States in their visual arts class. Students create clay sculptures and pots during their art class. At the same time the physical education teacher teaches Native American games and dances. The students learn how to perform the skills needed to play the games or perform the dances during the physical education class.

Action Figures

Visual Arts
Drawing action figures

Physical Education
Positions used in sports, gymnastics, and dance

Grade Level
4-6
The visual arts teacher presents a unit on drawing people in different positions. The students focus on the angles of the arms, legs, head, and torso and learn which joints of the body are bent or straight in the different positions. The students prepare for the art unit by selecting positions from sports, gymnastics, or dance that they could use in their drawings, such as a batting stance, a basketball foul shot, the beginning of a straddle roll, the backhand position in tennis, the preparation for a one-footed turn, or catching a fly ball. Some of the students can serve as athletic models while others observe the various angles of the body and note whether the joints are bent or straight.

Art History

Visual Arts
Study of visual arts from different time periods, such as the Renaissance, Middle Ages, ancient Egypt, early 20th century, or contemporary art

Physical Education
Creating or learning games and dances from a particular time period

Grade Level
4-6
The students are currently studying a particular time period in their art class. Several students are completing research for creating a scrapbook. The scrapbook will include sections about how people lived, the types of buildings, the clothing, the visual artists, the music, types of jobs, avenues of recreation, and other forms of entertainment of the era. To integrate this research with the physical education curriculum, the students also investigate the games and dances of the period. Students should pay attention to the depiction of games, dances, or actions in the artwork of the period.

From their observations they can create games and dances that represent the time period.

Interpreting Visual Arts Through Dance

Visual Arts
Interpreting ideas or emotions expressed in a variety of works of art

Physical Education
Interpreting ideas or emotions expressed in a variety of dances

Grade Level
2-6
The visual arts teacher presents the ways a work of art conveys emotions and ideas. During the physical education class students view videotapes of dances that convey different emotions or ideas and compare them to the works of art viewed in the art class. Students can also create dances that convey similar emotions or ideas to those viewed in the works of art.

Negative and Positive Space in Visual Arts

Visual Arts
Negative and positive space in three-dimensional art

Physical Education
Making straight, twisted, and curved shapes individually, with a partner, or in a small group

Grade Level
4-6
The visual arts teacher and the physical education teacher collaborate to teach a unit on how shape is defined through the use of negative and positive space in sculptures. In the art class students are introduced to the concept of positive and negative space through viewing and creating sculptures. During the physical education class students create body sculptures using straight, twisted, or curved shapes and identify the positive and negative use of space. Then, in pairs or small groups, students create sculptures that connect to one another. The connection is made by fitting a part of one person's shape into the negative space created by another person's shape or by attaching a part of one person's shape to a body part of another person. (The body is considered the positive space and the spaces between the body parts are considered the negative space.)

Tracing Body Shapes

Visual Arts
Drawing

Physical Education
Body shapes

Grade Level
PreK-2
Students make different straight, twisted, or curved body shapes while lying on the floor or standing. After exploring many different shapes, the students each choose a favorite shape. Next, working in pairs or small groups, one student lies down on a 3 foot × 5-foot sheet of paper and makes their shape; another student or students trace the shape using a crayon. When the shape is completed, the student who was traced stands and looks at the shape, while the other students take turns lying on the paper to see whether they can fit into the shape. One tracing is completed for each student. This lesson can also be accomplished with an overhead projector. One student makes a standing shape in front of the light, and a shadow of the shape is projected on a piece of paper taped to the wall. Another student traces the shape of the shadow.

Picture Dance

Visual Arts
Human figures in paintings and drawings

Physical Education
Creating a dance

Grade Level
3-6
Students view how various artists use human figures to show people working. The students create a dance using the shapes and actions shown in the paintings and drawings. The dance begins with the students posing in one of the positions in the painting or drawing. Next, the students create a sequence of work movements using the elements of time, space, and force. The dance concludes with the students returning to positions shown in the painting or drawing.

Texture Toss

Visual Arts
Texture in different art media

Physical Education
Throwing and catching

Grade Level
K-3
The physical education teacher and the art teacher agree to teach about texture at the same time in their respective disciplines. In the physical education class the students practice throwing and catching individually, in pairs, or in small groups. The students use a variety of objects that have different smooth and rough textures, such as foam balls, rubber balls, Frisbees, newspaper balls, marbles, yarn balls, tennis balls, bean-bags, basketballs, soccer balls, field hockey balls, or balloons. Students discuss how

the different textures feel and how the throw or catch is changed by the texture of the ball.

Theater Arts and Visual Arts

Masks

Theater Arts
Creating a character using a mask and an environment for that character

Visual Arts
Creating a mask relief that represents a mood or feeling using papier-mâché

Physical Education
Creating dance movements for the character wearing the mask

Grade Level
4-6

The theater arts, visual arts, and physical education teachers collaborate on an interdisciplinary unit of study based on the use of masks in African rituals. In the art class students create masks that reflect a specific mood or feeling and can be worn while moving. A theater artist is working with the students to create a scene that describes the purpose of the mask and the environment where it would be worn. In their physical education class the children create the movements and sequences needed to bring the scene to life. The three-discipline collaboration requires planning time for coordination of activities and can result in a grand performance for an audience.

Summary

Music, theater arts, and visual arts, like physical education, can be taught as discrete disciplines with their own body of knowledge, concepts, and skills. Each art form is unique and essential in the curriculum because of the particular avenues of perception that it develops. The arts teach children how to use verbal and nonverbal symbols to communicate and express their thoughts and feelings more effectively and to analyze and understand messages communicated to them. Connections can be made between any art form and other disciplines through the transfer of learning that occurs when students learn to apply the process, skills, and concepts used in a particular arts discipline to other areas. The interdisciplinary possibilities are infinite. The content standards for each of the arts disciplines include a specific standard that addresses developing relationships between art disciplines and with disciplines outside the arts.

The learning experiences describe how a student assumes the character of a circus performer and explores the movements characteristic of that performer; how the use of patterns in art parallels many activities involving throwing, catching, or bouncing; how tempo and rhythm come alive as twisted, straight, or round shapes; and how traveling along a pathway is all the more enjoyable with music, character, and illustration. The suggested ideas at the end of the chapter can serve as the genesis for wonderful learning experiences in music, theater arts, visual arts, and physical education.

Selected Readings

Allen, V. (1996). A critical look at integration. *Teaching Elementary Physical Education, 7,* 12-14.

Alperstein, C., and Weyl, R. (1992). *Arts for everykid: A handbook for change.* Trenton, NJ: New Jersey State Council on the Arts/Department of State and Alliance for Arts Education.

Ashlock, R.O. and J.O. Humphrey. (1976*). Teaching elementary school mathematics through motor learning.* Springfield, IL: Charles C. Thomas.

Association for Supervision and Curriculum Development. (1994). Teaching across disciplines. *Education Update. 36*(10), 1-4.

Atlanta Committee for the Olympic Games. (1994-95*). Olympic day in the schools* (Vols. 1-3). Atlanta, GA: Author.

Baker, K., and Wagner, J. (1977). *A place for ideas — Our theater.* New Orleans: Anchorage Press.

Banks, J. (1985). *Teaching strategies for the social studies.* New York: Longman.

Barnfield, G. (1968). *Creative drama in schools.* New York: Hart.

Belka, D. (1994). *Teaching children games.* Champaign, IL: Human Kinetics.

Benzwie, T. (1987). *A moving experience: Dance for lovers of children and the child within.* Tucson, AZ: Zephyr Press.

Boorman, J. (1973). *Dance and language experiences with children.* Don Mills, Ontario: Longman Press.

Boorman, J.(1987). *Pompous potatoes.*[cassette recording and instruction manual]. Edmonton, AB Canada: University of Alberta.

Brazelton, A. (1975). *Clap, snap, tap* [sound recording]. Freeport, NY: Educational Activities.

Brazelton, A. (1977). *Only just begun* [sound recording]. Freeport, NY: Educational Activities.

Bredekamp, S. (Ed.). (1987). *Developmentally appropriate practice in early childhood programs serving children from birth through age 8.* Washington, DC: National Association for the Education of Young Children.

Britannica. (1993). *Science system.* Berkeley: Lawrence Hall of Science, University of California.

Brophy, J., and Alleman, J. (1991). A caveat: Curriculum integration isn't always a good idea. *Educational Leadership, 49*(2), 66.

Bucek, L. (1992). Constructing a child centered dance curriculum. *Journal of Physical Education, Recreation and Dance, 63*(9), 43-48.

Buchoff, R., and Mitchell, D. (1996). Poetry workouts. *Strategies, 10,* 18-23.

Buschner, C. (1994). *Teaching children movement concepts and skills.* Champaign, IL: Human Kinetics.

California Department of Education. (1989). *Visual and performing arts framework.* Sacramento, CA: Author.

Cecil, N., and Lauritzen, P. (1994). *Literacy and the arts for the integrated classroom.* White Plains, NY: Longman.

Clements, R., and Osteen, M. (1995). Creating and implementing preschool movement narratives. *Journal of Physical Education, Recreation and Dance, 66*(3), 24-29.

College Board. (1983). *Academic preparation for college — What students need to know and be able to do.* New York: College Board Publications.

College Board. (1985). *Academic preparation in the arts — Teaching for transition from high school to college.* New York: College Board Publications.

College Board. (1996). The role of the arts in unifying the high school curriculum. *National Center for Cross-Disciplinary Teaching and Learning Newsletter, 2*(2), 2.

Collom, J., and Noethe, S. (1994). *Poetry everywhere.* New York: Teachers and Writers Collaborative.

Colvin, A., and Walker, P. (1996). Map out excitement. *Strategies, 9,* 26-29.

Cone, S., and Cone, T. (1998). *Moving across the curriculum: An interdisciplinary approach to physical education and dance.* Abstracts: EDA 1998 Convention. N. Kingstown, RI: Eastern District Association of the American Alliance for Health, Physical Education, Recreation and Dance.

Connor-Kuntz, F., and Dummer, G. (1996). Teaching across the curriculum: Language-enriched physical education for preschool children.

Adapted Physical Activity Quarterly, 13, 302-315.

Consortium of National Arts Education Associations. (1994). *National standards for arts education.* Reston, VA: Music Educators National Conference.

Cottrell, J. (1977). *Teaching with creative dramatics.* Skokie, IL: National Textbook.

Cratty, B. (1971). *Active learning: Games to enhance academic abilities.* Englewood Cliffs, NJ: Prentice Hall.

Cratty, B. (1973). *Intelligence in action.* Englewood Cliffs, NJ: Prentice Hall.

Cratty, B. (1985). *Active Learning: Games to enhance academic abilities.* Englewood Cliffs, NJ: Prentice Hall.

DePaola, P. (1975). *The cloud book.* New York: Holiday House.

DePice, D. (1996). Stirring imaginations: Connections among the disciplines. *NJEA Review, 69,* 36-39.

Dewey, J. (1934). *Art as experience.* New York: Perigu Books.

Eisner, E. (1980). Why public schools should teach the arts. *New York Education Quarterly, 11,* 2-7.

Eisner, E. (1988). *The role of discipline-based art education in America's schools.* Los Angeles: Getty Center for Education in the Arts.

Evans, J., and Brueckner, M. (1990). *Elementary social studies: Teaching for today and tomorrow.* Boston: Allyn and Bacon.

Feelings, M. (1971). *Moja means one.* New York: Puffin Pied Piper.

Fleming, D. (1987). Social studies goals: U.S. Department of Education style! *Social Education, 77,* 141-144.

Fogarty, R. (1991a). *The mindful school: How to integrate the curricula.* Palatine, IL: IRI/Skylight.

Fogarty, R. (1991b). Ten ways to integrate curriculum. *Educational Leadership, 49*(2), 61-65.

Fowler, C. (1988). *Can we rescue the arts for America's children?* New York: ACA Books.

Fowler, C. (1994). *Music: Its role and importance in our lives.* New York: Glencoe.

Fraser, D. (1991). *Playdancing.* Pennington, NJ: Princeton Book.

Freeman, S. (1984). *Books kids will sit still for.* Hagerstown, MD: Alleyside Press.

Friedlander, J. (1992). Creating dances and dance instruction: An integrated arts approach. *Jour-*

nal of Physical Education, Recreation and Dance, 63(9), 49-52.

Gallahue, D. (1993). *Developmental physical education for today's children.* Dubuque, IA: Brown and Benchmark.

Gardner, H. (1983). *Frames of mind: The theory of multiple intelligences.* New York: Basic Books.

Gega, P. (1994a). *How to teach elementary school science.* New York: Macmillan.

Gega, P. (1994b). *Concepts and experiences in elementary school science.* Columbus, OH: Merrill.

Gilbert, A. (1977). *Teaching the 3 Rs through movement experiences.* New York: Macmillan.

Gilbert, A. (1992). A conceptual approach to studio dance, PreK-12. *Journal of Physical Education, Recreation and Dance, 63*(9), 43-48.

Gillespie, J., and Nadea, C. (1996). *Best books for children.* New Providence, NJ: Bowker.

Graham, G. (1992). *Teaching children physical education.* Champaign, IL: Human Kinetics.

Graham, G., Holt/Hale, S., and Parker, M. (1993). *Children moving: A reflective approach to teaching physical education.* Mountain View, CA: Mayfield.

Greene, M. (1978). *Landscapes of learning.* New York: Teacher's College Press.

Heard, G. (1989). *For the good of the earth and sun.* Portsmouth, NH: Heineman.

Hoban, T. (1972). *Count and see.* New York: Macmillan.

Holt music: Scope and sequence. (1988). Austin, TX: Holt, Reinhart and Winston.

Horrigan, O. (1929). *Creative activities in physical education.* New York: Barnes.

Horwood, B. (1994). Integration and experiences in the secondary curriculum. *McGill Journal of Education, 29*(1), 89-102.

Huck, C. (1976). *Children's literature in the elementary school* (3rd ed.). New York: Holt, Reinhart and Winston.

Humphrey, J. (1965). *Child learning.* Dubuque, IA: Brown.

Humphrey, J. (1974). *Child learning through elementary school physical education.* Dubuque, IA: Brown.

Humphrey, J. (1987). *Child development and learning through dance.* New York: AMS Press.

Hunt, S. (1964). *Games and sports the world around.* New York: Ronald Press.

International Council for Health, Physical Education and Recreation. (1967). *ICHPER book of worldwide games and dances.* Washington, DC: Author.

International Reading Association. (1970). *Poetry and children.* Newark, DE: Author.

Jacobs, H.H. (1989). *Interdisciplinary curriculum: Design and implementation.* Alexandria, VA: Association for Supervision and Curriculum Development.

Jensen, T. (1971). Creative ropes. *Journal of Health, Physical Education and Recreation, 32* (5): 56-57.

Johnson, E., Sickels, E., Sayers, F., and Horovitz, C. (1977). *Anthology of children's literature.* Boston: Houghton Mifflin.

Johnson, L. (1976). *Simplified lummi stick activities PK-2* [sound recording]. Freeport, NY: Educational Activities.

Joyce, M. (1994). *First steps in teaching creative dance to children.* Mountain View, CA: Mayfield.

Kirchner, G. (1991). *Children's games from around the world.* Dubuque, IA: Brown.

Kunitz, S. (1985). *Next to last things.* Boston: Atlantic Monthly Press.

Kupka, C. (1982). *Windsails.* Modern Dance Technique Environments. [sound recording]. Waldwick, NJ: Hoctor Records.

Lamme, L. (1984). *Growing up writing.* Washington, DC: Acropolis Books.

Lee, M. (1993). Learning through the arts. *Journal of Physical Education, Recreation and Dance, 64*(5), 42-46.

Lima, C., and Lima, J. (1996). *A to zoo: Subject access to children's picture books.* New Providence, NJ: Bowker.

Mahan, C., and Sanders, C. (1996). The two minute mental workout. *Teaching Elementary Physical Education, 7*(6), 26-27.

Martinello, M., and Cook, G. (1994). *Interdisciplinary inquiry in teaching and learning.* New York: Macmillan.

Mathematics. (1995). Morristown, NJ: Silver Burdett Ginn.

Mathematics in action. (1994). New York: Macmillan/McGraw-Hill.

The mathematics experience. (1995). Atlanta, GA: Houghton Mifflin.

Maurer, R.E. (1994). *Designing interdisciplinary curriculum in middle, junior high, and high schools.* Boston: Allyn and Bacon.

McCaslin, N. (1990). *Creative drama in the classroom* (5th ed.). New York: Longman.

McElmeel, S. (1988). *An author a month for pennies.* Englewood, CO: Libraries Unlimited.

Memmel, R.(1953). Arithmetic through play. *Journal of Health, Physical Education and Recreation,* 24:31.

Michael Herman's Orchestra. (1980).*First folk dances* [sound recording]. LPM 1625. New York: RCA Victor.

Miller, A., and Whitcomb, V. (1969). *Physical education in the elementary school curriculum.* Englewood Cliffs, NJ: Prentice Hall.

Mittler, G., and Ragans, R. (1992a). *Exploring art.* Lake Forest, IL: Glencoe.

Mittler, G., and Ragans, R. (1992b). *Understanding art.* Lake Forest, IL: Glencoe.

National Art Education Association. (1991). *Your child and visual arts.* Reston, VA: Author

National Assessment Governing Board. (1994). *Arts education assessment and exercise specifications.* Washington, DC: Author.

National Association for Sport and Physical Education. (1992a). *Developmentally appropriate physical education practices for children.* Reston, VA: Author.

National Association for Sport and Physical Education. (1992b). *The physically educated person.* Reston, VA: Author.

National Association for Sport and Physical Education. (1994). *Developmentally appropriate practice in movement programs for young children, ages 3-5.* Reston, VA: Author.

National Association for Sport and Physical Education. (1995a). *Moving into the future: National standards for physical education.* St. Louis: Mosby.

National Association for Sport and Physical Education. (1995b). *Standards for beginning physical education teachers.* Reston, VA: Author.

National Council of Teachers of English and International Reading Association. (1996). *National standards for the English language arts.* Newark, DE: Author.

National Dance Association. (1994). *National standards for dance education: What every young American should know and be able to do in dance.* Reston, VA: Author.

Nebraska Department of Education. (1993). *K-12 visual and performing arts curriculum framework.* Lincoln, NE: Author.

New Jersey Department of Education. (1996). *New Jersey core curriculum standards.* Trenton, NJ: Author.

Nielsen, M.E. (1989, Fall). Integrative learning for young children: A thematic approach. *Educational Horizons,* pp. 18-24.

Orlando, L. (1993). *The multicultural game book.* New York: Scholastic Professional Books.

Padgett, R. (Ed.). (1987). *The teachers and writers handbook for poetic form.* New York: Teachers and Writers Collaborative.

Palmer, H. (1969). *Modern rhythm band tune.* [sound recording]. Freeport, NY: Educational Activities.

Palmer, H. (1973). *Enter Sunlight.* Movin. [sound recording]. Freeport, NY: Educational Activities.

Piaget, J. (1969). *Psychology of intelligence.* Totowa, NJ: Littlefield, Adams.

Pica, R. (1995). *Kids on the move.* Kennebunk, ME: Moving and Learning, Spring.

Pontious, M. (1986). *A guide to curriculum planning in music.* Madison: Wisconsin Department of Public Instruction.

Purcell, T. (1994). *Teaching children dance.* Champaign, IL: Human Kinetics.

Purcell, T. and Werner, P. (1996). *Teaching children through interdisciplinary programming.* Atlanta, GA: AAHPERD National Convention.

Raftis, A. (1991). *Dance in poetry.* Princeton, NJ: Princeton Book.

Ragans, R., and Rhoades, J. (1992a). *Exploring art: Teacher's manual.* Lake Forest, IL: Glencoe.

Ragans, R., and Rhoades, J. (1992b). *Understanding art: Teacher's manual.* Lake Forest, IL: Glencoe.

Rahn, M.L., Alt, M., Emanuel, D., Ramer, C., Hoachlander, E., Holmes, P., Jackson, M., Klein, S., and Rossi, K. (1995). *Getting to work module two: Integrated curriculum.* Berkeley: National Center for Research in Vocational Education, University of California.

Ratliffe, T., and Ratliffe, L. (1994). *Teaching children fitness.* Champaign, IL: Human Kinetics.

Rayala, M. (1995). *A guide to curriculum planning in art education.* Madison: Wisconsin Department of Public Instruction.

Science anyone. (1995). Orlando, FL: Harcourt Brace.

Science anytime. (1995). Orlando, FL: Harcourt Brace.

Science insights. (1996). Menlo Park, CA: Addison Wesley.

Sendak, M. (1963, 1988). *Where the wild things are.* Boston: HarperCollins.

Shaw, C.G. (1947). *It looked like spilled milk.* New York: Harper and Row.

Silver Burdett. (1974). *Music.* [Text and sound recording]. Morristown, NJ: Author.

Silvey, A. (Ed.). (1995). *Children's books and their creators.* Boston: Houghton Mifflin.

Social studies. (1986). New York: Harcourt Brace Jovanovich.

Social studies. (1991). Orlando, FL: Houghton Mifflin.

South Brunswick Township Public Schools. (1995). *Language arts curriculum K-6.* Monmouth Junction, NJ: Author.

South Carolina Department of Education. (1995). *South Carolina Science Framework.* Columbia, SC: Author.

State of Delaware Department of Public Instruction. (1997). *Visual and performing arts curriculum framework.* Dover, DE: Author.

Stevens, D. (1994). Integrated learning: Collaboration among teachers. *Teaching Elementary Physical Education,* 5(6), 7-8.

Stinson, S. (1988). *Dance for young children: Finding the magic in movement.* Reston, VA: American Alliance for Health, Physical Education, Recreation and Dance.

Temple, C., and Collins, P. (Eds.). (1992). *Stories and readers: New perspectives on literature in the elementary classroom.* Norwood, MA: Christopher-Gordon.

Umminger, W. (1963). *Supermen, heroes, and gods: The story of sport through the ages.* New York: McGraw-Hill.

U.S. Army Infantry School. (1971). *The orienteering handbook.* Fort Benning, Georgia: Author.

United States Olympic Committee. (1984). *The Olympics: An educational opportunity K-6.* Colorado Springs, CO: Author.

University of Illinois School Mathematics Project. (1995). *Everyday learning corporation.* Evanston, IL: Author.

Wall, J., and Murray, N. (1990). *Children and movement: Physical education in the elementary school.* Dubuque, IA: Brown.

Warren, L. (1975). *The theater of Africa: An introduction.* Englewood Cliffs, NJ: Prentice Hall.

Wasley, P. (1994). *Stirring the chalk dust: Tales of teachers changing classroom practice.* New York: Teachers College Press.

Weikart, P. (1989). *Rhythmically moving* [sound recording]. Ypsilanti, MI: High Scope.

Werner, P. (1971). *Effects of integration of physical education with selected science concepts upon science knowledge and selected physical perfor-*

mance skills of boys and girls at fourth, fifth and sixth grade levels. Unpublished doctoral dissertation. Indiana University, Bloomington, IN.

Werner, P. (1994a). *Teaching children gymnastics*. Champaign, IL: Human Kinetics.

Werner, P. (1994b). Whole physical education. *Journal of Physical Education, Recreation and Dance, 65*(6), 40-44.

Werner, P. (1996). Interdisciplinary programming in physical education: What goes around comes around. *Teaching Elementary Physical Education, 7*(4), 28-30.

Werner, P., Bowling, T. and Simmons, M. (1989). Combining the arts and academics. *Journal of Physical Education, Recreation and Dance, 60*(7): 55-57.

Werner, P., and Burton, E. (1979). *Learning through movement*. St. Louis: Mosby.

Whitin, D., Mills, H., and O'Keefe, T. (1991). Living and learning mathematics: Five stories and strategies for supporting mathematical library. Portsmouth, NH: Heineman.

Whitin, D., and Wilde, S. (1992). *Read any good math lately?* Portsmouth, NH: Heineman.

Wigginson, W. (1985). *The haiku handbook*. Tokyo: Kodansha International.

Wilcox, E. (1994). An interview with Susan M. Tarnowski. *Teaching Music, 2*(2), 44-45.

The world around us. (1991). New York: Macmillan/ McGraw-Hill.

Index

About the Authors

Theresa Purcell Cone has been a physical education and dance teacher at Brunswick Acres Elementary School in Kendall Park, New Jersey, since 1976. She is also a teacher and choreographer at the Princeton Ballet School. A past president of the National Dance Association (NDA), Theresa also authored *Teaching Children Dance* (Human Kinetics, 1994). She has received numerous awards, including the American Alliance for Health, Physical Education, Recreation and Dance (AAHPERD) Honor Award (1992); NDA's Presidential Citation (1996 and 1997); NDA's National Dance Educator of the Year (1989); and the Distinguished Alumni Achievement Award from Temple University (1995). Theresa earned her master's degree in dance education from Temple.

Peter Werner is a professor in the Department of Physical Education at the University of South Carolina. He has more than 20 years of consulting experience with classroom teachers and physical education teachers on the topic of interdisciplinary learning. He also has written many articles, made several presentations at national conferences, written three books, and conducted inservice workshops on the topics of interdisciplinary learning and academic integration. The author of *Teaching Children Gymnastics* (Human Kinetics, 1994), Peter earned his PED from Indiana University. In 1996 he received the Outstanding Alumni Award from the University of Wisconsin—Lacrosse, from which he received his bachelor's degree.

Stephen L. Cone is an associate professor in the Department of Health and Exercise Science at Rowan University in New Jersey. He has written dozens of articles for physical education publications, and he contributed a chapter on assessment to his wife Theresa's book, *Teaching Children Dance*. An American Council on Education Fellow in 1993-94, Stephen has held numerous leadership positions in HPERD organizations. He received a Presidential Citation from the National Dance Association in 1995 and the Honor Award from the Eastern District Association of AAHPERD in 1994. He earned his doctorate in motor learning and sports psychology from Texas A&M University.

Amelia Mays Woods is an associate professor of physical education at Indiana State University. She instructs elementary teaching majors on how to teach physical education, focusing on how to integrate movement with other subjects taught in the classroom. Amelia has written many articles on elementary and middle school physical education and has presented at state and national physical education conferences. A member of AAHPERD since 1988, she earned her doctoral degree in instruction and curriculum in physical education from the University of South Carolina.